T
ATTACKS

TERROR ATTACKS

by
ANNE WILLIAMS
and
VIVIAN HEAD

Futura

A *Futura* Book

First published by Futura in 2006

ISBN-13: 978-0-7088-0783-5
ISBN-10: 0-7088-0783-6

Produced by Omnipress, Eastbourne

Printed in Great Britain

Futura
An imprint of
Little, Brown Book Group
Brettenham House
Lancaster Place
London WC2E 7EN

Photo credits: Getty Images and Reuters

The views expressed in this publication are those of the author. The information and the interpretation of that information are presented in good faith. Readers are advised that where ethical issues are involved, and often highly controversial ethical issues at that, they have a personal responsibility for making their own assessments and their own ethical judgements.

CONTENTS

PART FOUR: 1970–1989

PART FIVE: 1990–2006

INTRODUCTION

Since September 11, 2001, the threat of terror attacks has become one of the most disturbing aspects of life in the 21st century. For those of us living in the more prosperous parts of the world, modern technology has, in many ways, made life easier and safer than ever before, whether in housing, transport, health care, communications, or through a huge variety of other services. Yet, increasingly, there is a sense that this ultra-modern, high-tech world is under threat: whether from environmental sources, such as climate change, or from human communities excluded from this rapid development, who now seek to destroy these benefits by whatever means they can. And, despite the rhetoric from Western governments about the benefits of our way of life, in terms of freedom, democracy and economic growth, many people feel a distinct sense of unease about the future. There is a sense that we do not really understand what is going on, either because we have not been told the truth, or because the issues are really too complex for any ordinary person to follow. But are they, in reality? Or do we just prefer to oversimplify, to make life easier for ourselves?

THE 'WAR ON TERROR'

In the aftermath of 9/11, President Bush delivered an address that proved to be a turning point in the history of Western democracy. He spoke of America launching a 'war on terror' and described an 'axis of evil' that the USA would seek to destroy. His use of these abstract nouns, 'terror' and 'evil', was highly significant. Firstly, by talking about 'terror' in the abstract instead of indicating the actual culprits behind the 9/11 attacks (a small group of militant extremists with limited global support) he gave himself carte blanche to wage war on any group that the USA might consider to be an enemy. In practise, this meant invading Afghanistan, and later Iraq – not as enemy nations who had committed aggressive acts against the USA, but as part of the new 'war on terror'. Secondly, by using the word 'evil', he gave the impression that there was no political issue at stake here: this was, in essence, a simple fight between the forces of good (America) and the forces of evil (al-Qaeda/The Taliban/Saddam Hussein/any anti-American or anticapitalist activist group).

While many may have agreed with Bush that both the precepts of Islamic fundamentalism and the regime of Saddam Hussein contravened some of our most basic assumptions in the West about respect for human rights, collapsing the differences between these two distinct approaches in the Arab world, and ignoring the political context of the conflict, gave his words a simplistic, ideological slant that many found both dishonest and dangerous. And, while in domestic terms Bush's strategy seems to have worked, at least in terms of getting him re-elected, globally his approach has done untold damage. For, by using these abstract terms, 'terror' and 'evil', Bush gave the impression that al-Qaeda was an enormously powerful Islamic organisation with millions of adherents across the world: a situation that, ironically, his 'war on terror' has helped to bring into being as more and more Muslims, in countries such as Pakistan, become alienated from the West and follow the path of Islamic fundamentalism. Thus, whether by mistake or design, Bush's 'war on terror' response to the 9/11 attacks has had the effect of plunging the Western and Arab worlds into a deepening global conflict whose battles are now being played out in terrorist attacks on the streets of our cities, instead of by soldiers fighting on the field of war.

POLITICAL CONFLICTS

As an example of this, let us look at the 2006 conflict in Lebanon. The ruling party in the southern area of the country is Hezbollah, listed as a terrorist organization by many countries in the West. Despite its brutality, Hezbollah has won the loyalty of the poverty-stricken people of the region by offering them resources such as housing, health care and social services. At the same time,

Hezbollah have been accused of kidnapping Israeli soldiers and firing missiles at Israeli targets across the border, causing the Israeli Defence Force to launch a series of attacks on the civilian population in Lebanon.

So who are the terrorists here? Is this a war, or a series of terrorist attacks? And in a situation where it is ordinary men, women, and children living in towns and cities who are first in the firing line, does it matter what you call it?

Contrary to what Bush would have us believe, this is not a simple situation in which the good fight the evil of 'terror': there is a long, extremely complex political background to this conflict that cannot be ignored if it is to be understood, let alone any solutions offered. And as with most conflicts, there appears to be only one simple aspect to the continuing unrest in the Middle East: that it is always the innocent who suffer, whoever the aggressors may be.

RESISTANCE OR TERROR?

Not surprisingly, Bush's stance has provoked a great deal of opposition, not just in Arab countries, but among millions of ordinary citizens in the West who find his policies arrogant, aggressive and narrow-minded. According to this oppositional point of view, the USA has oppressed the peoples of many countries around the world, either by direct military intervention or through economic and cultural imperialism. It has even, in some cases, involved itself in, or turned a blind eye to 'state terrorism', that is, terrorist attacks covertly sponsored by national governments. The formation of militant activist groups committing acts of terrorism in return is the desperate response of leaders among these oppressed peoples, who have no other way to bring the world's attention to their cause.

In many ways, the idea that terror attacks are committed on behalf of minority groups who do not have access to political power, and as such have some moral purpose, is a persuasive one. Certainly, there are situations in which resistance to an oppressor seems to be the only course of action, and there are many instances in history of courageous leaders taking a stand to defend their people, whether it be the French Resistance fighters in World War II or Nelson Mandela and the ANC in South Africa under apartheid.

Yet, when we look closely at contemporary terror attacks, we find that they do not always fit this pattern: often, terrorists have no mandate from the peoples they profess to fight for; they may even kill members of their own community or religious group; and, interestingly, they may even be well-off, wealthy individuals who have little in common with the oppressed peoples they apparently represent.

THE BILLIONAIRE TERRORIST

There can be no more obvious example of this than

the leader of al-Qaeda, Osama bin Laden, who, as the son of a billionaire businessman, seems on the face of it to have a background that has more in common with President Bush than with the poverty-stricken inmate of a Palestinian refugee camp. Yet bin Laden, a wealthy, well-educated individual brought up in the lap of luxury, sees himself as the saviour of the economically and culturally dispossessed around the world. In the same way, many other terrorist leaders, such as Carlos the Jackal and members of the Baader-Meinhof group, came from well-heeled backgrounds, and their crimes seemed as much rebellions against their privileged backgrounds as they were political statements.

THE SECOND-GENERATION SEPARATIST

Not all terrorist leaders, of course, were born with a silver spoon in their mouths. However, it is remarkable how many of them come from sections of their communities that are by no means the poorest or most oppressed. For example, it emerged that the perpetrators of the July 7, 2005, attacks in London were mostly from fairly well-integrated Asian families, and their parents, as first-generation immigrants, would have had far more problems to contend with in settling in to a new country than did their children, born and educated in Britain. Similarly, the suicide bombers in the 9/11 attacks in the USA were, on the whole, fairly well-educated young men with reasonably good prospects in terms of career, family and so on, rather than desperate Palestinan refugees sacrificing their lives in the hopes of a better future for their people.

Why should this be? Surely, those who have no hope for the future unless the status quo is changed are more likely to commit terror attacks than those who have many future opportunities in life? Yet that does not seem to be the case. Perhaps it is only the more settled, educated members of a minority group that become politicized, militant leaders who go on to commit terror attacks; or perhaps the experience of being expected to straddle two different value systems is a profoundly disturbing one for the second-generation immigrant. Whatever the truth, it is clear that the pathology of terrorism is one that we are only just beginning to trace, let alone understand. This is an area that must be looked at in terms of a whole series of issues, such as second-generation immigrant culture in different nations, the problems of separatism, of state funding for the religious schooling of minority groups, of generational conflict, of migration patterns and so on. Once again, there is no simple picture here, and no easy answers.

ACTIVIST OR THUG?

Allied to this question of the terrorist's cultural and economic background is that of motivation. To what extent is the terrorist a sober political realist with a clear aim in mind – however brutal the means to his or her end? And to what extent a mentally unstable individual with a pathological desire simply to kill, maim and harm, with no real grasp of politics at all?

Once again, the lines here are often blurred. For example, the IRA's long campaign of terror attacks, undertaken to secure a united Ireland independent of British rule, was clearly a strongly political campaign with specific military targets to begin with, which was to some degree effective in that it had local support in the country, and gains were made for the cause; yet, by the last stages of the campaign, it had become clear that the 'Provos', as they became known, were acting in a senselessly brutal, often mercenary manner, alienating any public support that they might once have had. In the same way, the terrorist Abu Nidal appears to have started out with a clear aim to improve the lot of the Palestinian people; however, he eventually became a brutal mercenary with a warped, sadistic personality, which caused him to be hated and feared among his own followers, as well as among his enemies. The same could perhaps be said of Chechen warlord Shamil Basayev, who may have been fighting to liberate his people from Russian rule, but whose own reputation for psychopathic brutality has become legendary in his country.

Ultimately, it seems that the psychology of such individuals, who live for the most part outside civilized society, remains largely unknown: the terrorist's journey from committed political activist to savage, deranged killer is yet another aspect of the phenomenon of terrorism that to date, has been under-researched.

THE WAY FORWARD

Given the fact that the issue of terrorism is not a simple one, as politicians both on the right and on the left would have us believe, what should our response to it be?

Most of us would agree that terror attacks are wrong: that killing people, especially defenceless citizens with no political connections, cannot be a way forward, whatever the injustices suffered by a group, people or nation. To this degree, terrorism is inexcusable: it is a breakdown of civilized human communication, in which the innocent are always targeted. It cannot, and must not, be tolerated: but, just as with any kind of conflict, if we are to stop it, we must make an effort to understand the root causes of it. If we do not, we risk an escalation of the violence, as we have already seen happen post 9/11.

SUICIDE BOMBERS

It seems that terrorism is the way war is often fought in the new millennium – with no formal agreements, no rules and no safeguards for the civilian population. The enormously complex global transport systems that we now have in place to carry literally millions of people around the planet ironically offer the 'freelance' terrorist many more opportunities for sabotage than at any other time in human history – especially if that terrorist is prepared to commit suicide in pursuit of his or her goal. We have only to remember the devastation wrought on the Twin Towers by two suicide bombers armed only with box-cutters to realize how much damage single individuals, with little in the way of arms or weapons, can do.

Of course, security can be tightened up, but the scale of the problem is enormous. Take the recent Mumbai train bombings of July 11, 2006, for example. In a situation where literally millions of people are travelling around a city daily, and a small group of terrorists are travelling with them, preparing to kill themselves along with their victims, it is difficult to see how security systems could ever effectively monitor and prevent such attacks.

STEPPING UP SECURITY

So what is the answer? Firstly, it is clear that increased security measures, important though they are, cannot be expected to solve the problem. Indeed, attempts to step up security have often ended in disaster, such as happened in the aftermath of the July 7 bombings in London, when an innocent victim, Charles de Menenez, was taken for a terrorist and shot to death on the London underground by police, in full view of the public.

Such acts can only increase the terror and anxiety felt by the ordinary people as they go about their business in our ever-expanding cities all around the world.

Secondly, the overblown, abstract rhetoric of the Bush administration has done nothing but cloud the issue; indeed, many feel that in exaggerating the scale of the problem for his own political purposes, Bush has created a profound rift between the Western and Islamic worlds, and one that has resulted in increased terror attacks. Similarly, the response of the political left has, in many cases, been over-simplistic: terror attacks around the world do not occur solely as a result of America's oppressive military, cultural and economic imperialism, although that is evidently a factor, but are a much more complex response to the modern world, in which individual psychopathology seems to play a large part.

CONCLUSION

To sum up, we cannot draw any meaningful conclusions about terror attacks in today's world unless we are prepared to discard the simplistic solutions of both the political right and left, and actually start to think independently. We need to ask ourselves questions, and to find out information.

What makes a terrorist? What actually goes on in the schools, mosques, training camps, cells and bomb factories of groups such as al-Qaeda? How does the kind of situation come about in which young people from relatively stable, economically secure backgrounds are prepared to kill themselves and others for a set of abstract beliefs? Is theirs a form of nihilism, or a perverted sense of idealism? And what is it in modern society that pushes second-generation immigrants into the arms of fundamentalist religious teachers – a sense of meaninglessness in the face of our consumer society? A feeling of exclusion? Or perhaps a type of psychological fragmentation that results when two value systems can no longer be held together? If so, is there anything we can do to change our Western way of life, to make it more inclusive, more human in scale, less aggressively materialist, perhaps more respectful of our differing spiritual needs?

Asking, and trying to answer, such questions is not to condone terror attacks. It is simply a way of trying to move forward, so that we can begin to understand the roots of the problem. We have seen that vowing to wage a 'war on terrorism' and finding scapegoats has only intensified the conflict. We now have to begin to think more creatively, and begin to find real solutions to what has become a new form of global warfare, waged by terrorists on the streets of our cities, and in the airspace of our nations, rather than by soldiers on the battlefield.

THE ORIGINS
OF TERRORISM

The word 'terrorism' actually entered into the European language in the wake of the French revolution of 1789. Robespierre felt that terror was a justifiable means to oust those who opposed his rule. The first true recording of the word was in the *Académie Française* in 1798, where it was listed as a 'system or rule of terror'. However, the origins of terrorism can be traced back to early recorded history when it was described as a group of people who attempted to scare, or rather terrorize, people into their own religious way of life.

Two early terrorist groups were the Zealots and the Sicarii. The Zealots were a group of Jewish men who quite openly attacked Roman and Greek authorities in an effort to get the message over that they were not wanted as ruling bodies. The second group were the Sicarii, also Jews, but they resorted to murdering fellow Jews who had slipped from their religious faiths.

Another fanatical group who were motivated by political/religious fervour were the Assassins. Having been suppressed by the Mongols in the 13th century, the Assassin leaders, realizing that their band of men were too small to go into battle, chose to use terror to enable them to maintain their religious autonomy by instilling fear into their enemies.

The true concept of the structured use of terrorism came to the fore in the 1870s, with the activities of the Russian revolutionaries. Characters of note are Nechayev (also Nechaev), a Russian revolutionary figure associated with the Nihilist movement and anarchism and known for his single-minded pursuit of revolution by any means necessary, including political violence. Mikhail Bakunin was one of the intellectual founding fathers of Anarchism and was often thought of as Marx's historical rival. A special place in the history of Russian terrorism belongs to a small band of revolutionaries known as Narodnaya Volya ('The People's Will') who used the word 'terrorism' proudly. They developed certain ideals that were to become the hallmark of subsequent terrorism in many other countries.

Terrorism, as we know it today, possibly dates back to the mid-19th century when an Italian revolutionary, Carlo Pisacane, conjectured that terrorism could deliver a message to an audience and draw attention to, and support for, a cause. But one thing is for certain, since the horrific events of September 11, 2001, terrorism is now on the minds of many people who previously had possibly never given it a second thought.

*We must try to find ways to starve the
terrorist and the hijacker of the oxygen of
publicity on which they depend.*

MARGARET THATCHER

Examples of early modern terrorism are the Ku Klux Klan, who formed after the American Civil War in 1865 with the main aim of resisting reconstruction. Another band of terrorists were the Young Bosnians who had Archduke Franz Ferdinand assassinated in 1914, which ultimately led to the outbreak of World War I.

It probably wasn't until the 1960s that terrorism as we know it today came into prominence, with the formation of the PLO (Palestine Liberation Organization) and the IRA (Irish Republican Army). These groups, and others like them, used violence against civilian populations in an effort to effect change for either religious or ideological reasons. One memorable example is 'Bloody Friday', the name given to July 21, 1972, due to bombings by the Provisional Irish Republican Army in and around Belfast, Northern Ireland, aimed at causing economic damage. A total of 22 bombs were planted and, in the resulting explosions, nine people were killed and a further 130 seriously injured.

The success of the Irish terrorist activities caught the eye of other nations, and realizing that it could have a very strong impact on a variety of issues, they started to fund terrorist groups from within their own governments. Syria, Libya and Iran were just a few of the countries who were prepared to sponsor terrorism. Of course very few people, apart from the Russian Tsar killers, would actually call themselves terrorists, but there are many common denominators in their so-called organizations. Most claim that their actions are as a direct result of an upsurge of public feeling, and for some naive reason, they believe that the use of violence or bullying will somehow transform the political scene in a favourable way. Possibly one of the most horrifying aspects of terrorism today is the fact that innocent civilians are becoming entangled in the web of violence. Hopefully it is the strong revulsion of the ordinary person against acts of terrorism that will eventually be the terrorists' downfall.

As there are common factors, it is possible to put some sort of definition to the word terrorism. The definition according to the Oxford Dictionary is:

terrorism [noun] the unofficial or unauthorized use of violence and intimidation in the pursuit of political aims.

There are definitely three key elements to terrorism – violence, fear and intimidation – and each of these elements produces terror in its victim. The statement, 'One man's terrorist is another man's freedom fighter', has become not only a common phrase, but also one of the most difficult obstacles in coping with terrorism. Other organizations have their own interpretations of terrorism.

Firstly, the United States Department of Defence defines terrorism as:

> *The calculated use of unlawful violence or threat of unlawful violence to inculcate fear; intended to coerce or to intimidate governments or societies in the pursuit of goals that are generally political, religious or ideological.*

The FBI's definition of terrorism is:

> *Terrorism is the unlawful use of force and violence against persons or property to intimidate or coerce a government, the civilian population, or any segment thereof, in furtherance of political or social objectives.*

The US Department of States defines it as:

> *Premeditated, politically motivated violence perpetrated against noncombatant targets by subnational groups or clandestine agents, usually intended to influence an audience.*

Finally the British Government's definition in 1974 was:

> *. . . the use of violence for political ends, and includes any use of violence for the purpose of putting the public, or any section of the public, in fear.*

Whatever definition we put to the atrocities of terrorist acts, whether it be those of an individual or a group of terrorists, the results are the same: terrorism is offensive and must end. The Terrorism Research Centre, Inc., which was formed in 1996, hit the nail on the head by saying, 'Terrorism is a criminal act that influences an audience beyond the immediate victim'.

During the 1960s the UN General Assembly tried to find some form of prohibition on terrorist activities, but their progress was slow because some states felt that terrorism in response to real grievances was justified. The UN was therefore limited in its power, but it drew up a series of 12 inadequate international conventions between 1963 and 1999. It only succeeded in passing a law to prohibit the hijacking of aircraft and the taking of diplomatic hostages.

Terrorists always plan their attacks to obtain the greatest publicity, choosing targets that typify what they themselves oppose. How effective the attack is relies not in the act itself, but in the public's, or indeed the government's, reaction to it. As an example the Black September Organization killed 11 Israelis at the 1972 Munich Olympic Games, making the Israelis the immediate victims. The true target, however, was the estimated one billion people watching the televised event.

As the 1990s progressed and concern about terrorism increased, the United States and several other nations became involved in a 'War on Terror', which has subsequently sent military units into Afghanistan in an effort to uncover al-Qaeda, and a large coalition force into Iraq to overthrow supporters of Sadaam Hussein. President George W. Bush announced to the United States in 2001 that he would be 'resolute in his determination to wipe out terrorism' – and yet it is more evident today than at any other time in recorded history.

Terry Waite, CBE, a British humanitarian and author, is best remembered for his work as a hostage negotiator and was himself held hostage in Lebanon for 1,760 days before being released on November 18, 1991.

> *The terrible thing about terrorism is that ultimately it destroys those who practise it. Slowly but surely, as they try to extinguish life in others, the light within them dies.*
>
> TERRY WAITE

PART ONE

EARLY TERRORISM

JING KE, THE MASTER ASSASSIN

The reason why China suffers bitterly from endless wars is because of the existence of feudal lords and kings.

QIN SHI HUANGDI

Qin Shi Huangdi was the founder of the Qin dynasty and was renowned for being a violent and brutal man. He became the first emperor of unified China in 221 BC and, at the time when he assumed power, the country had been in turmoil for over 200 years. This period of history became known as the Warring States Period. Before this time China was divided into numerous small kingdoms, or *fiefdoms*, but during the Warring States period seven dominant kingdoms emerged – Qin, Yan, Qi, Qu, Yan, Han, Zhao and Wei – of these Qin was the most powerful.

After such a violent and tumultuous period, the people were ready to accept Huangdi's vision of a unified China with open arms. But their excitement was to be short-lived because the emperor not only used violence in his drive to unify China, but he also resorted to the slaughter of thousands of innocent people who he felt were not true to his cause.

The Kingdom of Zhao plays a very significant role in the life of the emperor, as this is where the King of Qin was raised and where he first met his life-long lover and confidante, Lady Zhao. Lady Zhao was a commoner and a servant to the emperor's family. She was a simple, but elegant woman, and possibly the only person who shared the emperor's vision. When Lady Zhao heard of the emperor's dream of a unified China she decided to sacrifice her dream of leaving the Qin palace and returning to her homeland in order to support her lover. But despite her loyalty, ironically, it was the emperor's brutal destruction of Zhao and the murdering of the children of Zhao that destroyed their relationship. The killing of the Zhao children is testimony of both the emperor's brutality and his inability to keep his promise to the one person he truly loved.

At the commencement of his rule, the emperor's vision for a unified China was genuine, wishing to bring an end to war and build one big empire where everyone spoke the same language and used the same currency. To avoid the anarchy of the Warring States Period, Qin Shi Huangdi and his prime minister, Li Si, completely abolished feudalism. They divided the empire into 36 provinces to be run by three governors – one civilian, one military, one moderator – all of whom could be dismissed by the emperor at any time. The emperor ordered that all members of the former royal houses of the conquered states to move to Xianyang (the capital of Qin) so that they could be kept under tight surveillance for rebellious activities. Huangdi also developed an extensive network of roads and canals, which provided easy access to the various provinces in the hope of promoting trade to his new empire. These also meant that there was an easy route if he needed to send his military section to any rebellious provinces too.

During his reign the Chinese script was unified. The new script was developed by Li Si, which he called the 'small seal script'. This was based on the script already used in the Qin State, and the emperor ordered that the new script was made mandatory, thus abolishing any previous scripts. Edicts written in this new script were carved on the walls of the sacred mountains that surrounded China, making sure that his people followed his law.

Qin Shi Huangdi continued to expand his military power, and he fought neighbouring nomadic tribes to the north and northwest in a constant effort to increase his empire. Although his army managed to subdue the tribes, the battles were inconclusive and to prevent the Xiongnu from encroaching on the northern frontier any further,

Huangdi ordered the construction of an enormous, defensive wall. This new wall linked several walls that were already in existence during the time of the Warring States. The construction of the new wall caused the death of thousands of men, and it was the forerunner of the present Great Wall of China. In order to build the great wall, the roads and the canals, Huangdi had to force peasants to do manual labour, and he believed that all his subjects should suffer in order that he live in relative peace. He suppressed freedom of thought and burned all Confucian literature, and through his constant cruelty and lack of compassion for his people Qin Shi Huangdi soon made many enemies.

JING KE

Qin Shi Huangdi had by this time conquered the states of Han and Zhao and was now threatening the state of Yan, to the northwest of his Empire, along the coast. Prince Dan, who was the son of the King of Yan, felt that their military were not strong enough to defend the state, and decided the best way to solve the problem was to assassinate the Emperor Huangdi. He already held a grudge against the emperor, because he had been captured by him and held prisoner in the Qin province for five years before be managed to escape.

About this time, Prince Dan befriended a young man by the name of Jing Ke, who was a native of the province of Wei but had journeyed to Yan. In

Yan he had formed a good reputation as he was always prepared to assist anyone in need and was well accepted by the local people. Jing Ke and Prince Dan got on well right from their first meeting, and the Prince soon decided that it was this young man who should carry out the assassination of his arch rival. In an effort to win Jing Ke over, the prince had a luxurious palace built for him and made sure that he had everything he wanted. The prince visited him every day and made sure that his favourite chariot was always available to him. The prince even had his favourite horse slaughtered and the liver cooked for Jing Ke, as it was one of his favourite dishes. All this attention worked, and Jing Ke felt that he would be willing to do anything for his friend.

Meanwhile, the Qin troops were starting to mass along the southern border of the Yan state. Prince Dan went to see his friend Jing Ke and told him of his fears that the state of Yan would soon be overthrown. Tentatively he suggested to Jing Ke that he felt the only way to save his state was to kill the emperor of Qin. To his surprise Jing Ke replied that he had already been thinking about doing the same thing, but felt that it would be very hard to gain access to the emperor. He asked the prince for two things – a map of the Dukang district, an area which Huangdi longed to possess, and the head of a man named Yan Yuqi. Apparently Yuqi had defected from Qin to Yan and was on the emperor's most wanted list. Jing Ke felt that if he offered the emperor these two items he would most certainly be granted an audience.

While the Prince prepared the map, Jing Ke himself went to see Yan Yuqi and told him of the assassination plot. As a loyal subject Yuqi was willing to sacrifice himself to save Yan and took a knife to his own throat. Prince Dan gave his friend a dagger with a poisoned blade and assigned another well-known warrior, Qin Quyang to accompany him on his mission.

When the pair arrived in the State of Qin it wasn't long before the news got to the emperor and they were offered an audience. However, when they actually confronted Huangdi, Jing Ke lost his nerve and his hands started to tremble uncontrollably. This aroused the emperor's suspicion, but Jing Ke recovered his composure and told him that it was just the fact that he was totally overawed to be in the presence of such a famous emperor.

Carrying a wooden box containing the severed head and a map scroll with the poisoned dagger rolled up inside it, Jing Ke approached the emperor. As he approached him and unrolled the map, the dagger was revealed and caused the emperor to take a step back. However, Jing Ke lunged at him, grabbed his sleeve and pointed the dagger towards him. The emperor moved swiftly and as he jerked away the dagger only managed to make a tear in the sleeve of his garments. The emperor hid behind a pillar with Jing Ke still determined to complete his task.

Because Huangdi had always been prepared for an attempt on his life, he had ordered that no one, not even his own retainers, could enter the throne room carrying any sort of weapon, so consequently he had very little protection. However, the emperor's personal physician attempted to get between them with his bag of medicine, and this gave the emperor a little more time. In this instant the emperor pulled out his own sword and managed to sever Jing Ke's left leg. In a last effort to assassinate the emperor, Jing Ke threw his dagger at him, but unfortunately he missed. Hearing the commotion the guards rushed in from outside the throne room and killed both Jing Ke and his accomplice, and consequently their plot to assassinate the emperor of Qin failed.

After this incident the emperor was incensed and drove his forces down to Yan. On reaching its capital the following year, Huangdi forced the Emperor of Yan to have his own son, Prince Dan, put to death and by the year 222 BC, the state of Yan had been completely wiped out by the state of Qin.

THE ASSASSINATION
OF POMPEY

> *At this his behavior Pompey had great
> indignation; Hyrcanus also and his friends
> made great intercessions to Pompey; so he took
> not only his Roman forces, but many of his
> Syrian auxiliaries, and marched against
> Aristobulus.*
>
> FLAVIUS JOSEPHUS

Gnaeus Pompeius Magnus (Pompey the Great) was
born in 106 BC in the Northern Italian town of
Picenum. His father, Pompey Strabo, was an
accomplished general, and by the age of 17, Pompey
took an active interest in his father's campaigns and
was already building a foundation for his own military career. He proved to have extraordinary valour
and a remarkable strength of character, even at such
a young age.

Pompey made his first military mark when he
was serving Sulla in the first major Roman civil war,

against the forces of Marius in Africa. For the speed and success of his commission, Pompey was honoured with the name of Magnus (meaning 'the Great'), and for one who had never held office this was indeed a great distinction. His next command took him to Spain, where he fought against the brave rebel Sartorious. Although the battle was not a clear-cut victory, because the opposing army only retreated following the murder of Sartorious, Pompey still returned to Rome in triumph.

On his return to Italy Pompey and Marcus Licinius Crassus, who conducted the bulk of the operation, were successful in bringing an end to the Servile War instigated by the slave Spartacus. Pompey was now the idol of his people as well as his army, and he was elected consul in the year 70 BC, serving alongside Crassus. Despite fears of a new military dictatorship Pompey received special powers, even though he was deeply distrusted by the Senatorial class. But seeing a truly capable general who had the power to march on Rome, the Senate tolerated him, albeit reluctantly.

In 67–66 BC, Pompey performed a noble service to the republic by clearing the Mediterranean Sea of pirates, who had overrun the area for many years. In the next four years, 65–62 BC, he conquered Mithridates VI of Pontus, Tigranes the Great, King of Armenia, and Antiochus XIII of Syria. He also subdued the Jewish nation and captured Jerusalem. On his return to Italy he disbanded his army and in 61 BC entered Rome in triumph for the third time.

Following a disagreement with the Senate Pompey formed a close alliance with Julius Caesar, and the two men, together with Crassus, formed a coalition commonly called the 'First Triumvirate'.

Pompey married Caesar's daughter Julia, which should have created a strong bond between the two men, but the liaisons between them were personal, tenuous and short-lived. The following year Caesar went to Gaul and rose in esteem as a warrior and a statesman. Pompey, meanwhile, spent his time in Rome making no great advances in his career. Jealousies soon came to the surface, as Pompey could not bear to have such a strong rival. When Julia died in 54 BC, one of the main links between Caesar and Pompey broke, and the rift between the two men grew wider. Pompey returned to the comfort of his former friends, the aristocracy. They, like Pompey, had a strong desire to strip Caesar of his command. Caesar was immediately ordered to lay down his office and return to Rome. He agreed to do this provided Pompey would do the same. The Senate insisted on an unconditional resignation, ordering him to immediately disband his army, otherwise he would be declared a public enemy. But Caesar ignored their command and crossed the Rubicon in 49 BC, consequently defying the Senate and its armies, both of which were under Pompey's command.

Pompey withdrew his forces to Brundisium (now Brindisi) and then moved on to Greece. Caesar, in the meantime, made himself master of Italy and defeated a strong army in Spain commanded by Pompey's legates, and then he crossed the Adriatic to attack Pompey. Pompey, who had managed to gather a strong army, was victorious in the opening encounters, but was finally defeated at Pharsalus in 48 BC. Pompey managed to survive the conflict unscathed and made his escape to Egypt.

Upon his arrival in Egypt, Pompey's fate was decided by three counsellors of the boy king, Ptolemy XIII. Pompey waited offshore for the king's decision, but the counsel and Ptolemy argued the cost of offering him refuge due to the fact that Caesar was already en route to Egypt with his army. The decision was made to murder Pompey, so that they could ingratiate themselves with Caesar.

On his 58th birthday, September 29, Pompey was enticed to come to the shore to meet a supposed audience. Among the welcoming party Pompey spotted two of his old comrades-in-arms from his earlier, glorious battles. What he didn't know was these two men were to be his assassins.

While Pompey rested in his small boat, preparing a speech he had made for the boy king, the two men stabbed him in the back with a sword and a dagger. His naked body was decapitated and left unceremoniously on the shore. His friend, Philipus, arranged a simple funeral pyre and cremated Pompey's body on a pile of broken ship's timbers.

When Caesar arrived a few days later, he was presented Pompey's head and ring in a basket as a welcoming present. But rather than being pleased with his gift, Caesar was angry that his former ally and son-in-law had been murdered by traitors. When offered the head, Caesar simply turned his head in disgust, and on being given Pompey's signet ring, which was engraved with a lion holding a sword, he burst into tears.

Out of revenge he deposed Ptolemy, executed his regent Pothinus and then elevated Cleopatra to the throne of Egypt. Caesar gave Pompey's ashes and ring to Cornelia, who took them back to his estates in Italy. At Caesar's request, Pompey was later deified by the Senate in the year 45 BC.

THE ASSASSINATION OF JULIUS CAESAR

If you must break the law, do it to seize power: in all other cases observe it.

JULIUS CAESAR

Using his position as a general and a politician of the late Roman republic, Gaius Julius Caesar managed to extend the Roman Empire quite extensively. In January of 49 BC, Julius Caesar led his army across the Rubicon river in Northern Italy and thereby plunged the Roman Republic into civil war. Within three months Caesar had taken control of the entire Italian peninsula, and in Spain he had defeated the legions who were loyal to Pompey.

Caesar pursued Pompey to Greece and soon crushed the forces of his enemy, although Pompey managed to escape to Egypt unharmed. Again Caesar followed him and was rewarded by being presented his rival's head on a platter as a token of friendship. Before he left Egypt he appointed Cleopatra as his surrogate ruler of the region. His remaining rivals in North Africa were defeated in 47 BC, and Caesar returned to Rome with his authority now firmly established.

Caesar continued to consolidate his power and proclaimed himself the dictator of Rome in 44 BC. This undermined the power of the Republic and also paved the way for a system of monarchy that was headed by emperors.

The position of dictator had always been a temporary position, but in 44 BC Caesar took the title for life. He used this extra power to carry out much-needed reform, relieving debt, making the senate larger, building the Forum Iulium and also revising the calendar. But along the way he made enemies – many of them republicans who had been spared – who despised his new-found dictatorial powers. Led by Brutus and Cassius, a diverse group of conspirators formed against him and started to plot his demise. Sixty members of the newly formed Senate quickly decided that the only way to resolve their grievances was to assassinate Caesar.

The members of the Senate met in secret at each other's houses to discuss various proposals of how to execute their plan. Suggestions were put forward that they should wait until he was on his favourite walk along the Sacred Way, or alternatively they should wait until the elections when he had to cross a bridge, from which he could be pushed. Another plan was to wait for a gladiator display, where there would be no suspicion aroused if people were seen to be carrying arms. The majority opinion, however, was to kill him while he sat in the Senate. As non-Senate members were not permitted, it meant that Caesar would be without allies at the next sitting, and it would also be easy for his conspirators to hide their daggers beneath their loose, flowing togas. Finally, this was the plan that they all agreed on.

Alarmed by rumours that had been going round about Caesar, his friends tried to talk him out of going to the Senate house. His doctor also advised against him going, due to the fact that he was suffering from a spell of dizziness, which Caesar was prone to from time to time. Another reason for Caesar not to attend, was the fact that his faithful wife, Calpurnia, had been frightened by a vivid dream in which her beloved husband had been killed. So determined was she to stop him, that she physically clung to his leg and begged him not to leave the house. However, his so-called friend Brutus, one of the main conspirators, asked him if he was the sort of ruler who would pay attention to the meaningless visions of a woman or listen to the gossip of stupid men. He said to Caesar that it would be an insult to the Senate if he were not to attend, and he told his friend that the Senate had been in session waiting for their ruler since early that morning. The words of an old friend (or so he presumed), persuaded Caesar and he left.

BAD OMENS

Before Caesar entered the Senate chamber, his priests brought up the victims for him to make what would turn out to be his very last sacrifice. However, the omens were very clearly not in his favour. After repeated unsuccessful sacrifices, the priests told Caesar that they could not see the divine intent as there was some evil spirit hidden within the sacrificial victims. Caesar was annoyed at their proclamation and informed them that he would abandon divination until sunset.

The conspirators that were present were delighted with this turn of events, although Caesar's friends convinced him to put off the meeting of the Senate until the following day due to the unhappy circumstances. Caesar agreed to this, but as he turned to leave some attendants ran up to him begging him to come to the Senate as it was already full. Brutus approached his friend and said, 'Come, good sir, pay no attention to the babblings of these men, and do not postpone what Caesar and his mighty power has seen fit to arrange. Make your own courage your favourable omen.' Caesar was convinced by these words and followed Brutus, in silence, into the Senate.

The Senate rose in reverence for his position when they saw Caesar enter. Those who were actually involved in the plot to kill Caesar made sure that they stood close to their victim. Tillius Climber, whose brother had been exiled by Caesar, stood directly next to him and, under the pretext of a simple request from his brother, approached the ruler. Cimber grabbed the front of Caesar's toga and held him tight, which annoyed the dictator.

The conspirators took advantage of the situation and made their move. They quickly removed their daggers from their sheaths and all dashed angrily at Caesar. The first man to strike him with the point of his dagger was Servilius Casca, who sunk the blade deep into Caesar's left shoulder just above the collar-bone. Caesar stood up and tried to defend himself against his attackers, but Casca shouted out to his brother in Greek, who then came forward and drove his dagger deep into his ribs. Cassius followed this with a slash to his face, while Decimus Brutus pierced his side. Each one made a bid to make their mark on Caesar – determined that it should be their wound that finally killed him.

Caesar, gasping for breath from his many wounds, fell at the foot of Pompey's statue. Each Senate member seemed to want to have a part in the downfall of the dictator, and as he lay under the statue there was not one member who did not strike his body. Eventually, wounded 35 times, Caesar took his last breath.

His death took place on the March 15 (the Ides of March) between 11.00 a.m. and 12.00 p.m., 44 BC. The assassination of Caesar sparked off yet another 14 years of civil war before his great-nephew and heir, Octavian, managed to establish a permanent monarchy in a more acceptable form.

THE ZEALOTS

*To attempt the destruction of our passions is
the height of folly. What a noble aim is that of
the zealot who tortures himself like a madman
in order to desire nothing, love nothing, feel
nothing, and who, if he succeeded, would end
up a complete monster!*

DENIS DIDEROT

The Zealots are a Jewish faction who can be traced
back to the revolt of the Maccabees in the 2nd
century BC. The term 'Zealot', in Hebrew *kanai*,
means one who is jealous on behalf of God. The
Zealots were organized into a party during the reign
of Herod the Great (37–4 BC), whose idolatrous
practices the group resisted, and who bitterly
opposed Roman rule and taxation. They were also
known as the Sicarii after the name of the daggers
(*sicae*) that they carried hidden underneath their
cloaks. The term Zealot technically applies to a
person who belonged to a Jewish sect who resisted
any Roman authority and other Jews that collab-
orated with Rome. For many generations the

Zealots resisted the Emperor's authority by means of violence. Their dream would be to have an all-powerful messiah who would lead their great holy army, destroy the Roman overlords and re-establish Jewish rule into Israel.

THEIR BELIEFS

The beliefs of the Zealot movement were quite simple and were broken down into four simple rules:

1. God alone was to be served.
2. God alone was their ruler, neither Rome nor Herod were legitimate authorities.
3. Taxes were to be paid only to God.
4. All foreign rule over the Jews was unscriptural. Serving Rome, whether in worship, slavery, or paying taxes, was a sin against God.

The Zealots believed that no matter what forces they used to support their beliefs, God would always be on their side, and they would triumph in the end. This strong belief led to their reputation for incredible bravery and tolerance towards suffering.

THE SICARII AND HEROD

The Sicarii, the dagger bearers of the Zealots, were a band of violent nationalists who were prepared to undertake assassination and murder in a campaign to set Palestine free. Bands of Zealots and Sicarii were formed in protest against this misrule, and their members pledged to kill any disloyal Jew. They worked swiftly by mingling in street gatherings, stabbing their appointed victims from behind, and disappearing in the chaos of the resultant crowd. The Zealots first used violence for the sake of punishing the crimes of idolatry and bloodshed that had been committed by Herod. It was the introduction of Roman institutions such as the gymnasium, the arena, and above all, the trophies or images to which homage was to be paid, that truly incensed the Zealots.

Ten citizens of Jerusalem banded together and swore vengeance against Herod. Concealing daggers under their robes, the ten men entered the theatre where Herod was supposed to be, with one thought in their head: to slay the enemy. However, Herod had many followers who kept vigil and was consequently informed of the conspirators plan to kill him, so he managed to escape. The conspirators were not so lucky, however, and they were tortured to death, glorifying in their martyrdom. Followers of the Zealots sympathized with them, hunted down the spy who had reported the plan to Herod, and literally tore him to pieces.

Later, towards the end of Herod's life, he once again angered the Zealots by placing a large golden eagle over the great gate of the Temple. Two Zealot masters, Judah ben Sarifai and Mattathias ben Margalot, ordered their disciples to sacrifice their own lives rather than allow this violation of their beliefs. The two masters, with the help of 40 other young men, used all their strength to pull down the golden eagle. Herod was so incensed by their actions that he ordered that they all be burnt to death.

JUDAS, ZEALOT LEADER

Despite Herod's efforts to quash the Zealot movement, their spirit could not be crushed. Following his death, the Romans appointed a series of governors called procurators, each one apparently more cruel and corrupt than the previous leader. People cried out for revenge and would not settle until the matter was resolved.

There were several robber bands in Judea, all of whom wanted to appoint one of their members as king. Judas, the son of Hezekiah (a robber-captain), took matters into his own hands and organized his forces for a revolt against the dynasty of Herod. Judas's teachings and his zeal influenced his followers, who were basically fanatics, waging war on all who opposed them. They exhibited extreme bravery, enduring sieges and torture rather than call anyone 'lord' other than God. And so it was under the leadership of Judas and his family that the Zealots became an aggressive and relentless political party.

There were groups of rebel Zealots and Sicarii everywhere, killing Romans and any Jews who co-operated with them. The priesthood became more dependent upon the Romans for their support and safety, and in so doing became more and more corrupt. The Zealots's popularity grew day by day, driving the common people towards their radical approach. It was quite apparent that the Roman administration was in a state of disorder, while the Zealots and Sicarii flourished. The people knew that the time was right for a revolt to free them from the political oppression they had suffered for too long.

BLOODY REVOLT

While Emperor Nero was throwing Christians and Jews alike to the lions, violence was flaring up in Judae. There was a conflict in Caesarea between Jews and Gentiles over activities that had been taking place in the synagogue. There was a public outcry when a Gentile offered a pagan sacrifice next to the entrance of the synagogue, causing the authorities in Jerusalem to ban the act of sacrifices. Florus, the governor from Caesarea, entered Jerusalem with troops and took a large amount of gold from the temple treasury. When people gathered to try and stop them, Florus simply unleashed his troops on the innocent civilians causing the death of more than 3,500 people. Hundreds of women and children were raped, whipped and even crucified. The reaction was so strong, that mobs swarmed the streets and forced the legionnaires out of their city.

Meanwhile, taking the Roman garrison by surprise, the Zealots occupied the Masada fortress. From here they managed to distribute large amounts of weapons, and due to the frenzy raised by the revolt even the nonpolitical Pharisees joined the Zealot movement by their hundreds.

Violence even mounted within the Zealot group itself when Eleazar, a Zealot leader, who had ordered the slaughter of all Roman prisoners remaining in the city, assassinated the Zealot leader Menahem. At this point the revolt reached its climax.

Hearing of the violence against fellow Romans in Jerusalem, the Gentiles in Caesarea fought against the Jews, and within a single day 20,000 Jews were slaughtered, regardless of age or sex. This slaughter was repeated in other parts of the empire, until an estimated 50,000 were killed in Alexandria alone. Literally the land was running with blood.

Nero acted quickly, ordering his leading general, Vespasian, to end the Jewish problem once and for all. Vespasian's army numbered more than 50,000 men and together they took several towns by force, destroying Gamla completely, where the Zealot movement was originally formed. Men were either crucified or executed, while the women and children were sold into slavery. Once again Galilee was in the hands of the Romans. Vespasian went on to conquer the coast and the lands east of Judea, and then took Jericho and Emmaus, which guarded the eastern and western approaches to Jerusalem, leaving the city isolated without any strongholds.

Vespasian became emperor in AD 68 due to the suicide of Nero. He handed over his duties as general to his son Titus, who was then left to finish the campaign against Jerusalem.

In the city of Jerusalem the situation was chaotic. Zealots had converged on the city, taking control of Temple Mount and appointing their own priest. When the Sadducee priests tried to resist, the Zealots responded by killing them along with 8,500 of their supporters. Jerusalem was in a complete state of confusion and terror under the reign of the Zealots. Titus and his army did not arrive in Jerusalem until the spring of AD 70. However, even the presence of his army in the city didn't stop the killing between the rival Jewish factions. They killed for food, they killed for money and they killed if anyone even contemplated surrender. Many of those who did surrender were crucified outside the walls of the city so that anyone who was thinking of turning against the Zealots could watch their fellow men die in agony. Eventually famine took its toll on Jerusalem, and it is estimated that more than 600,000 bodies were thrown out of the city.

At the end of the revolt the Jews' holy city and Temple were completely destroyed. A few of the remaining Zealots took refuge at Herod's fortress of Masada, hoping to outlast the Romans. Titus's legion built a fortified wall 20m (6ft) high and more than 3km (2 miles) in length around the fortress. However, the Zealots felt safe in their stronghold and Herod had left extensive storehouses filled with food and water, so they were able to stay there for a long period of time. Over the next seven months, the Romans built a siege ramp against the western side of the mountain. When the ramp was complete a battering ram was hoisted to the top, and the Roman soldiers rammed a hole into the side of the fortress wall. Still the Zealots fought back by fortifying their walls with timber, but the Romans simply set these on fire.

That night the Zealots, along with their leader, Eleazar from Gamla, had a meeting and argued that the only course of action was a mass suicide pact. They knew what the Romans would do to their women and children if they succeeded in breaking into their fortress, and rather than serve anyone other than God, they were prepared to make the ultimate sacrifice.

Every single man killed his family, while ten more were chosen to kill the Jewish soldiers. They chose one out of the ten to kill the remaining Zealots, and then he took his own life, and in so doing the band of revolutionists had the last word and stole victory over the Romans. Only two old women and five children survived the revolt to tell the world their horrific tale.

MODERN-DAY SICARII

The city of Medellin in Colombia has been documented as being one of the most dangerous cities in America. Living there are a modern-day equivalent of the Sicarii, an army of hitmen or 'sicarios', drawn from the poor neighbourhoods in the outer reaches of the city. A drug trafficker named Pablo Escobar formed these squads of hitmen, and in a city of two million, there were an estimated 4,000 violent deaths in 2005. The sicario philosophy was that it was better to live fast and die young, and taking advantage of this, Escobar used these desperate men to do his dirty work, wiping out rival drug dealers, politicians, judges, policemen or indeed anyone that crossed his path.

ALI IBN ABI TALIB

*He who has a thousand friends has not a
friend to spare, and he who has one enemy
will meet him everywhere.*

ALI IBN ABI TALIB

Ali ibn Abi Talib was an early Islamic leader who
was born in Mecca in the Hijaz region of central
western Arabia, *c.*599. Ali was a direct cousin of the
Holy Prophet, Muhammad, and he was raised by
him and brought up like his own son. He lived in an
atmosphere of virtue and piety that was to have a
lasting effect on the young boy. He grew with a
passionate love for truth and Allah and later proved
to be a fearless fighter.

Ali truly loved the Holy Prophet as his own
father and would do anything for him without
bounds. One night when the Holy Prophet was due
to leave for Medina, they discovered that his house
was surrounded by bloodthirsty men of the
Quraish. The Prophet asked Ali if he would sleep in
his bed and cover for him while he crept stealthily
away. Ali was only too pleased to do this for his

beloved Muhammad, and he was even more thrilled that between them they had succeeded in outwitting the Quraish who were waiting to kill the Prophet.

The following morning when the Quraish realized they had been outwitted by a young boy, they decided to make him pay with his life for the part he had played. However, Ali stood unnerved by the threat of death and, shocked by his courage, the Quraish decided to let him go. Ali wanted to follow the Holy Prophet to Medina, but before he could do this he was given the dangerous job of returning all the goods and properties which had been entrusted to Muhammad for safekeeping, to their original owners. Ali also survived this risky mission and then set off for Medina to join the Prophet.

Medina was a small community of Muslim immigrants who were at first extremely poor. They had no land, no houses and basically lived on the charity of the Madinans who had converted to Islam. Ali lived among the peasants and shared in their poverty and hardships.

Ali first proved himself as a soldier in the year 624, when he fought at the Battle of Badr. The emigration of the Holy Prophet to Medina had turned the enemies from Mecca more hostile, and they were constantly thinking how they could overthrow him and put an end to Islam. The Battle of Badr was the most important of the Islamic battles of Destiny and for the first time the followers of the new faith were put to a serious test. This battle laid the foundation of the Islamic State and made the Muslims a force to be reckoned with.

Although Ali already had a very close tie with Muhammad, following his part in the Battle of Badr and his ultimate success, the Holy Prophet offered his daughter, Fatima, to Ali in marriage. She was his youngest and favourite daughter, and Ali realized what a great honour this was. They raised two sons, Hasan and Hussain, both of whom the Holy Prophet loved as his own sons.

Ali stood firm in his support of Muhammad during the years of persecution of Muslims in Mecca and for the ten years that he led the community in Medina, Ali was extremely active in his cousin's armies. He led parties of warriors on raids, carrying messages and obeying the Prophet's orders. Ali became a person of authority and standing within the Muslim community and his skill with a sword put fear in the heart of his enemies.

During the battle of Ohud, Ali stood bravely beside the Prophet. However, the battle did not go well because Muslim archers had left one of the passes undefended, and soon the soldiers were running in fear. A rumour spread quickly that the Messenger of Allah had been killed, and in the midst of all the confusion the Prophet fell into a deep pit that the enemy had covered with twigs and grass. Ali, with no regard for his own safety, pulled him out with the aid of two fellow soldiers. Ali himself had received 17 wounds in this battle, but he and his faithful Fatima tended the wounds of his Prophet before tending to his own needs.

After the fifth year of fighting, all the enemies of Islam joined together and led an enormous army against Medina. The Holy Prophet started to take precautions and ordered that a deep, wide trench be dug around the city to act as fortification. This proved to be successful for a while, until a feared Arabian warrior by the name of Abdwood succeeded in jumping the trench on his horse. Not one of the Prophet's men dared faced this man, but Ali came forward and offered him a fight. It took Ali only a few minutes to overcome his opponent and cut off his head. Ali once again proved that he would stop at nothing in his protection of Muhammad and his unfaltering belief in Allah.

DEATH OF MUHAMMAD

In 632, following several months of ill health, Muhammad returned to his quarters, following prayers at a mosque, and died. Before his body was barely cold, a gathering of Muslims swore allegiance to a man named Abu Bakr as the new leader of the Muslim community. Ali had many supporters, friends and followers who believed that he should have succeeded Muhammad, but Ali had not even been informed of the meeting, nor had his name even been mentioned as the future Caliph.

It is customary when a new Arab chief is declared that the whole community had to give their declaration of allegiance to the new leader. Ali accepted the chosen Caliph without question, but the Shia's believed it should have rightfully gone to Ali as he was the closest and most loyal subject to the late Muhammad. Although Ali had declared Abu Bakr as the Leader, a group formed calling themselves the Shi'tes, who pledged their allegiance to Ali and stated that they wanted him to be the First Caliph. This was when the Muslims ultimately divided into two branches based on their political issue towards this matter – the Shi'tes and the Sunni.

DEATH OF CALIPH UTHMAN

In the year 656, the third caliph, Uthman was murdered in his own house in Medina while reading the Qur'an. The murder was carried out by rebellious Muslim soldiers. From what was once a small, poor town, Medina had now grown into a large city and was in fact capital of an empire that stretched from Africa to Central Asia. The city fell into chaos, and some Muslims turned to Ali for assistance, urging him to seek the caliphate. Ali initially refused their request, as having been horrified by the assassination of Uthman, he did not want to be seen profiting from the situation in any way. However, his supporters pressed him further until Ali finally agreed to be proclaimed caliph.

Some of his opponents at that time claimed that he had been instrumental in the murder of Uthman to further his own cause, but of this there is no proof. Ali was revered by the Sunnis as the last truly exemplary successor of Muhammad, and they held him in very high esteem.

One of Ali's first acts as caliphate was to quell a rebellion led by two eminent associates of Muhammad, who had been edged on by his widow, Aisha. According to the Shi'tes she disliked Ali intently and had tried very hard to stop him being advanced to the position of caliphate.

The resultant fighting culminated in the Battle of Basra. After the battle Ali inspected the battlefield and was distressed to see body after body piled up, the plain literally being soaked with their blood. He felt sickened by the deplorable sight of Muslims having killed Muslims and consequently did not celebrate the victory. Instead he ordered three days of mourning.

After the days of mourning were over, Ali and his men entered the city of Basra. He declared amnesty for the people of Basra, against the wishes of his own men, and asked them to assemble in the city's mosque. Ali made a proclamation that they were all free to return to their homes and that no action would be taken for their sins or any part they had taken in the battle. Aisha, on the other hand, had felt the strain of the battle and humiliation at the failure of her mission. She was escorted back to Medina, where she was offered a pension so long as she took no further part in politics.

Soon after the battle, honestly believing that

many of Uthman's troubles were due to the men that he employed, Ali dismissed several governors, some of whom were relatives of Uthman, and replaced them with trusted aides. He then transferred his capital from Medina to the Muslim city Kufa, in what is now known as Iraq. The governor of Syria, Mu'awiyah, raised an army and marched against Ali, claiming vengeance for the murder of Uthman. A long battle ensued in July 657 near the Euphrates. The Battle of Siffin was turning in Ali's favour, until members of the opposition decided to pin copies of the Qur'an to the tips of their swords, claiming that:

The matter ought to be settled by reference to this book, which forbids Muslims to shed each other's blood.

Ali's soldiers laid down their swords and refused to fight and demanded that the issue be referred to arbitration. Ali and his followers are said to have disagreed over the choice of advocate for Ali, which greatly injured his cause and weakened him in the eyes of his men.

DEATH OF ALI

Ali was attacked on the 19th of Ramadan while performing morning prayers in a mosque in the city of Kufa. Ali suffered a mortal head wound, and the legend says that the sword was tainted with poison.

As he fell Ali was heard to cry, 'By the Lord of Ka'bah, I have succeeded!'

Ali died three days after receiving the head wound and mystery still surrounds the place of his burial. If he had been buried according to Islamic law he would have been interred simply, quickly and close to the place where he died. But many believe that Ali was so concerned that his grave would be desecrated by his enemies, that he requested friends to bury him in a secret location.

THE LAST WILL OF ALI IBN ABI TALIB

Imam Ali's last will to his sons Imam Hasan and Imam Hussain was made after an attempt on his life by Ibn Muljam and it read as follows:

❑ *My advice to you is to be conscious of Allah and steadfast in your religion. Do not yearn for the world, and do not be seduced by it. Do not resent anything you have missed in it. Proclaim the truth; work for the next world. Oppose the oppressor and support the oppressed.*

❑ *I advise you, and all my children, my relatives and whosoever receives this message, to be conscious of Allah, to remove your differences and to strengthen your ties. I heard your grandfather, peace be upon him, say: 'Reconciliation of your differences is more worthy than all prayers and all fasting.'*

❑ *Fear Allah in matters concerning orphans. Attend to their nutrition and do not forget their interests in the middle of yours.*

❑ *Fear Allah in your relations with your neighbours. Your Prophet often recommended them to you, so much so that we thought he would give them a share in inheritance.*

❑ *Remain attached to the Qur'an. Nobody should surpass you in being intent on it, or more sincere in implementing it.*

❑ *Fear Allah in relation to your prayers. It is the pillar of your religion.*

❑ *Fear Allah in relation to His House; do not abandon it as long as you live. It you should do that you would abandon your dignity.*

❑ *Persist in jihad in the cause of Allah, with your money, your souls and your tongue.*

❑ *Maintain communication and exchange of opinion among yourselves. Beware of disunity and enmity. Do not desist from promoting good deeds and cautioning against bad ones. Should you do that, the worst among you would be your leaders, and you will call upon Allah without response.*

❑ *O Children of Abdul Mattaleb! Do not shed the blood of Muslims under the banner: The Imam has been assassinated! Only the assassin should be condemned to death.*

❑ *If I die of this stab of his, kill him with one similar stroke. Do not mutilate him! I have heard the Prophet, peace be upon him, say: 'Mutilate not even a rabid dog.'*

THE ASSASSIN
MOVEMENT

It is a common myth that the word 'assassin' comes from the Arabic word haschishin *for hashish user.*

The Assassin movement or Hashshashin, also known as the 'new propaganda' by its own members, was formed c.1090 when al-Hasan ibn-al-Sabbah established a stronghold in the mountains at Alamut, a region south of the Caspian Sea. The Assassins were a religious sect with a cult following, who specialized in terrorizing the Abbasid elite with politically motivated assassinations. Their motives were most definitely for personal gain and a desire for vengeance. Their own name for the sect was *al-da'wa al-jadida*, which means 'the new doctrine', but among themselves they simply referred to their group as *fedayeen*, which literally means 'he who is ready to sacrifice their life for a cause'.

From their mountain stronghold, al-Hasan and his scant group of followers inspired terror out of all proportion to their numbers. Recruits into the Assassins were promised 'paradise' in return for giving their life in action. To convince them that this was true al-Hasan would have new recruits drugged with materials such as hashish, and then they would be taken to a garden containing beautiful women and a fountain of wine. On arrival at the garden they were awakened from their drug-induced state and told that this is what they would find at the end of their journey if they remained loyal to their leader and cause.

The Assassins had a system of terrorists as well as secret agents who were positioned in enemy camps and cities. They worked closely with leaders of the Muslim states, and they gained a reputation as a reliable source to kill important persons in enemy states. One of the most important of the Muslim allies was the Seljuq ruler of Aleppo, Ridwan. It was with his help that the Assassins were able to set themselves up in the Syrian mountains, where several fortresses were erected. Here they managed to form their own state, and it is said that their influence over Aleppo and his people was immense, and that effectively they ruled the politics and economy of his state for a couple of decades.

The members of the Assassins were organized into classes according to their intelligence, courage and trustworthiness. The highest position held was the Grand Master, and below him were the Grand

Priors, each in charge of a particular district. After these came the ordinary propagandists, and at the lowest level of order came the *fida'is*, who would readily kill at the order of the Grand Master. They underwent both intense physical and educational training. The devoted followers sought martyrdom and followed orders with unquestioned devotion, orders which often included assassination. In fact they became so skilled in the use of the dagger that it is said that they almost made assassination an 'art'.

Out on a mission, the Assassins generally worked alone, and it would be very rare to see more than two working as a team. They usually dressed up as tradesmen or ascetic religious men and spent much of their time in a city in an effort to get well acquainted with the area, as well as the daily routines of their future victim. The actual murder was always performed with a dagger and in full public view, and they often chose to carry out the assassination inside a mosque on a Friday when it was full of worshippers. By doing it this way, the information about the assassination was soon widespread, which increased the fear of the people, and the Assassins' inherent power over them. Because they chose to carry out the act in public, it was normal for the Assassin himself to be killed immediately after the murder by guards of their victim.

Information regarding this secretive group of assassins is quite limited because all Assassin books and records were destroyed when the fortress was eventually seized in 1256. It is known, however, that the Assassins mainly targeted Sunni Muslims and in the year 1092 the Muslim world was plunged into terror with the assassination of an illustrious sultan by the name of Nizam-al-Mulk.

Saladin, a great Muslim leader, whose real name was Salah al-Din Yusuf, considered himself as a title-holder of the Sunni orthodoxy, and on two occasions in the mid-1170s the Assassins attempted to take his life. The first attempt took place while Saladin was besieging Aleppo, and a number of Assassins penetrated the camp of Ayyubid on a cold wintry day. However, their plan was foiled when the emir of Abu Qubasis recognized some of the men from the sect. Feeling suspicious about their presence on his land, Qubasis approached the men, but they killed him before he had time to question their activities. The Assassins continued in the quest to reach Saladin, but the alarm had already been raised, and although members of his entourage were slain, Saladin managed to escape unharmed.

A second attempt was made on his life during the siege of the town of Azaz. Several of the Assassins disguised themselves as members of Saladin's army and even distinguished themselves in several military operations. Saladin decided to reward some of his soldiers for bravery and arranged an inspection of his artillerymen. As he walked among his men, an Assassin sprang from the ranks and struck Saladin with a dagger, but the blow only glanced off his steel helmet. Saladin managed to throw his attacker to the ground, where he was cut to pieces by his loyal men. A second, third and fourth Assassin came forward in an attempt to kill their target, but these two were overcome by Saladin's men, although several of his emirs were killed in the struggle. After these attempts Saladin decided to increase his security arrangements and started to sleep in a wooden tower that could only be reached by a rope ladder, which was pulled up by the occupant, making him a much more difficult target.

Incensed by these unsuccessful attempts made on his life, Saladin decided to attack the Assassin stronghold of Masyaf. However, after several mysterious warnings from the Grand Master himself, Saladin lifted the siege and attempted to maintain good relations with the sect. Legend has it that the sect's leader, referred to as the 'Old Man', actually stole into Saladin's tent, leaving a poisoned cake and a note on his chest as he slept, with the message 'You are in our power'. Another account is that a letter was sent to Saladin's maternal uncle, swearing that the entire royal line would be wiped out. Maybe these were just idle threats, but whatever the truth is behind these mysterious threats, Saladin certainly heeded these warnings and took no further action.

It appears that Christians were largely untouched by the Assassins, and it was not until the middle of the 12th century that they had even heard of the strange sect. However, Raymond II of Tripoli and

Conrad of Montferrat, King of Jerusalem, were both victims of their attacks. It is thought that the assassins of Conrad could possibly have been hired by Richard the Lionheart.

Conrad was attacked by two Hashshashin, who, dressed as monks, stabbed him in the side and back when he was returning home after visiting his friend, Philip, Bishop of Beauvais. Apparently they had waited six months for an opportune moment to carry out the assassination. He was taken home by his guards, who managed to kill one of his attackers and capture the other. Conrad received the last rites before dying of his wounds and on his deathbed, he urged his wife Isabella to give the city over to Richard the Lionheart, although this story has been disputed. According to Saladin's envoy the two Assassins confessed under torture that Richard was the instigator, and this was widely believed among the Franks, especially when Richard's friend Count Henry of Champagne married Conrad's widow and succeeded to the throne. This information is of course impossible to prove as fact. If, however, Saladin was responsible he did not live to profit from his action because he died the following year, in March.

The Assassins made a firm footing in Syria, and watched the consolidation of the fragmented states and the old Fatimid Empire of Cairo into a single state with great apprehension. They preferred that the Arab states of Syria remain fragmented so that they could play their potential enemies off one another, ensuring that their own power remain on a similar level to that of their rivals.

Following the capture of Masyad in 1260 by the Mongols, the Mamluk Sultan Baybars in 1272 dealt the Syrian branch of the Assassins a final blow. Following that attack, the Assassins were estimated to be around 150,000 in number, but they were sparsely scattered through Syria, Persia, Zanzibar and India and went by the name of Thojas or Mowlas.

THE MODERN EQUIVALENT

There have been comparisons made between the historical Assassin movement and al-Qaeda, possibly because the similarity between their tactics of using terror and political assassinations, and also their promise of reaching 'paradise' following their mission. Al-Qaeda, like the Assassins, is a truly secretive society whose leaders are purportedly hiding in mountain hideouts, with martyrdom as one of their key tactics. However, the Assassins, unlike al-Qaeda, were not known to target innocent civilians.

PART TWO

1600–1899

THE
GUNPOWDER PLOT

Remember remember the fifth of November
Gunpowder, treason and plot.
I see no reason why gunpowder, treason
Should ever be forgot . . .

More than 400 years after the event the Gunpowder Plot and Guy Fawkes are still remembered. The nursery rhyme above continues to remind us why on the night of November 5 bonfires are lit in almost every town and village in Britain, accompanied by a spectacular display of fireworks. But how many people really know why we follow this ritual and burn an effigy, or 'guy', on this day each year.

In truth the Gunpowder Plot of 1605 was nothing short of a desperate, but failed, attempt by a group of English Catholics to kill James I of England, his family, and as many of the Protestant aristocracy as they could in one attack. This attack was aimed at the Houses of Parliament during the State Opening, at which they hoped to create the most carnage.

Following the death of Queen Elizabeth I in 1603, Catholics in England, who had been persecuted under her rule, had hoped that James I, her successor, would be more tolerant of their beliefs. But much to their horror, James I proved no more tolerant than the previous Queen, and so it was that a band of men, 13 in total, decided that violence was the only answer to make their cause heard.

THE CONSPIRATORS

Under the leadership of a man named Robert Catesby, a small group banded together. Among his fellow conspirators were:

Guido (Guy) Fawkes
Thomas Wintour
Thomas Percy
Thomas Bates
Christopher Wright
Robert Wintour
John Grant
John Wright
Robert Keyes
Ambrose Rookwood
Sir Everard Digby
Francis Tresham

In May 1604, Thomas Percy rented a house that was adjacent to the House of Lords. Their plan was to dig a tunnel underneath the foundations of the House of Lords and plant some gunpowder. Guido Fawkes, or Guy as he has become better known, was an explosives expert with considerable military experience. He had been introduced to Robert Catesby by a man named Hugh Owen. Although their plans to blow up the Houses of Parliament were known by a Jesuit priest, Father Henry Garnet – as he had learned of the plot through confession – he felt bound not to reveal their activities to the authorities. Despite his pleadings and protestations, the plot went ahead, but Garnet's opposition to the plan still did not prevent him from later being hanged, drawn and quartered for treason.

For a while the group of men laboured away digging a tunnel to come out underneath the Houses of Parliament. However, the men were not used to such physical exercise and their progress was exceptionally slow. During the summer of 1604 London was hit by a particularly severe bout of the plague, and as a result the Opening of Parliament was suspended until 1605. By Christmas Eve the men had still not dug their tunnel anywhere near to the Houses of Parliament, and when they learned that the Opening had been still further postponed to October 3, the plotters decided to take advantage of the time and row the barrels of gunpowder up the River Thames from Lambeth and conceal it in their rented house. It was then that they heard by pure chance, that there was an empty coal cellar coming up for lease in a prime location.

Abandoning their original plan, in March 1605, Thomas Percy, using connections he had in the Royal Court, was able to rent the cellar, which turned out to be directly under the House of Lords. Fawkes, posing as Percy's servant under the pseudonym 'John Johnson', filled the underground storeroom with 36 barrels of gunpowder. He secreted them underneath a pile of coal and wooden sticks that had been stored there for use as fuel when the weather turned cold. The barrels themselves contained more than 800 kg (1,800 lbs) of gunpowder and, had everything gone to plan, not only would it have destroyed the entire Houses of Parliament, but it would have blown out windows in the surrounding area within a 1km (½ mile) radius.

Everything was in place, and all the conspirators had to do now was to sit and wait. They decided it would be safer to split up as it would only cause suspicion if they were regularly seen together. So they left London in May and went to their various houses, or to different parts of the country to bide their time. The plan was to all meet up again in September, but once again they learned that the Opening of Parliament was to be postponed further.

Possibly the group of men had made their plans too early, or perhaps it was because of the many delays, but it would appear that their eventual downfall would be one of their own men Francis Tresham, who spilled the beans.

Just ten days before the Opening of Parliament, Lord Monteagle received a letter that read:

> *My lord, out of the love I bear for some of your friends, I have a care for your preservation. Therefore I would advise you, as you tender your life, to devise some excuse to shift of your attendance of this Parliament, for God and man hath concurred to punish the wickedness of this time. And think not slightly of this advertisement but retire yourself into your country, where you may expect the event in safety, for though there be no appearance of any stir, yet I say they shall receive a terrible blow, the Parliament, and yet they shall not see who hurts them . . . This counsel is not to be contemned, because it may do you good and can do you know harm, for the danger is past as soon as you have burnt the latter: and I hope God will give you the grace to make good use of it, to whose holy protection I commend you.*

Although the writer of this letter has never been identified for certain, Francis Tresham was Lord Monteagle's brother-in-law and was most likely to have been the perpetrator.

Concerned about the contents of the letter Lord Monteagle showed it to Robert Cecil, the Earl of Salisbury and Secretary of State. Thinking at first that it was just a hoax, the Privy Council were slow to have the vaults under the House of Lords searched. Therefore, it wasn't until the evening of November 4 that the cellar was searched, firstly by the Earl of Suffolk and then, later the same evening, by Sir Thomas Knyvett. Keeping his composure until the end, Guy Fawkes casually let the officials into Percy's rented cellar. Still posing as Mr John Johnson, Fawkes was searched and found to be carrying a watch, slow matches and touchpaper. It didn't take long for them to uncover the gunpowder barrels, and Guy Fawkes was taken into custody. Far from denying his intentions, Fawkes stated quite proudly that their sole purpose had been to destroy the King and his Parliament.

Fawkes was taken into the bed chamber of the King, who assembled all his ministers even though it was one o'clock in the morning. During his interrogation, Fawkes never once tried to make a secret of his intentions, and he maintained an attitude of defiance throughout. Later the same morning Fawkes was summoned again and questioned about his accomplices, in particular the involvement of Thomas Percy. When he wasn't forthcoming, Fawkes was taken to the Tower of London and interrogated further with the use of torture. At this time the use of torture was forbidden unless under direct instructions from the monarch or the Privy Council. In a letter dated November 6, King James I stated:

> *The gentler tortours are to be first used unto him,* et sic per gradus ad maiora tenditur

> *[and thus by increase to the worst], and so*
> *God speed your goode worke.*

Fawkes was strong to the end and resisted giving any information until he eventually succumbed to the torture on November 8 by giving the names of his fellow conspirators. He made a full statement about their plot on November 9, and on November 10 he gave a signed confession, although his signature was barely legible due to his terrible state following his sessions on the torture rack.

As soon as Robert Catesby and Thomas Wintour learned that their plans had been foiled, they fled to Warwickshire to meet up with the remainder of the party. Failing to rally any support for their Catholic cause, they only managed to stay in hiding for a few days in the houses of friends and sympathizers. On the third day they were captured in a bloody raid on Holbeche House in Staffordshire. Catesby, Percy and the two Wright brothers were both killed, while Thomas Wintour and Ambrose Rokewood, who had both been wounded in the raid, were taken away to London to be questioned. The remainder were captured a few days later, although Robert Wintour managed to stay at large for about two months, before being captured at Hagley Park.

The conspirators were tried on January 27, 1606, in Westminster Hall. All of the men pleaded not guilty with the exception of Everard Digby, who attempted to defend himself by saying that it was because the King had gone back on a promise regarding Catholic tolerance. The trial only lasted one day and the verdict was never in doubt – guilty as charged. The trial was very popular as a public spectacle and there are records that people paid as much as 10 shillings to attend. Four of the conspirators were executed in St Paul's Churchyard on January 30 and the following day Fawkes, Winter and a number of others who had been implicated in the plot were taken to the Old Palace Yard in Westminster, where they were hanged, drawn and quartered. Francis Tresham the only one of the original 13 left alive, died while still a prisoner in the Tower of London.

IMPACT OF THE PLOT

For the Catholics living in England the Gunpowder Plot truly backfired, as it halted any moves towards Emancipation of the Catholics. It would be another 200 years before the Catholics would receive equal rights.

Of course most people remember Guy Fawkes and the Gunpowder Plot by celebrations that take place on November 5, or Bonfire Night as it has now become known. An Act of Parliament was passed to appoint that date in each year as a day of thanksgiving for 'the joyful day of deliverance', and this Act remained in force until 1859. Legend says that on November 5, 1605, the people of London celebrated the defeat of the plot by lighting fires and holding street parties. It is still a custom in Britain to let off fireworks and burn an effigy of Guy Fawkes on November 5, and in certain areas, for example Lewes and Battle in East Sussex, there are extensive processions to accompany an enormous bonfire.

The Houses of Parliament are still searched today by the Yeoman of the Guard before any Opening of Parliment, which since 1928 has been held in the month of November. However, this is upheld today due to a rather quaint custom rather than to stop any serious antiterrorist precaution.

The original cellar in which Guy Fawkes placed his gunpowder barrels was damaged by fire in 1834, and it was totally destroyed when they rebuilt the Palace of Westminster in the 19th century. The lantern that Guy Fawkes carried to light his way to the cellar can be seen in the Ashmolean Museum in Oxford.

THE BOSTON
TEA PARTY

*I shall therefore conclude with a proposal
that your watchmen be instructed, as they
go on their rounds, to call out every night,
half-past twelve, 'Beware of the East India
Company'.*

FROM A PAMPHLET SIGNED BY 'RUSTICUS', 1773

The Boston Tea Party was a demonstration by
American colonists against Great Britain's decision
to put a heavy tax on tea. Britain's part in both the
French and Indian War had been a very costly
exercise, so when the war came to an end in 1763,
King George III and his government needed to find
ways of recouping their losses. They looked at
taxing the American colonies and a series of actions,
including the Stamp Act of 1765, the Townsend
Acts of 1767 and the Boston Massacre of 1770,

angered the colonists and strained the relationship of the two countries. The final straw was Britain's attempt to tax tea, which spurred the colonists into action. The incident, known as the Boston Tea Party, took place on December 16, 1773, and is said to have been a contributory factor to the American Revolution.

The colonies refused to comply with the levies enforced by the Townsend Act, saying they had no obligation to pay taxes to a government in which they had no representatives. One of the main protesters was a man named John Hancock. Parliament decided to retract the taxes, with the exception of the duty they had imposed on tea.

In the year 1773, Britain's East India Company was sitting on enormous stocks of tea that they were unable to sell in England, and it was on the verge of going bankrupt. In an effort to save the company, the government passed the Tea Act, which gave them the right to export its merchandise directly to the colonies without having to pay any of the taxes imposed on the Americans. This meant that they could undersell the American merchants and monopolize the colonial tea trade.

Naively, the British government thought this would appease the situation because Americans would now be able to get their tea at a cheaper rate. However, what they overlooked was the fact that the colonists were not prepared to pay the duty on imported tea, because then they would be agreeing to unrepresentational taxation. Even though tea was a staple diet to the colonists, they were not fooled by the British government's ploy, and when the East India Company sent shipments of tea to Philadelphia and New York, the colonists would not allow their ships to land.

The only place the ships were allowed to dock was Boston, because there the East India Company had the assistance of the British-appointed governor, who arranged for the tea to be landed with the aid of British armed ships. The inhabitants of Boston were furious after failing to turn back three ships – the *Dartmouth*, the *Eleanor* and the *Beaver* – in the harbour, and it all came to a head on the evening of December 16, 1773.

The Tea Act required that the requisite tax be collected within 20 days of a ship's arrival in port, which made December 16 the deadline. It was at this time that a man named Samuel Adams came to the fore. He began to question the fairness of the laws imposed by the governor, who was appointed by the British government. Adams and his father spent several years trying to prevent British officials from taking their home and land. Adams believed the colonists had a right to elect their own government officials, and he began to convince others about their rights for fairness, justice and representation. He wrote newspaper articles and essays and promoted his ideas at taverns and meetings. As a result he formed the Country Party, which included farmers who supported his ideas.

Adams kept public passion high by holding

meetings in the Old South Meeting House, and as many as 5,000 people filled the surrounding streets. At one of these gatherings, a resolution was adopted that asked the consignees to return the tea to England. However some of the tea agents were relatives of the governor and refused to comply. On December 16, the owner of the *Dartmouth*, who sympathized with their plight, agreed to sail his ship back to England. This opportunity to ease tensions was abruptly ended, however, when British officials denied permission for the ship to clear the port and began preparations to seize the vessel for non-payment of tax.

This was when the men took the matter into their own hands. Three groups of 50 Boston residents – calling themselves the Sons of Liberty – burst out of the Old South Meeting House and headed towards Griffin's Wharf. Masquerading as Mohawks they passed through a large crowd of spectators that had gathered on the docks and boarded the three ships waiting at the wharf. The ships were loaded with hundreds of crates of tea, and the raiders opened all the hatches and took out the tea chests and threw them overboard, first cutting and splitting the chests open with their tomahawks. By 9 o'clock that evening they had opened 342 crates of tea and thrown the contents into the water of the Boston Harbour. Even though the harbour was surrounded by British armed ships, no attempt was made to stop the raids. After rampage, the leader of the groups made the men remove their shoes, wash and sweep the decks, and also made the first mate agree to say that the Sons of Liberty had only destroyed the tea and nothing else. The whole event was remarkably peaceful and the next day, the raiders even sent a man to one of the ships to repair a padlock that had been broken the evening before.

The following morning it was discovered that large quantities of the tea were still floating on the surface of the water, and to prevent the possibility of any of it being saved, a number of small boats were rowed out into the harbour and the inhabitants beat the surface of the water with their oars so that the tea was thoroughly drenched in sea water.

Soon the news of the Boston Tea Party spread and other seaports followed their example and held similar acts of resistance.

When the people of Boston refused to pay for the tea they had destroyed, the British government responded by closing the port of Boston. On top of this, in 1774, they introduced the Restraining Acts, or Coercive Acts as they were popularly known in England, which sparked off new resistance up and down the coast of America. It was these new acts, instigated by Lord North with the backing of George III, which led to the American Revolution. Some members of parliament voiced their opinions that these stern measures would lead to something far worse, but their advice went unheeded.

The Boston Tea Party, however, was not a futile reaction to Britain's unfair taxes because it received a lot of backing and served to rally support for revolutionaries in the 13 colonies. These colonies were eventually successful in their fight for independence.

Samuel Adams continued to represent the people of Boston, and ultimately became president of the Massachusetts Senate. He voted for the Constitution in 1788, and he strongly supported the need for a bill of rights. He spent the rest of his life as a voice for reform. Adams died in Boston in 1803. His strong belief in independence and his ability to persuade support for the cause of freedom earned him the name 'the Father of the American Revolution'.

JOHN BROWN'S FIGHT AGAINST SLAVERY

John Brown's zeal in the cause of freedom was infinitely superior to mine. Mine was as the taper light; his was as the burning sun. I could live for the slave; John Brown could die for him.

FREDERICK DOUGLASS

John Brown is remembered as being a man of action; a man who declared eternal war on slavery; a man who would not be deterred from his mission of abolishing slavery; a man who would let nothing stand in his way.

John Brown was born on May 9, 1800, into a deeply religious family. His father was a vehement abolitionist and when John was only five the family moved from Torrington, Connecticut, to northern

Ohio, an area that would become famous for its anti-slavery views. The views of his father had a lasting effect on the young Brown, who believed that his main education came from his own life experiences. He had very little formal education, and when he did go to school he hated all the restraints that went along with it. Often brawling with fellow classmates, Brown spent a lot of his youth in solitude, and when he was only 12 years old his family entrusted him with the safe transportation of their cattle hundreds of miles away. He was a lone soul and resolutely carried out his task until they arrived safely at their destination.

One incident in Brown's adolescence had a very profound effect on him. As usual Brown had been travelling around the country, and in the year 1812 he stopped at a house to ask the master if he would be kind enough to give him a meal and a bed for the night. While he was in the house Brown met a small black slave boy who was a similar age to himself. He watched in horror as the scantily clad youth was verbally abused by the man who had been kind enough to take Brown in. Brown was confused: why should the man show him kindness, and yet beat this young black boy who was so obviously an orphan?

In 1820 Brown married Dianthe Lusk and for most of their married life they lived on the western slopes of the Alleghenies, where Brown worked as a tanner. Together they had seven children, but she died during the birth of their eighth. In 1833 he married his second wife, Mary Ann Day, with whom he had 13 more children, although only six lived to be adults.

During his adult life Brown had always been involved in the abolitionist movement, although his feelings did not run very deep in the early years. He started to become more and more involved, but he was frustrated with how little action the movement actually took towards freeing slaves. In 1839 a black preacher spurred him into action by telling him of all the verbal abuse and injustice that he had put up with over the years. It was after that conversation with the preacher that John Brown decided to dedicate his life to fighting slavery, and to do this he enlisted the help of his entire family.

It was at this point in his life that Brown knew what his mission was to be, and with each tale of torment he heard, his determination grew stronger. Wanting to learn more about the abolition movement, in 1845 Brown started studying the history of the insurrection. After just one year of studying it is thought that the attack that took place at Harper's Ferry later in his life was already starting to formulate in his head.

Despite his contributions to the antislavery cause, Brown did not emerge as a significant figure until 1855, when he followed five of his sons to the Kansas territory. This new territory offered brand new land and a call for:

*All lovers of freedom who desired homes in a
new region to go there as settlers, and by their
votes save Kansas from the curse of slavery.*

DU BOIS 127

When Brown was on his way to Kansas he stopped to take part in an antislavery convention in New York State. It was here that he solicited weapons and funds, and where he managed to obtain guns, ammunition and swords from sympathetic free-state supporters. Once in Kansas, Brown became a leading figure in the fight against slavery, and the immediate result was conflict and bloodshed. From the very moment he entered the territory, John Brown was itching for a fight and on May 21–22, 1856, a group of proslavery agitators attacked the town of Lawrence, burning buildings and killing two men.

The following year Brown went to a proslavery town and brutally killed five of its settlers in retribution for another attack. For the remainder of that year Brown and his sons continued to fight for their cause. It is estimated that between November 1855 and December 1856 around 200 men were killed and about two million dollars' worth of property was destroyed in the territory.

For fear of being caught Brown went into hiding. Meanwhile two of his sons, who weren't even involved in the fighting, were arrested. They were eventually set free but were apparently severely mistreated during their confinement. This only added fuel to the fire, and made Brown more committed to being at the centre of the abolitionist movement.

GATHERING FORCES

By November 1856, Brown was running out of funds and had to return to the East Coast. He travelled around New England for the next couple of years gathering as much money together as he could. He befriended a prominent Boston merchant by the name of Amos Adams Lawrence, who contributed a considerable amount into his fund. Brown was also introduced to several influential abolitionists who agreed to offer him financial support for his activities, and they were the ones who would eventually provide the funds for Harper's Ferry. These supporters became known as the Secret Six and the Committee of the Six. Over the years Brown often asked for their assistance, but it is unclear as to how much these supporters actually knew. Brown spent the entire summer of 1856 gathering funds, weapons and recruits, and in August he and his supporters fought with settlers at Osawatomie, where his son Frederick was killed.

I will die fighting for this cause. There will be no peace in this land until slavery is done fore.

In early 1857 Brown headed east with plans to invade the south. He gathered more supporters and started vigorous training. He held meetings with eastern abolitionists, and in early 1858 Brown sent his son John Jr to find out more about the country around Harper's Ferry, which was the site of a Federal arsenal.

RAID ON HARPER'S FERRY

On June 3, 1859, John Brown arrived at Harper's Ferry and, using the name of Isaac Smith, he rented a farmhouse in nearby Maryland. He waited patiently for his recruits to join him, but there were fewer than he had expected. In August he met with a man named Frederick Douglass, one of the foremost leaders of the abolitionist movement, and told him of his plans to raid Harper's Ferry. Douglass had many reservations about Brown's plan and declined any offer to join his mission.

Brown's final band of men only numbered 21 (16 white and five black), ranging in age from 21 to 49. On the night of October 16, 1859, Brown and 18 of his men set out for Harper's Ferry, leaving three men behind to guard the farmhouse. The plan was to raid the armoury, a large complex of buildings, which they estimated to contain around 100,000 muskets and rifles. Brown planned to seize the weapons and distribute them among the local slaves before they headed south, hoping this would encourage a general revolution.

At first the raid went well, and the band of men met no resistance as they headed into town. They cut telegraph wires so that no alarm could be raised and entered the armoury easily, as it was only being guarded by one watchman. Next they rounded up hostages from surrounding farms, one of whom, Colonel Lewis Washington, was the great-grand-nephew of George Washington. They spread the news to the local slaves that they would soon be free and told them to be ready to leave. However, things started to go awry when a Baltimore and Ohio train pulled into the town. Seeing the band of men, the train's baggage master attempted to warn his passengers, but Brown's met shouted at him to stop and then opened fire.

Their first victim was the baggage master himself, Hayward Shepherd, who ironically was a free black man not affected by any of the restrictions of slavery. For some unexplained reason, following the killing of Shepherd, Brown allowed the train to continue its journey, and consequently the news of the raid on the armoury reached Washington by the next morning.

Back at the armoury, Brown's men took prisoner an armoury clerk, John Daingerfield, who had arrived for work. He was taken to the guardhouse where he joined the other hostages.

News had spread like wildfire of the men holding the armoury and local residents including farmers and shopkeepers, and militia came out in force and held the men in the armoury by firing from high points behind the town. Some of the locals were shot, and of course it was impossible for them to get hold of any further arms or ammunition as the arsenal was being closely guarded by Brown's men. By noon a company of militiamen blockaded the bridge, which was Brown's only escape route. Brown decided to move his men and prisoners into the engine house, which was a small brick building next to the armoury. They barricaded the doors and windows and knocked holes in the brick walls so that they could fire at the encroaching army. Completely surrounded and outnumbered Brown begrudgingly sent his son Watson and another of his men out carrying a white flag of surrender. But the crowd were angry and they shot them, which caused another bout of shooting, in which Brown's son Oliver was wounded. By nightfall Brown's group of men were trapped in the engine house, and all but five were wounded. That night 90 marines arrived from Washington to assist in the fight against Brown.

By the morning of October 18 the engine house, which later became known as John Brown's Fort, was surrounded by the marines. They were informed that if they surrendered their lives would be spared, but Brown refused and said that he would prefer to die than give up. The marines stormed the building, using sledge hammers and a makeshift battering ram to break down the door. During the ensuing chaos one of the marines, a Lieutenant Green, cornered Brown and thrust him so hard with his sword that his body actually left the ground and broke the soldier's sword. His life was spared, however, because the sword luckily struck his belt. Brown fell forward from the force of the attack, and Green subsequently struck him several times wounding his head.

In total, Brown's men killed four people and wounded a further nine. Ten of Brown's men were killed, including his two sons Watson and Oliver, seven were captured along with Brown, and five managed to escape, including his son Owen.

Brown and his men were held in the office at the armoury and questioned for three hours before being taken to a jail at Charles Town to await trial.

TRIAL AND SENTENCE

It was October 27 when a doctor pronounced that Brown was fit enough to stand trial. He was charged with murdering four whites and a black, conspiring with slaves to rebel and with treason against Virginia. Following a week-long trial, and 45 minutes of deliberation, the jury at Charles Town found John Brown guilty on all three counts. He was sentenced to be hanged in public on December 2, 1859, along with four of his men.

Following the hearing of his sentence, Brown was allowed to make one last address to the court:

> . . . I believe to have interfered as I have done
> . . . in behalf of His despised poor, was not
> wrong, but right. Now, if it be deemed
> necessary that I should forfeit my life for the

> *furtherance of the ends of justice, and mingle*
> *my blood further with the blood of my*
> *children, and with the blood of millions in*
> *this slave country whose rights are*
> *disregarded by wicked, cruel and unjust*
> *enactments, I submit: so let it be done.*

The month that Brown spent in jail awaiting his forthcoming hanging, he received and sent letters. A friend of Brown's from Kansas, Silas Soule, somehow managed to gain access into the prison, but when he tried to rescue his friend, Brown told him that he was ready to die as a martyr and Silas left him to his fate. The letters that Brown wrote were soon picked up by the local press, and his unfaltering beliefs and support for abolition gained him increasing numbers of supporters in the North, while infuriating the population of the South.

Brown's loyal wife joined him for his last meal on December 1, but when they denied her permission to spend the night with her husband, it was the only time that John Brown was seen to lose his composure throughout the whole ordeal.

On the morning of December 2, Brown wrote a final letter to his wife which included his will, and then sat down and read his Bible. At 11 o'clock he was escorted through the crowds. Among the crowds was John Wilkes Booth, who is best known today as the assassin of President Abraham Lincoln. He had borrowed a militia uniform and stood guard during the execution. Brown refused the offer of a minister at the final hour, due to the fact that he had consistently rejected the ministrations of proslavery clergy. On his way to the gallows, Brown handed his jailer a note which read:

> *I John Brown am now quite certain that the crimes of this guilty land: will never be purged away; but with Blood.*

Drawing strength from his own principles, John Brown was hanged at 11.15 a.m. As a last gesture of Southern contempt his body was placed in a basic wooden coffin with the noose still around his neck.

THE LEGEND

News of John Brown's exploits shocked the nation. Many praised him for his fight against slavery, while others considered he had committed an evil crime. Many of Brown's friends sent letters to Governor Wise of Virginia, but he chose to ignore them. The end of slavery of the United States came with the end of the Civil War in 1865. The war was fought to decide whether or not to allow slavery into the new territories and also in an effort to prevent the southern states from leaving the Union and forming an independent nation. People throughout the North gathered to mourn Brown, and church bells tolled throughout the region at the hour of his execution.

John Brown was buried in North Elba and was

considered a hero among abolitionists. Already a legend, in 1861 a song was written about him called 'John Brown's Body', which was set to the music of an old hymn:

John Brown's body lies a-mouldering in the grave,
John Brown's body lies a-mouldering in the grave,
But his soul goes marching on.

Chorus:
Glory, glory, hallelujah,
Glory, glory, hallelujah,
His soul goes marching on.

He's gone to be a soldier in the Army of the Lord,
He's gone to be a soldier in the Army of the Lord,
His soul goes marching on.
Chorus:

John Brown's knapsack is strapped upon his back,
John Brown's knapsack is strapped upon his back,
His soul goes marching on.
Chorus:

John Brown died that the slaves might be free,
John Brown died that the slaves might be free,
His soul goes marching on.
Chorus:

The stars above in Heaven now are looking
    kindly down,

The stars above in Heaven now are looking
  kindly down,
His soul goes marching on.
Chorus:

POGROMS IN ODESSA

We saw a procession of peasants and townspeople, led by priests, carrying crosses and banners and images. We lived in fear till the end of the day, knowing that the least disturbance might start a riot, and a riot led to a pogrom.

MARY ANTIN (1881–1949)

The Russian word *pogrom* literally means 'an outbreak of mass violence directed against a minority religious, ethnic or social group'. The *Oxford English Dictionary* records the first use of the word on March 17, 1882, when the *Times* stated 'That the *Pogromen* [riots against the Jews] must be stopped . . .' and gave the full definition as 'an organized massacre in Russia for the destruction or annihilation of any body or class: orig. and esp. applied to those direction against the Jews'.

Before 1881 anti-Jewish violence in the Russian Empire was hardly ever heard of, being confined largely to the ever-expanding area of Odessa. In Odessa, two rival ethnic communities, the Greeks and the Jews, lived side by side and it was obvious that it wouldn't be long before there would be some form of friction.

It was the assassination of Tsar Alexander II in 1881 that threw the Russian government into chaos and directly preceded the first major outbreak of pogroms. The first pogrom flared up in Elizavetgrad when the new Tsar Alexander III blamed the Jews for having murdered his father. He issued a decree instructing the people to beat and plunder the Jews. Thousands of Jewish homes were destroyed, many families were reduced to exceptional poverty, women were sexually assaulted, and many men, women and children were injured in the frenzied attacks. After Elizavetgrad, a wave of pogroms spread throughout the southwestern regions, and in the first year there were at least 200 such riots.

The authorities turned a blind eye to the pogroms, feeling that the pogromists were justified in their actions, and the riots continued for more than three years. It was widely believed by many of the Jewish contemporaries that the pogroms could possibly have been organized or directed by the government itself, given their wide range and duration. However, in 1882 the new tsar, believing that the pogroms were not the result of revolutionary fervour but the action of the Jews themselves, issued a series of harsh restrictions on the Jewish community. These laws prohibited new Jewish settlement outside towns, or *shtetles*, prohibited Jews from buying property in the country, and also banned Jews from trading on Sundays or any Christian holidays. These new laws, instead of preventing further pogroms, instigated a new spread of violence and regular pogrom outbreaks lasted until June 7, 1884, culminating in a particularly vicious one in Nizhnii Novgorod, where the victims were killed with axes and thrown from the rooftops.

Situated at the centre of Odessa was the marketplace, and it was here that the pogroms of 1871 and 1881 took place. Throughout the market, Jewish stallholders were beaten, their stalls, stands and shops raided, and their goods were either stolen or destroyed. The pogrom spread to other parts of the city where the Jews were known to live or where they had businesses, schools and synagogues. The rioters broke into their houses, smashing windows, forcing doors open, destroying furniture and ripping open feather pillows and mattresses, a somewhat traditional, if pointless, element of the pogroms. Once again the government seemed to turn their backs on these outbursts, and only occasionally did they send an army in to dampen down the hostility.

An even worse wave of pogroms broke out during the years 1903–06, in which an estimated 2,000 Jews were killed and many more wounded. *The New York Times* described the first Kishinev pogrom that took place during Easter 1903 in the following way:

> *The anti-Jewish riots in Kishinev, Bessarabia, are worse than the censor will permit to publish. There was a well laid-out plan for the general massacre of Jews on the day following the Russian Easter. The mob was led by priests, and the general cry, 'Kill the Jews', was taken up all over the city. The Jews were taken wholly unaware and were slaughtered like sheep. The dead number 120* [Note: the actual number of dead was 47–48] *and the injured about 500. The scenes of horror attending this massacre are beyond description. Babes were literally torn to pieces by the frenzies and blood-thirsty mob. The local police made no attempt to check the reign of terror. At sunset the streets were piled with corpses and wounded. Those who could make their escape fled in terror, and the city is now practically deserted of Jews.*

The worst pogrom in the history of Jewish Odessa took place in October 1905, after Tsar Nicholas II was forced to sign the October Manifesto, which created a constitutional monarchy. At this time there were an estimated 175,000 Jews living inside the city of Odessa. The program enveloped the whole of the city and spread from the central streets to the outlying districts, predominantly Moldovanka, which was known to have a large and impoverished Jewish population. The riot lasted for three days and nights, and the frenzied crowds robbed shops, destroyed houses, tortured and killed Jews with knives, daggers and firearms, in fact nobody was spared, not even the women, elderly or children. This pogrom took 299 victims, the youngest of whom was one year old and the eldest 85. Thousands managed to escape to the city's hospital, which was surrounded by solid stone walls, and this was where the wounded were brought for treatment. Following this last pogrom there was a considerable increase in the emigration of Jews out of Odessa.

Pogroms continued during the Revolution of 1917 and the ensuing Russian Civil War, and it is estimated that a further 70,000 to 250,000 Jewish civilians were slaughtered in the atrocities throughout the former Russian Empire. After the Civil War pogroms slowly died out, but anti-Semitism still persists in certain areas to this very day.

LASTING EFFECT

The horrendous pogroms of the 1880s caused public outcry throughout the world and, along with the harsh laws that had been imposed, they were instrumental in the mass emigration of Jews. Around two million Jews fled the Russian Empire between the years 1880 and 1914, many of whom made the United States their home. Also as a result of the pogroms, Jews became more politically active. The Bund, otherwise known as the General Jewish Labour Union, and the Jewish participation in the Bolshevik movements were a direct repercussion to the riots. Pogroms were also instrumental in the forming of *Hibbat Zion*, a pre-Zionist movement advocating the revival of Jewish life in the Land of Israel. Its adherents worked towards the physical development of the land and founded agricultural settlements in Palestine. By the time the First Zionist Congress met in 1897, they had already begun to transform the face of the Holy Land.

ASSASSINATION OF TSAR ALEXANDER II

*It is better to abolish serfdom from above than
to wait for it to abolish itself from below.*
ALEXANDER II OF RUSSIA

Alexander was the eldest son of Tsar Nicholas I and
was born on April 17, 1818, in Moscow. His mother
was Charlotte of Prussia, daughter of Frederick
William III of Prussia. In his early years he showed
no aptitude towards politics, and indeed right up
until the time of his accession in 1855, he showed no
real potential for the duties required in his future role.

During his early years, poverty was rife in St
Petersburg, compared to the riches of the royal
court. Freedom of thought or indeed political
innovation or initiative were not encouraged and
both personal and official censorship was rife. Any
criticism of the authorities was considered to be a
very serious crime.

The young Alexander was educated in the same
way as other young affluent Russians, and the topics

included a small amount of knowledge on a great many subjects. Alexander showed no interest at all in military affairs, which was a great disappointment to his father, who had a great passion for the military. In fact his hard, demanding father considered his son too soft for his forthcoming role.

Alexander married Princess Marie of Hesse on April 16, 1841. She was the daughter of Ludwig II, and after their marriage she became known as Maria Alexandrovna. They had six sons and two daughters before her premature death in June 1880. Less than a month after Maria's death, Alexander formed a morganatic marriage with his mistress, Princess Catherine Dolgoruki, with whom he had already had three children.

Alexander became the Tsar of Russia on the death of his father in 1855, and he fought hard for peace after the fall of Sevastopol, with the help of his trusted counsellor, Prince Gorchakov. The Crimean War had made Alexander realize that Russia was no longer a great military power, and that their economy was no match for the industrialized nations such as Britain and France. Alexander also had in his mind to eradicate serfdom in Russia, but the nobility were opposed to this move.

Alexander eventually got his own way and passed his Emancipation Manifesto in 1861, which proposed laws that would give freedom to the serfs. He publicly announced that personal serfdom would be abolished and that peasants would now be allowed to buy land from their landlords. The

State would pay the landlords for the land, which they in turn would get back from the peasants through a payment scheme called redemption payments, which consisted of 49 annual payments.

During that year Alexander introduced many other reforms, and in 1864 he allowed each district to set up an authority called a Zemstvo. This gave the local councils power to provide roads, schools and medical services, which gave everyone a better standard of life. Alexander encouraged the expansion of industry and the railway network, and he introduced reforms that improved the municipal government.

However, through his new reforms Alexander made many enemies among the liberals and radicals, who wanted a parliamentary democracy with the power of freedom of speech. The reforms in agriculture did not appease the peasants and workers who wanted even better conditions. Radicals started to form secret societies and there was a rumour of revolutionary agitation. Alexander felt compelled to adopt severe and repressive measures to quell the revolutionaries.

In 1876 a group of reformers formed an organization called Land and Liberty. Their main aim was to fight for the peasants and their rights to own agricultural land. It was a punishable offence in Russia to criticize the government so the group held their meetings in secret. The men were influenced by the writings of a man named Mikhail Bakunun, who had published literature demanding that the government handed over agricultural land to the peasants. Some of these reformers even favoured terrorism to obtain reform, and this led to several assassination attempts on Tsar Alexander II.

ATTEMPTS ON HIS LIFE

The first attempt made on Alexander's life was in 1866 in the city of Petersburg, by a man named Dmitry Karakozov. The tsar had a narrow escape on this occasion, and to commemorate his survival he held a competition to design a magnificent gate for the city. Viktor Hartmann, an architect, painter and costume designer, won the competition, but the gate was never to be built.

The second assassination attempt took place on the morning of April 20, 1879, when Alexander was walking towards the Square of the Guards Staff. He was confronted by a 33-year-old student, Alexander Soloviev, with a revolver in his hand. The tsar turned quickly and ran, and even though Soloviev fired several times, he never hit his target. Soloviev was subsequently sentenced to death and hanged on May 28.

Although the student was acting independently, there were plenty of revolutionary groups who were keen to see Alexander dead. Hoping to incite a social revolution, a radical group placed some explosives on the railway line from Livadia to Moscow, but the tsar didn't get on the train as planned and so their attempts were futile. Another failed attempt took place on the evening of February 5, 1880, when the same band of revolutionaries placed some explosives underneath the dining room of the tsar's Winter Palace. On this occasion the tsar was late for supper and was therefore unharmed by the explosion, which turned out to be rather less powerful than the revolutionaries had intended anyway.

However, March 1, 1881, proved to be a different story. Alexander was travelling through the snow to his Winter Palace in St Petersburg. The tsar was accompanied by guards, and next to the coach driver sat an armed Cossack and another six followed on horseback. By coincidence it was the day that the tsar had signed a document granting the first ever constitution to the Russian people, but this was not known to the group of radicals calling themselves 'Narodnaya Volya' or 'The People's Will'. On a street corner near the Catherine Canal, they hurled the first of their hand-made bombs at the tsar's carriage. The missiles missed the carriage and landed among the Cossacks instead. The tsar was unhurt, but he was insistent that he wanted to get out of the carriage to check the condition of his wounded guards. While he was standing with the wounded Cossacks, another terrorist by the name of Ignacy Hryniewiecki threw his bomb and this time it hit the target. The blast was so great that Alexander died instantly, as did the bomber himself. Of the other conspirators, Nikolai Sablin committed suicide before he could be arrested and Gesia

Gelfman died in prison. The remainder were hanged on April 3, 1881.

Alexander's assassin was a Pole, and it is theorized that Hryniewiecki wanted to resolve the issue of Russification by the assassination of the tsar. Russification was a process that the Russians had instigated to eradicate the Polish language in public places, schools and offices.

Alexander's importance lies chiefly in his efforts to modernize Russia. He certainly had a great influence through his position as autocratic ruler and through his Great Reforms, although they didn't always achieve what they set out to do. Alexander II, perhaps unknowingly, did much to hinder his own policies of reform, which finally set Russia on the road to revolution.

HAYMARKET SQUARE RIOT

Our verdict this morning cheers the hearts of tyrants throughout the world, and the result will be celebrated by King Capital in its drunken feast of flowing wine from Chicago to St Petersburg. Nevertheless, our doom to death is the handwriting on the wall, foretelling the downfall of hate, malice, hypocrisy, judicial murder, oppression and the domination of man over his fellowman. The oppressed of earth are writhing in their legal chains. The giant Labor is awakening. The masses, aroused from their stupor, will snap their petty chains like reeds in the whirlwind.

HAYMARKET MARTYR ALBERT PARSONS'
LAST WORDS TO HIS WIFE

The Haymarket Square Riot, which took place in Chicago, Illinois, on May 4, 1886, is the inception of the international May Day observances. Although the causes of the riot are still not fully known, it is believed that it was the division between the business and working classes in the late 19th century that probably brought about the disaster.

Prosperity was starting to return to the city of Chicago following the years after the Great Fire, but many activitists were annoyed that the wealth was staying in the hands of the privileged few. Companies such as the McCormick Reaper Works experienced constant unrest among their workers over their working conditions, the paltry amount of pay and the long hours they were required to work. There was no doubt, especially in the slaughter-houses, that men were working six days a week, 10–12 hours a day, for very little remuneration. In 1886 strikes and protests had become common-place, and bad feeling had been brewing since the end of the Civil War. Trade Unions began to form to protect the rights of the worker, and many of the organizers were blatant socialists, which helped spark the event that was to change the face of the labour movement forever.

Violence erupted on May 3, 1886, during a meeting of strikers at the McCormick Reaper Works, and as a result anarchists turned Chicago into a city just waiting to boil over. On the evening of May 4, a meeting was called to protest against the action the police had taken against striking employees at the McCormick factory the day before. In the ensuing scuffles the police had killed one man and injured many others. The workers had been striking in an effort to reduce their working day to eight hours.

They expected around 20,000 to turn up for the meeting, but the rain had kept many of them indoors. In truth only around 2,500 rather tired spectators showed up to listen to speeches from Albert Parsons, Samuel Fielden and August Spies, all three of whom were considered to be dangerous anarchists by the city authorities. Despite this, Mayor Carter Henry Harrison issued a permit to allow the meeting to take place, believing that there would be no real reason for concern. Others in authority were not so sure, and in response to local businessmen 600 police officers were put on duty that night in West Chicago. Police Inspector John Bonfield told his men to be prepared for a riot. Believing that the trouble might be citywide, he arranged for a further 100 police officers to be on hand should they be required.

The rally began at Haymarket Square at around 8.30 p.m. The crowd were fairly subdued, partly due to the wet weather, and when Mayor Harrison rode his horse through the crowds, he was satisfied that it was going to be a peaceful gathering. He told Inspector Bonfield to send his reserve officers home. However, Bonfield wasn't convinced that there wouldn't be trouble and ignored the Mayor's request.

The rally was starting to draw to a close at around 10 o'clock, and Inspector Bonfield, accompanied by 176 policemen, went in rather heavy-handedly, demanding immediate dispersal of the remaining 200 workers. Without warning, a crude hand-made bomb was thrown into the police column from a foyer in Des Plaines Street. Officer Mathias Degan was killed in the blast and six other officers were seriously wounded. The police, who were initially stunned, quickly responded by firing wildly into the fleeing crowd of workers. This random firing continued for up to five minutes and in the ensuing chaos six officers were killed and at least 60 others injured. Medical evidence later showed that most of the injuries received by the police were caused by their own bullets.

Following the days of the riot, despite the Mayor's pleading for calm, Bonfield and Police Inspector Michael Schaak decided to take the matter into their own hands. They were determined to find the person or persons responsible for the throwing of the bomb, or who had made the bomb in the first place. The police started a reign of terror among the working class citizens of Chicago. Hundreds of well-known anarchists and socialists were rounded up, beaten and interrogated at all hours of the night. They were so determined to get their man that they forced false confessions by using violence. Of course, by this time, whoever the real bomber was, had probably faded away into the distance anyway. Out of all the men the police arrested, 31 were named in criminal indictments and eight were held for trial.

Out of the eight that were charged with causing the riot, seven of them received the death sentence, with the eighth being sentenced to 15 years in prison. They were all sentenced on conspiracy charges to incite violence that led to the subsequent deaths of the police officers. The sentencing sparked more outrage in labour circles and resulted in protests around the world, making the defendants into international political heroes. The eight men appealed to the state supreme court, but their appeal got them nowhere.

One of the men, Louis Lingg, tried to kill himself by blowing himself up, and mortally wounded he died soon after. Four of the men charged, August Spies, Albert Parsons, George Engel and Adolph Fischer, were hanged on November 11, 1997. Two of the men had their sentences commuted to life imprisonment and one remained in prison even though there was no firm case against him.

In 1893 Judge Altgeld was chosen as the Democratic candidate for the office of governor in the state of Illinois. Unlike his predecesor, Altgeld looked at the defendants' appeals claiming that they had not received a fair trial, and they were subsequently pardoned. Judge Altged was criticized by the media, calling him an 'anarchist' for pardoning the three labour union activists, an act which made him very unpopular and one which risked his political career. John Peter Altgeld simply said he was doing what he thought was right, and that he fought for the underdog, won, and paid the price of what sometimes comes with justice. He was criticized and hated by many for what he did.

On May 4, 1889, the city of Chicago erected a monument of a police officer in Haymarket Square. For many years the police were seen as the victims of the riot, but with the formation of the labour unions opinions started to change. The statue was defaced in the 1960s, blown up twice, repaired, and finally it was moved to the Chicago Police Training Academy.

A second monument was erected in German Waldheim Cemetery, Illinois, and it depicts Justice preparing to draw a sword while placing a laurel wreath on the brow of a fallen worker. At the base of the statue are the final words of August Spies just before his execution:

> *The day will come when our silence will be more powerful than the voices you are throttling today.*

On the other hand, the inscription below the monument of the police officer reads:

> *In the name of the people I command peace.*

But somehow peace has not been very forthcoming since its dedication in 1889.

PART THREE

1900–1969

THE *LOS ANGELES TIMES* BOMBING

'Sons of Duty,' they were defenders of
Industrial Freedom under Law. When they
died they were exercising their inalienable
and constitutional rights as American citizens,
empowered to labour freely, without menace
and without fear, in the performance of their
duty to themselves, their families, their journal
and their kind.

INSCRIPTION ON THE MONUMENT TO
THE VICTIMS OF 'THE CRIME OF THE
CENTURY'

The *Los Angeles Times* (also known as the *LA Times*) is a daily newspaper published in Los Angeles, California, and is the second largest metropolitan newspaper in the United States. The paper was first published on December 4, 1881, under the name *Los Angeles Daily Times*, but the company was soon experiencing major financial difficulties.

Its saviour was Colonel Harrison Gray Otis, a former Union Army lieutenant. As soon as he heard that the newest Los Angeles newspaper was for sale, he headed for the city. He managed to scrape together $6,000 and bought a quarter interest in 1882, and the Mirror Company, who printed the paper, gave him the job as Editor. In October 1882, Otis and his family moved from Santa Barbara in California and established a home in Los Angeles, and for a weekly salary of $15, Otis wrote the editorials and much of the local news. His wife Eliza contributed columns about women, morals and religion.

Otis soon turned the newspaper's fortunes around and made it a financial success. In 1884 he bought out the remaining three-quarters of the newspaper, and also the printing company, and formed the Times-Mirror Company.

Otis was a powerful man who hated unions, and he was a staunch Republican. This was often reflected in the paper's contents, both in the news and editorial pages, and because of his views he made many enemies along the way.

RETRIBUTION

On October 1, 1910, a bomb exploded by the side of the *Los Angeles Times* building. The force of the blast weakened the second floor of the three-storey building, which caused it to collapse on top of the office workers below. Fire quickly spread throughout the building, and by the time the fire services managed to get the flames under control, 21 of the newspaper's workers had been killed and many more seriously wounded. One of the survivors said, 'Frames and timbers flew in all directions. The force of the thing was indescribable'. Many of the employees had tried to escape the flames by jumping out of the windows without any safety nets to catch them. At the end of the day all that was left of the *Los Angeles Times* building was a pile of smouldering debris.

Another bomb exploded, this time at the home of Harrison Gray Otis. A third bomb was found at the home of the secretary of the Merchants and Manufacturers Association, but the experts managed to diffuse the third bomb before it caused any damage.

The police were sure that the bombings were the work of one specific group, and Otis himself blamed organized labour and dubbed it 'The Crime of the Century'. Organized labour retaliated by blaming Otis, asking, 'Are his own hands clean?' The President of the American Federation of Labor (AFL) denied any participation by their union in the tragedy, arguing that urban terrorism would actually do labour's cause more harm than good.

William J. Burns, a famous detective, was hired to make a full investigation. Going on a hunch, Burns was led to the International Association of Bridge and Structural Iron Workers (BSIW), which was located in Indianapolis, Indiana. Suspecting the union's secretary, John J. McNamara, Burns set up a trap in a Detroit hotel on April 12, 1912. His ploy worked and he arrested McNamara, his brother James, and another accomplice by the name of Ortie McManigal. In a suitcase owned by McManigal, Burns had discovered guns and six lock mechanisms, which were similar to the type used in the Los Angeles bombing. McManigal became the key witness and Burns succeeded in personally turning him against the McNamara brothers. Burns had McManigal secretly transported to Chicago, where he confessed that he had been hired by John McNamara to plant dynamite at dozens of anti-union work sites around the country, and that the *Times* bombing was the work of John's brother, James. The brothers were subsequently arrested and charged with murdering the 21 workers at the *Los Angeles Times*.

This sparked off an outrage as many people believed that it was just another attempt at damaging the reputation of the trade union movement, which was starting to gain strength. Clarence Darrow, an eminent American lawyer, was asked to defend the McNamara brothers. Darrow had defended several trade union leaders arrested during industrial disputes, and he had also become involved in the campaign against child labour and capital punishment. In 1906–07 Darrow successfully defended William D. Haywood, leader of the Industrial Workers of the World (IWW), when he was charged with murdering Frank R. Steunenberg, the former governor of Idaho. Despite his reputation for winning his cases, Darrow was reluctant to take the case because he felt the prosecution's case against the brothers was too strong. Although many of the trade unionists believed that the brothers had been framed, Darrow discovered that the police did have a considerable amount of evidence that they could use against the two men. Darrow felt sure that the brothers would be found guilty and executed and for this reason he convinced the brothers to change their plea to guilty. After much discussion the McNamara brothers agreed to admit their guilt in exchange for a prison sentence.

Their guilty pleas were entered before the selection of the jury selection was complete. John, the older brother, was sentenced to 15 years in prison, while James, who had actually planted the bomb, was sentenced to life. Some of the brothers' supporters in the trade unions claimed to be shocked by their confessions and were vastly disappointed that Darrow had not performed with his usual enthusiasm, although he did, in fact, save the men from execution, which was his prime concern.

REPERCUSSIONS

The McNamara case lead to heavy losses and declines in membership for all Los Angeles unions. Labour union efforts to turn Los Angeles into a union town in the early part of the 20th century failed miserably. The AFL was seriously hurt by the public backlash and received strong criticism for supporting the McNamara brothers. The public felt justified in their criticism for not only had the brothers taken 21 lives when they blew up the Times building, but they had also been instrumental in destroying the labour movement in Los Angeles.

As for the newspaper itself, Otis Chandler remained with the *Los Angeles Times* until 1980. In 2000 the Times-Mirror Company was purchased by the Tribune Company of Chicago, Illinois, ending one of the last examples of a family-controlled metropolitan daily newspaper in the United States. John Carroll, former editor of the *Baltimore Sun*, was brought in to modernize the appearance of the publication, and today it is the nation's fourth-largest newspaper, with an average weekday circulation of approximately 850,000.

ASSASSINATION OF ARCHDUKE FRANZ FERDINAND

What is the good of your speeches? I come to Sarajevo on a visit, and I get bombs thrown at me. It is outrageous.

ARCHDUKE FRANZ FERDINAND

The assassination of Archduke Franz Ferdinand, heir to the Austro-Hungarian throne, and his wife Sophie on June 28, 1914, started a series of diplomatic events that were instrumental in provoking World War I.

Franz Ferdinand, the eldest son of Carl Ludwig, was born in 1863. He had a difficult childhood that was plagued with illness, and his family never really expected him to survive into adulthood. However, Ferdinand was much stronger than his family had anticipated, and by his 13th birthday, his ill health was just a distant memory. He joined the Austro-Hungarian army in 1883 and proved his worth by working his way up from Captain to General in a relatively short period of time.

Ferdinand first met Sophie von Chotkovato in Prague in 1888, and it was here, at a dance, that the couple fell in love. Although Sophie was descended from a noble Bohemian family, she was not considered to be an elligible partner for the future Archduke. Ideally, a suitable marriage partner needed to be a direct descendant of the House of Hapsburg or from one of the ruling dynasties of Europe. However, Ferdinand insisted that he would marry no other woman, and to avoid undermining the stability of the monarchy, Emperor Franz Josef offered him a solution. He told Ferdinand that he would be allowed to marry Sophie as long as it was stipulated that her descendants would not be allowed to succeed to the throne. He was also informed that his wife would not be allowed to accompany him in the royal carriage, or even sit beside him in the royal box.

The wedding went ahead even though the only members of Ferdinand's family to attend were his stepmother, Maria Theresia, and her two daughters. Despite this rocky start, the marriage was a success and they had three children – Sophie, Maximilian and Ernst.

In 1896 at the age of 51, Franz Ferdinand became heir to the throne following the death of his father. In the years leading up to his reign, Ferdinand's relations with Kaiser Wilhelm and the other Archdukes was at times hostile. However, the bitterness eventually subsided and Ferdinand started to take a more serious role in the activities of the government. His first major appointment was as Inspector of the Army, which made him realize the Kaiser's army was in poor shape, thus giving him the chance to reshape it. He promoted naval expansion and modernized the military, and he soon became a popular man with the armed forces. His reputation spread, and Franz Ferdinand was invited to Sarajevo, the capital of Bosnia and Herzegovina, to make an inspection of the Austro-Hungarian troops there.

THE BLACK HAND AND EVENTS LEADING UP TO THE ASSASSINATION

Both Bosnia and Hertzegovina were provinces just south of Austria, which, up until 1878, had been governed by the Turks. The disposition of land lost by the Turks during their disastrous war with Russia was settled in 1878 with the Treaty of Berlin. Bosnia was now populated primarily by three groups – Croats (Roman Catholics), ethnic Serbs and Muslims. Many of the Bosnian-Serbs had a strong desire to unite their lands with that of their Serb associates across the river, a desire which was shared by many of the people in Serbia. In October 1908, Austria annexed Bosnia and Herzegovina directly into the Austro-Hungarian empire, removing any hopes that Turkey might have of reclaiming their territories. The Serbs were not happy about this takeover, and through this unrest a secret society was formed called the Black Hand (*Ujedinjenje ili Smrt*) in Belgrade. They undertook the work of an older sect called The People's Defence (*Narodna Odbrana*), which included anti-Austrian propaganda within Serbia, sabotage, espionage and political murders. The society included many people of high ranking, including government officials, professional people and army officers.

When the Black Hand heard that the Archduke Franz Ferdinand was due to visit Sarajevo in June of 1914, they made plans to assassinate him. To add fuel to the fire, Ferdinand had supported a strong stance against Serbia during the Balkan Wars. The Black Hand appointed three of their members, who were trained and equipped for their forthcoming assignment. They were the three young Bosnians Gavrilo Princip, Nedjelko Cabrinovic and Trifko Grabez.

The movements of the Black Hand were well known to the Serbian government as they had members among their midst, but when Prime Minister Pasic heard of the plot to kill the Archduke he realized that he had a major dilemma. If he did nothing and they succeeded in their mission, the implications of the secret society and the Serbian government would be obvious, and it could even lead to war with Austria. However, if he were to warn the Austrians of the plot he would be seen as a traitor by his own people. Pasic made a weak attempt at having the assassins intercepted at the border, but when that failed he decided to try and warn Austria in a diplomatic way that would not expose the Black Hand.

The Serbian Minister to Vienna, Jovan Jovanovic, was given the job of warning the Austrians, and he told the Austrian Minister of Finance, Dr Leon von Bilinski, that it would be a good idea to convince the Archduke not to visit Sarajevo. However, Bilinski either did not understand or decided to take no action on the matter, and the visit was to go ahead.

Meanwhile the three trainees had made their way back to Sarajevo accompanied by a fourth man, Danilo Ilic. He had joined the group of his own choice and had brought three other recruits along with him. Between them they had four Serbian army pistols and six bombs, which had been supplied from Serbian army arsenals.

THE VISIT TO SARAJEVO

Franz Ferdinand decided to accept the invitation to inspect the troops in Sarajevo, as it had been a long time since a prominent official from Hapsburg had made such a visit. As the trip coincided with this 14th wedding anniversary, he decided to take his wife Sophie along with him. Although at home she was not allowed to ride in the same carriage as her husband, the same rule did not apply in cities such as Sarajevo, and so she was able to share her husband's car. Franz Ferdinand certainly knew that the visit could be a little dangerous, but his security was quite minimal as he felt restricted with the presence of security men round him all the time. Another reason was that he didn't want a cordon between himself and the crowd as he wanted to be able to greet them properly and, for the most part, Ferdinand was received warmly by the Bosnian people.

Sunday, June 28, 1914, was a bright and sunny morning, and at around 10.00 a.m. the party left Philipovic military camp, following Ferdinand's inspection of the troops. The motorcade itself consisted of six cars, and they were heading towards the City Hall for a reception being hosted by the Major of Sarajevo. The Archduke, his wife and General Potiorek travelled in an open Viennese sports car along the chosen route, a wide avenue called Appel Quay. The Archduke requested that the car be driven slowly so that he could look at his surroundings and greet the crowds waiting to see him. Crowds had lined the avenue and were cheering the royal couple, but little did they know that among the crowd were seven young assassins who had all taken up their appointed positions along the route.

As the procession reached the central police station, a tall young man, Cabrinovic, hurled a hand grenade directly at the open-top car. The grenade bounced off the folded roof of the Archduke's car and landed in the street, exploding underneath the car that was following them. It wounded several officers and about 20 people in the crowd. The driver of the Archduke's car started to accelerate away to reach the relative safety of the town hall.

However, Franz Ferdinand ordered his driver to stop as he wanted to see who had been injured in the attack. The imperial car was now a sitting target, and it was then that they noticed Sophie's neck had been grazed – apart from that she appeared unhurt.

The Archduke was now in an outraged mood, and on arriving at the town hall confronted the Mayor, claiming that the whole situation was outrageous. The Mayor was perplexed as he was completely unaware of what had taken place. After he had calmed down Franz Ferdinand asked to be taken to see one of the officers who had been wounded by the grenade, and who had been taken to the local military hospital. The prearranged visit to a local museum would then proceed as planned. Sophie, who had not originally intended to visit the museum, insisted that she now accompany her husband on the remainder of his tour.

Once again the cars set out along Appel Quay, but this time at speed. However, neither the driver of Franz Ferdinand's car nor the Mayor's had been informed of the change of plan. When the first car turned right at the corner of Appel Quay and Franz Josef Street and the second car followed, General Potiorek shouted angrily to the driver of the third car that he was making a mistake. The driver braked sharply and came to a halt, at which point a young Bosnian man, Gavrilo Princip, seized the opportunity and took out a revolver. A policeman desperately tried to grab the gun out of the young man's hand, but he was struck by someone nearby in the crowd. Princip stepped out from the crowd and only a few paces away from the stationary car, fired twice at the occupants. The first bullet struck the Archduke in the jugular vein, and the second entered his wife's abdomen. Sophie sank to the floor with her face between her husband's knees. The Archduke's last words were, 'Sophie, Sophie, don't die. Stay alive for the children', before he passed into unconsciousness. The car shot off at speed towards Governor Potiorek's official residence, but they were too badly injured and were dead before arrival.

Although Franz Ferdinand was not popular in Vienna, little did anyone know that his death would raise issues of such far-reaching significance – four years of bloodshed and the death of millions. The murders of Franz Ferdinand and Sophie brought Austro-Serbian tensions to a head. Trouble had been brewing between Serbia and Austria for many years, and this was the final straw.

Investigations into the assassinations at Sarajevo, turned to the Serbian secret society headed by 'Apis', a somewhat shadowy figure who was head of the Serbian military intelligence.

The reasons behind the double assassinations will never really be known, but extreme Serbian nationalists regarded Franz Ferdinand with fear because he favoured concessions to the South Slav minority on Austro-Hungary. The Black Hand thought that these concessions might not be advantageous to Serbia's position and therefore decided the Archduke should be eliminated. Vienna knew that it would be a long time before there would be any conclusive proof of the assassins and decided to act based on the mass of circumstantial evidence available to them.

As Vienna took a hard line against Serbia, the other powers in Europe started to take sides. The original squabble between Vienna and Serbia grew out of all proportion and within 30 days of the death of Franz Ferdinand and Sophie there was a World War!

What has been said is that Princip and the Black Hand secret society assassinated the one person in the Hapsburg family who was concerned with the future of Austria-Hungary. Archduke Franz Ferdinand, using the Dual Monarchy, made every effort during his reign to create a more peaceful affiliation between the different nationalities of the world.

WALL STREET BOMBING

Remember we will not tolerate any longer.
Free the political prisoners or it will be sure
death for all of you.

AMERICAN ANARCHIST FIGHTERS

Although there had been previous terror attacks in the United States during the late 19th and early 20th centuries, the Wall Street attack was different because it was aimed at the public and it was intended to kill a large number of people. In the early part of 1920 the American economy was in a bad way due to high unemployment and the sharp rise in inflation. The solid walls of the New York Stock Exchange, the Sub-Treasury, the Assay office and J.P. Morgan's bank stood for stability, and the workers were completely unaware of what was about to hit them on September 16, 1920.

It was not uncommon to see a horse and cart on New York streets in 1920, although most were not as ramshackle as the one that pulled up outside the

Assay office at 23 Wall Street at around noon. The driver, knowing that he had little time to spare, stepped down from the carriage and walked briskly away.

The Trinity Church bells could he heard indicating that it was midday. Everything in Wall Street was bustling as usual and then the dilapidated old wagon with its tired old horse delivered its lethal cargo – an extremely large quantity of explosives, in total 45 kg (100 lb) of dynamite. There was an ear-shattering explosion, followed by flames and smoke, which plumed high into the sky. Windows shattered in buildings throughout a 1 km (H mile) radius and pieces of glass and iron tore their way through anything that got in their path. Building awnings were burnt to ashes within seconds and hundreds of people and cars were literally blown away by the force of the blast. There was carnage everywhere. The people who had survived the blast looked on in horror as Wall Street literally ran red with the blood of the victims. A single horse leg lay on the steps of a building nearby, and a woman's head, still wearing a hat, was stuck to the wall of another. Mutilated bodies lay everywhere and hundreds of office workers were running in panic away from the site of devastation. A bell could be heard ringing from the Stock Exchange building, signifying that they had ceased trading – the first time trading had ever been stopped by violence.

Within minutes of the explosion, policemen, firemen and ambulances raced to the scene of the blast by any method of transport available. Even troops from the 22nd Infantry, who were garrisoned on Governor's Island, marched their way through Lower Manhattan. People began to help the injured, ferrying them to the nearby Broad Street Hospital. Order was very quickly resumed as the emergency services laid out the bodies on the pavement and covered them with white sheets. By nightfall the death toll stood at 31, with hundreds more injured.

SEARCH FOR THE CULPRIT

William J. Flynn, head of the Federal Bureau of Investigation (FBI), was asked to lead the enquiry, and he arrived in New York that night. At first the officials felt that it might just have been an accident, with a car colliding with a wagon that was carrying dynamite, and the explosives were indeed the type used for demolition work. But the dynamite had been wired to a timer and wrapped with many small pieces of iron. Added to that there had been several eyewitnesses who reported seeing an Italian-looking man jumping down from a horse and cart and running away from the scene, and they soon realized that something far more sinister had taken place. A chocolate peddler, Lawrence Servin, who had been knocked unconscious by the blast, was able to give a good description of the man once he had regained consciousness. He told them that the man he had seen on the horse and cart was:

. . . dark-complexioned, unshaven, wiry man, probably 35 or 40 years old, and dressed in working clothes and a dark cap. He seemed to be about five feet six inches tall. He had dark hair.

Suspicion immediately fell on anarchists, who had recently been behind an unsuccessful campaign of letter bombs aimed at Jack Morgan, of J.P. Morgan & Co., which was at the time the world's most powerful financial institution. Then the police had their next clue when a message was found in a post box just one block away from Wall Street, which read:

Free the political prisoners. Or it will be sure death for all of you.

The note was signed 'American Anarchist Fighters'. The previous day two of their members, Nicola Sacco and Bartolomeo Vanzetti, had been arrested for bank robbery and murder. The police felt that perhaps there was a connection between this and the explosion.

The Wall Street Stock Exchange opened for business as usual the following morning at 10.00 a.m. prompt. All the debris had been cleared away and any broken windows covered with tarpaulins. This made the job of searching for clues difficult for the investigating officers, who had to track down where the debris had been taken as it might contain vital clues. Outside the damaged Wall Street building thousands of patriotic New Yorkers gathered and sang *America the Beautiful*, everyone was defiant and wanted to show the world that business was as usual.

During the next few weeks the police investigations spread further and further afield. William Flynn asked for the help of blacksmiths, harness makers and livery stable owners to assist in the reconstruction of the wagon used in the bombing. They also attempted to track down the blacksmith who had made the horse's shoes, but their determination did not lead to any vital clues.

Meanwhile prominent New York businessmen hired security men to guard their homes and J.P. Morgan, who was away in Europe at the time of the attack, hired his own private detective in an effort to find the anarchist. No group or person ever came forward and claimed responsibility for bombing Wall Street and the FBI's leads simply fizzled out. No charges were ever filed in the bombing, and even though the authorities were pretty sure it was the work of anarchists, they could never gather enough evidence. In the year 1940 the FBI rendered the case inactive. The final toll of the attack was 33 dead, 400 wounded and $2 million of damage to property.

At a time when New York was considered to be the financial capital of the world, the attack could have been far worse with the loss of a large percentage of paper wealth and gold. As it was, it did nothing to halt the economic rise of the capital. Although J.P. Morgan & Co. is no longer in existence, 23 Wall Street still bears the scars of the bomb.

THE HEBRON
MASSACRE

> *The racial strife was begun by the Arabs, and
> rapidly developed into a conflict of great
> violence between Arabs and Jews, in which
> the Arab majority, who were generally the
> aggressors, inflicted most of the casualties.*
> HAYCRAFT COMMISSION SUMMARY REPORT

Throughout the 1920s tension had been brewing
between the Palestinian Jews and Arabs. The mandate government took no action to alleviate the
situation, and the resulting riots did an enormous
amount of damage to the Zionist cause. The Arabs
of Palestine were dominated by two clans – the
Husseinis and the Nashashibis. The Husseinis controlled the Palestine Arab Executive and Supreme
Muslim Council and the Nashashibis became the
mu'aridan, or the opposition.

HAJ AMIN AL-HUSSEINI

Haj Amin al-Husseini was appointed Mufti of Jerusalem by the British in 1921, and he was the most prominent figure in Palestine during the Mandatory period. Al-Husseini was born in 1893 in Jerusalem and served in the Ottoman Army during World War I. His appointment as mufti was, in itself, controversial as he had been sentenced to ten years imprisonment by the British for inciting riots in 1920. However, al-Husseini served none of the ten years, and he fled to Transjordan, where he was later given amnesty by Herbert Samuel, first high commissioner of Palestine. Samuel was a British Jew, and it was his decision to appoint al-Husseini as mufti, with the promise that he would use his influence as a high official to quell any further disturbances. In the following year he expanded his already significant powers by being appointed Supreme Muslim Council and he soon established himself as the pre-eminent Arab power in Palestine. Al-Husseini did not keep his promise to the high commissioner when he helped to incite the series of pogroms, which lasted from 1936 to 1939, in which hundreds of Jews were killed.

TENSION MOUNTS

There had been a long-running dispute between Muslims and Jews over access to the Muslim Wall in Jerusalem, and in the summer of 1929 the situation grew steadily more and more volatile. The riots began when al-Husseini falsely accused Jews of defiling and endangering local mosques, including Al Aqsa. The call went out to the Arab masses: 'Izbah Al-Yahud!' – 'Slaughter the Jews!' The prime reason for the discontent was the proximity of the Al Aqsa mosque to the wailing wall. Islamic law states that only Muslims may pray in the proximity of a mosque while prayers are being held in the mosque itself. The Muslims claimed that the prayers at the wailing wall were disturbing the prayers of the Muslims and that action must be taken to stop the Jewish sector.

Propaganda literature started to appear stating that the Jews were getting ready to take control of the holy places, and it told the Muslim people to come to Jerusalem to defend their rights. A demonstration organized by the Supreme Muslim Council took place on August 16, 1929. They marched to the wailing wall, where they proceeded to burn prayer books and the humble notes that had been left in the cracks of the walls by the worshippers.

Haj Amin al-Husseini helped to foment the Arab hatred by accusing the Jews of endangering the mosques and the other holy sites of Islam. On August 22, 1919, leaders of the Yishuv (the Jewish settlement in Palestine) had a meeting with the British Deputy High Commissioner to warn him that they feared widespread riots. However, the British officials placated them by saying they were completely on top of the situation. However, the following day the worst riots seen in the area erupted and lasted for a full seven days.

On Friday, August 23, inflamed by false rumours that two Arabs had been killed by Jews, Arabs started to attack the Old City of Hebron. The violence quickly spread to other parts of Palestine, but Hebron definitely caught the worst of the action with at least 68 people killed. The carnage was horrendous, with the gangs actually slicing off their victim's body parts. Some of the victims caught up in the violence were American students who had come over to study at the famous yeshiva.

On the following day, as early as 8 o'clock in the morning, Arabs started to gather in mobs. They were armed with knives, axes and clubs. They ransacked the homes of the Jews and destroyed their property, and with only one single police officer in Hebron, they met with no opposition. He called for reinforcements, but to his disgust he did not get any backup for a further five hours.

Rabbi Slonim attempted to shelter as many as the Jewish population as he could, and when the Arab rioters found out they offered him a deal. They told him that if he handed over all the Ashkenazi yeshiva students over to the Arabs, they would spare the lives of the remainder of the Sephardi community. When Rabbi Slonim refused to comply with their request, he was killed instantly. By the end of the day, 55 Ashkenazi and 12 Sephardi Jews were slaughtered.

Many Arabs not involved in the rioting tried to

shelter the Jews, and a total of 19 families saved dozens, possibly hundreds of Jewish people. Warding off the rioters with swords, many of the families hid the Jews in their cellars until they could be escorted to safety to the police station in Beit Romano. On the morning of August 24, not only did the police station turn into a refuge for the fleeing Jews but it also acted as a synagogue, where the Orthodox members said their morning prayers. Not long after they had completed their prayers, the inhabitants of the police station heard noises outside the building. Thousands of Arabs had gathered from Hebron and they were shouting, 'Kill the Jews! Kill the Jews!' trying their hardest to break down the doors. The Arabs besieged Beit Romano for three days before eventually giving up.

Although the worst of the fury flared up in Hebron, the rioting was also very bad in Safed, another religious community, which was once a centre for kabbala. The Jewish quarter was burned down, leaving hundreds without homes, and almost 24 Jews were killed. Throughout Jerusalem and the surrounding area, the violence continued for seven days until in total 133 Jews and 116 Arabs were killed, and 339 Jews and 232 Arabs were injured. When the massacre was finally over, the surviving Jews were forced to leave their home city and settle in Jerusalem. During the following years the Arabs had found pogroms were an effective political tool because of the lack of British response towards violence directed at the Jewish population.

However, as a direct result of the rioting throughout Palestine, the British established a Commission of Inquiry, with the intent of determining the cause of the violence. They formed the Shaw Commission, headed by Sir Walter Shaw, which introduced policies that they hoped would prevent any further violence from erupting in Palestine.

Through their investigations the Shaw Commission found that the pogroms occurred due to:

> *. . . racial animosity on the part of the Arabs, consequent upon the disappointment of their political and national aspirations and fear for their economic future.*

Basically the report claimed that the Arabs were afraid of being displaced by Jewish immigrants, and they feared political domination by a group who, they felt, seemed to have some form of funding from outside of Palestine. The Commission also blamed the ambiguity of British statements that had been made to both Arabs and Jews, and it recommended that in future the government clearly define its intentions for Palestine. Also on the Commission's recommendation, immigration was halted until they could find a resolution to the problem.

Of course the Arabs were very pleased with the outcome of the Shaw Commission as it was considered to be very much in their favour. However, on the other side of the counter there was a strong outcry from Jews all over the world.

Although a few Jewish families returned to Hebron in 1931, the community never re-established itself, and by the end of 1936 there were no Jews remaining in Hebron.

Haj Amin al-Husseini's part in the 1929 riots was a matter of controversy at the time. The Jewish Agency, which was originally formed for the singular purpose of rebuilding the Jewish national home in the Land of Israel, charged him with inciting the violence. The Shaw Commission, however, were not in agreement with their decision and concluded that:

> . . . *no connection has been established between the Mufti and the work of those who either are known or are thought to have engaged in agitation or incitement . . . After the disturbances have broken out the Mufti co-operated with the Government in their efforts both to restore peace and to prevent the the extension of disorder.*

THE BOMBING OF KING DAVID HOTEL

Israel is still the only country in the world against which there is a written document to the effect that it must disappear.

MENACHEM BEGIN

The bombing of the King David Hotel in Jerusalem on July 22, 1946, was the largest attack against the British government of Palestine in the history of the Mandate, when Palestine was administered by Britain. The attack was carried out by a militant Zionist group called the Irgun, which was headed by Menachem Begin.

The hotel was built by the Moseri family, members of a wealthy Jewish establishment. It was a luxurious seven-storey building with 200 rooms, and it was opened to the public in 1931. In 1938, the Mandatory government took over one entire wing of the hotel for the British Military Command, and later it also served as the headquarters of the Criminal Investigation Department. The King

David Hotel was chosen because of its prime location and because it was easy to safeguard against attack. A military communications centre was set up in the basement area, and so that they could link the hotel to an army camp based on the south side of the hotel, they added an extra door on the side of the building. Only about one-third of the original hotel was now available for civilian use.

THE ATTACK

On June 29, 1946, British troops unexpectedly entered the premises of the Jewish Agency and confiscated large quantities of documents. These documents disclosed details about the Agency's operations, including intelligence activities in Arab countries. The documents were taken back to the King David Hotel, where they were going to be analyzed by the CID. At around the same time, an estimated 2,500 Jews from all over Palestine were placed under arrest.

The Irgun, a secret Jewish organization, saw the hotel as a military building and decided they would use it as their target for vengeance and also as a way of destroying the documents stolen by the British. Begin, the leader of the Irgun, was sent a coded letter by the chief of the Haganah General Headquarters, Moshe Sneh, with clear instructions to blow up the King David Hotel. The operation was delayed on several occasions at the request of the Haganah, due to the ever-changing political situation.

The terrorists assembled on the morning of Monday, July 22, 1946, and were briefed about their mission. The first group of 'porters' travelled to the hotel by bus and waited at the side entrance to help unload the milk churns from the van. The next band of terrorists left in a van loaded with seven milk churns, each one containing 50 kg (110 lb) of explosives. The leader of the operation, Yisrael Levi (Gidon), was dressed as a Sudenese waiter, while all the other members were dressed as Arabs to avoid arousing too much suspicion. The van drove through the streets of Jerusalem with a tarpaulin over the back to cover the milk churns and the other occupants. They stopped at the side entrance of the hotel, which is where food was taken in for the café in the basement.

One British officer standing nearby, was suspicious of the group of Arab men and started to ask a few questions. He was shot, and a policeman stationed at the tradesman's entrance also suffered the same fate when he challenged the Irgun men. The gang hurried to the basement, searched all the rooms and then made all the kitchen workers assemble in one room. Then they returned to the van and took the milk churns into the restaurant, placing them beside the pillars, which were directly beneath the military section of the hotel. Gidon then set the fuses to go off in 30 minutes and ordered his men to get out of the hotel. The staff were told to leave in another 10 minutes to avoid getting hurt.

When they ran from the hotel two of the Irgun men were wounded by guards, and one of them, Aharon Abramovitch, later died of his wounds.

Two women fighters who were waiting nearby were told by Gidon to carry out their part of the mission, which was to go the nearest telephone booth and phone the hotel receptionist and the *Palestine Post*, giving the following message:

> *I am speaking on behalf of the Hebrew*
> *underground. We have placed an explosive*
> *device in the hotel. Evacuate it at once – you*
> *have been warned.*

The French Consulate, which was adjacent to the hotel, was also issued a warning, telling them to open their windows to avoid being damaged by the forthcoming explosion.

Twenty-five minutes after the warnings were given a devastating explosion shook the King David Hotel that reverberated throughout Jerusalem. The entire south wing of the hotel was destroyed. For some unknown reason the warnings were not heeded, which accounted for the large number of people who were trapped in the debris. Rescue workers started searching the rubble immediately in the desperate hope of finding survivors. Road blocks that had been set up by the Jews hindered the Royal Engineers, who were stoned and jeered at as they attempted to get to the scene of the explosion with heavy lifting equipment.

Rescue workers toiled for the next three days and nights, each shift working eight hours at a time. Most were totally exhausted, and even those that could hardly stand refused to give up looking for survivors. From the rubble the rescuers only managed to save six people. Due to the unstable condition of the building the use of mechanical equipment had to be limited, and it wasn't until the last hope of finding anyone alive that they started to dig away at the wreckage. At the end of a week they had removed 2,000 lorry loads of rubble and had recovered 91 bodies. It was the height of summer and the stench of decaying flesh made their job even more unbearable.

Not all of the 91 people killed were members of the British Military. Among the dead were 15 Jews who had been working at the hotel.

REPERCUSSIONS

For years afterwards the British denied that they had received any warnings about the forthcoming explosions. However, in 1979 a member of the British Parliament produced evidence that the Irgun had in fact issued just such a warning. He said that a British officer had overhead other officers joking in the King David Hotel bar about a Zionist threat. The officer who had overhead the conversation left the hotel straight away and survived.

The Irgun issued an initial statement stating that they were the group responsible for the attack, but blamed the deaths on the fact that their warnings went unheeded.

Just a few hours after the explosion the British army commander in Palestine issued a publication that instructed that any Jewish place of entertainment, for example, restaurants, shops and even Jewish homes, were out of bounds to all British military soldiers and officers. The publication ended with the following sentence:

> *The aim of these orders are to punish the Jews*
> *in a way the race dislikes as much as any,*
> *namely by striking at their pockets.*

This communication reached the ears of the Irgun's intelligence service, which they immediately made public knowledge. The tone of the letter greatly embarrassed the British government due to its anti-Semitic tone, and the order was duly rescinded just two weeks after it was issued. This did unrepairable damage to the British cause in Palestine and made them realize that their term of Mandate was coming to an end.

The following year, on July 22, 1947, the Irgun issued a second statement saying:

> *On July 1 – two days after the British raid*
> *on the National Institutions and on our towns*
> *and villages – we received a letter from the*
> *headquarters of the United Resistance,*
> *demanding that we carry out an attack on the*

*centre of government at the King David Hotel
as soon as possible . . .*

*Execution of this plan was postponed several
times – both for technical reasons and at the
request of the United Resistance. It was
finally approved on July 22 . . .*

*Notwithstanding this, days later, Kol Yisrael
broadcast a statement – in the name of the
United Resistance – abhorring the high death
toll at the King David caused by the actions
of the 'dissidents' . . .*

*We have kept silent for a whole year. We have
faced incitement, such as this country has
never before known. We have withstood the
worst possible provocations – and remained
silent. We have witnessed, evasion, hypocrisy
and cowardice – and remined sillent.*

*But today, when the United Resistance has
expired and there is no hope that it will ever
be revived . . . There are no longer valid
reasons why we should maintain our silence
concerning the assault against the centre of
Nazi–British rule – one of the mightiest
attacks ever carried out by a militant
underground. Now it is permissible to reveal
the truth; now we must reveal the truth. Let
the people see – and judge.*

The British, whose popularity had now dwin-
dled, and seeing the situation quickly spiralling out
of hand, decided to terminate their Mandate and

withdrew their forces from Palestine by May 1948. On the news of their withdrawal the Jewish provisional government declared the formation of the state of Israel, and the provisional government said that it would grant full civil rights to all within its borders, whether they were Arab, Jew, Bedouin or Druze. The declaration stated:

> *We appeal . . . to the Arab inhabitants of the state of Israel to preserve peace and participate in the upbuilding of the State on the basis of full and equal citizenship and due representation in all its provisional and permanent institutions.*

By creating this new state it meant that any inhabitants inside the newly formed state of Israel, whether they were Palestinian Jews or Palestinian Arabs simply became known as Israeli.

THE QIBYA MASSACRE

The orders were utterly clear – Qibya was to be an example for everyone.

EXCERPT FROM ARIEL SHARON'S DIARY

The massacre that took place in Qibya, a village on the Arab West Bank, in October 1953, also became known as the 'Qibya Raid' or 'Qibya Operation'. The massacre was a result of clashes between the borders almost directly after the signing of the armistice in 1949, which divided the new Jewish state of Israel from other parts of Mandate Palestine. Israel was being heavily infiltrated by a band of Palestinians, and it appeared that the Arab Legion in Jordan were either unwilling to curb the infiltration or unable to stop it.

ARIEL SHARON

Ariel Sharon has always been a controversial figure, and for the majority of his career he fought for the maximum political rights for the Jews and the minimum for the Palestinians. His enemies described him as a leader with a dangerous obsession, believing that whatever action he took for his own cause was justifiable.

When Israel was formed Ariel Sharon was a platoon commander in the Alexandroni Brigade. He was promoted to company commander in 1949 and finally in 1951 to intelligence officer. After a couple of years' break, while he studied history and Middle Eastern Culture at the University of Jerusalem, he returned to active service under the rank of major. He became the leader of Israeli's special forces unit, Unit 101. This Unit, under the encouragement of Sharon, carried out a series of raids against the Palestinians and neighbouring Arab states, which, it is claimed, was to improve the Israeli image and morale. However, this caused much bloodshed and in 1951, 137 Israelis, the majority of whom were civilians, were killed by Palestinian infiltrators. The following year the death toll was 162, and in 1953 a further 160 met their fate. On October 12, 1953, an innocent Jewish woman and her two children were killed by the infiltrators in the Israeli town of Yahud, and it was after this appalling attack that the Israeli government decided to retaliate.

ATTACK ON QIBYA

On the evening of October 14, 1953, a raid was

carried out on the Jordanian village of Qibya. It started with an artillery barrage until the Israeli troops could get close enough to the village itself. They laid landmines on the approaching roads to prevent any Jordanian troops from joining in the action. When the Israelis received no further resistance from the village, they placed explosives directly outside many of the houses and, after warning the residents to leave their homes, they detonated their bombs. During a six-hour killing spree the troops murdered a total of 69 people, blew up more than 40 houses, a school, a water pumping station, a mosque, a police station and a telephone office. By dawn, considering their attack was complete, the Israeli troops withdrew with not one single casualty – the village of Qibya had been totally defenceless. The remainder of the population of Qibya, around 2,700 people, had evacuated under the instructions of Ariel Sharon's forces.

When the rescue forces entered the village the following day, of the 42 bodies recovered, 38 of them were innocent women and children. One man, who had survived the massacre, had lost 11 members of the family. There was carnage everywhere, and bullet-ridden bodies lay near the doorways and inside the houses, which, despite the rumour that they had been warned to leave, proved that the inhabitants had been forced to stay inside their homes until they were blown up around them.

AFTER THE MASSACRE

After the appalling, and seemingly needless, massacre of Qibya, condemnation by the United Nations Security was swift in coming. On October 16 the UN issued a statement expressing the deepest sympathy for the victims of Qibya and telling the surviving population that they would do everything in the power to bring the perpetrators to justice.

Of course for many years the world has known who was responsible for the massacre and yet no legal action has ever been taken. In fact, Ariel Sharon, has rarely been criticized for giving instructions to his Unit 101 to destroy the village of Qibya, even though his orders categorically stated 'destruction and maximum killing'.

Another appalling fact is that Qibya was not the only large-scale killing that was instigated by Sharon. Almost 30 years later, in 1982, he was the person who ordered the abhorrent atrocities that occurred at Sabra and Shatilla, the Southern Lebanon refugee camps. Here, the total of people killed were believed to have been between 800 and 3,000 civilians. The Palestinians described the action as 'genocide'.

The reason for the attack was to route out the Lebanese Christian Phalangist militia, who the Israelis believed had avoided evacuation from Beirut by hiding among the refugees. They believed that there were possibly as many as 200 armed men in the camps with a generous stock of ammunition.

As soon as the scale of this massacre was published in the world press, with photographs of the refugee's bodies having been brutally murdered, Israeli was held directly responsible. The Israeli public were appalled and a huge demonstration of around 300,000 people took place on September 25, 1982. They demanded for the immediate resignation of Prime Minister Menaheim Begin and Ariel Sharon and insisted on an immediate investigation of the tragedy.

In his autobiography, Ariel Sharon wrote that, although he deeply regretted the civilian casualties at Qibya,

> *. . . it was now clear that Israeli forces were again capable of finding and hitting targets far behind enemy lines.*

Although Unit 101 was disbanded, it did, however, continue to take part in retaliatory action on military targets, but this time under the name of the 202nd Paratroop Brigade.

Even at the end of his career Ariel Sharon was still commanding 'death squads', and he has never been indicted for any of his crimes. Prime Minister Sharon suffered a brain haemorrhage on January 4, 2006, and Ehud Olmert took over as Acting Prime Minister.

BOMBING OF 16TH STREET BAPTIST CHURCH

We had been trying to win the hearts of white Southerners, and that was a mistake, a misjudgement. We realized that you have to hit them in the pocket.

WYATT TEE WALKER

Birmingham, Alabama, was one of the most segregated cities in the United States in the 1960s, and it was also the place where a violent branch of the Ku Klux Klan lived. Since the end of World War II, the city had seen a lot of prejudice against its black community. An event that took place on Sunday, September 16, 1963, proved to be a turning point in the civil rights movement at that time, and it put an end to segregation in the south.

The 16th Street Baptist Church in Birmingham was a three-storey building and the largest black church in Birmingham. Due to its prime position in the town it was often used to hold meetings and a rallying point for many civil rights activists. So it wasn't by accident that the Ku Klux Klan made this church their target. The church itself was built in a Byzantine-style with two domed towers and a large basement, which served as the meeting place for influential activists, even attracting names such as Martin Luther King.

Two members of the Ku Klux Klan, Bobby Frank Cherry and Robert Edward Chambliss (also known as 'Dynamite Bob') moved stealthily towards the 16th Street Baptist Church in the early hours of Sunday morning. Underneath a set of steps at the side of the church, the two men planted 19 sticks of dynamite and then left as quickly as they had come.

At approximately 10.15 a.m., 80 children were starting to assemble in the basement of the church to hear prayers on the church's Youth Day. Suddenly there was a tremendous explosion, which blew a hole in the wall at the back of the church, destroyed the steps and destroyed all the stained glass windows – with the exception of one, which depicted Jesus Christ leading young children. Five cars that were parked behind the church were also badly damaged or destroyed, and the windows in a building opposite were completely blown out.

The callous attack on innocent victims took the lives of four young girls – Addie Mae Collins, Carole Robertson, Cynthia Wesley and Denise McNair – and a further 22 victims were badly injured.

One 14-year-old girl who survived the blast described what happened when the bomb went off as follows:

> *I heard something that sounded, at first, a little like thunder and then just this terrific noise and the windows came crashing in. And then a lot of screaming, just a lot of screaming and I heard someone say, 'Hit the floor'. And I remember being on the floor . . . and it was real quiet.*

The nation was stunned and outraged by the attack, which sparked a spate of violence in Birmingham city, with two more young African-American children dead by nightfall. Johnnie Robinson, who was 16, was shot by police when he threw stones at a car carrying white people, and 13-year-old Virgil Ware was killed by two white people riding on a motorcycle.

The governor of Alabama, George Wallace, was accused by local civil rights activists of arranging the killings. The former Birmingham police commissioner, Eugene Connor, made matters even worse by saying to a large crowd of people at a citizen's meeting, that if they wanted to blame anyone they should blame the Supreme Court. He also put forward that it could possibly be the African- Americans themselves who could have detonated the bomb intentionally to bring attention to their cause.

However, a witness eventually came forward and said he could identify Robert Chambliss, a member of the Ku Klux Klan, as the man who had placed the bomb under the steps of the church. Chambliss was arrested and charged with murder and possession of explosives. Following a trial on October 8, 1963, he was found not guilty of murder and charged with six month's imprisonment and a fine for the possession of the dynamite.

It was more than a decade before the file on the 16th Street Baptist Church bombing was reopened. Bill Baxley, the attorney general of Alabama, asked to see the original FBI files on the case and soon found that they had indeed accumulated a large amount of evidence that had not been brought to light in the first trial. Chambliss was tried once again in November 1977, and with the new evidence, he was found guilty of murder and given a life sentence. He died in Alabama prison on October 29, 1985, having never publicly admitted that he had taken any part in the bombing.

After the case was opened several more times, it wasn't until May 17, 2000, that the FBI eventually announced that the bombing had been the work of the Ku Klux Klan splinter group known as the Cahaba Boys. They claimed the bombing had been the work of four men, Robert Chambliss, Herman Cash, Thomas Blanton and Bobby Cherry. Cash was already dead, but Blanton and Cherry were arrested and tried. So it was 38 years after the bombing of the church that Thomas Blanton and

Bobby Cherry were found guilty of the deaths of the four girls and given a life sentence. Bobby Cherry, who right up until his death in November 2004, always denied that he had had any part in terror attack on the Baptist church.

A song entitled *Birmingham Sunday* was composed by Richard Farina and recorded by Joan Baez to commemorate the aftermath of the tragedy, and in 1997 a documentary called *4 Little Girls,* which was directed by Spike Lee, was nominated for an Academy Award.

BIRMINGHAM SUNDAY

Come round by my side and I'll sing you a song
I'll sing it so softly, it'll do no one wrong
On Birmingham Sunday, the blood ran like wine
And the choir kept singing of freedom

That cold autumn morning no eyes saw the sun
And Addie Mae Collins, her number was one
At an old Baptist church, there was no need to run
And the choir kept singing of freedom

The clouds they were gray and the autumn winds blew
And Denise McNair brought the number to two
The falcon of Death was a creature they knew
And the choir kept singing of freedom

The church it was crowded but no one could see
That Cynthia Wesley's dark number was three

Her prayers and her feelings would shame you and me
And the choir kept singing of freedom

Young Carol Robertson entered the door
And the number her killers had given was four
She asked for a blessing, but asked for no more
And the choir kept singing of freedom

On Birmingham Sunday the noise shook the ground
And people all over the earth turned around
For no one recalled a more cowardly sounds
And the choir kept singing of freedom

The men in the forest, they asked it of me
How many blackberries grew in the blue sea
And I asked them right with a tear in my eye
How many dark ships in the forest

The Sunday has come and the Sunday has gone
And I can't do much more than to sing you this song
I'll sing it so softly, it'll do no one wrong
And the choirs keep singing of freedom

The church itself was repaired and is still functional today, remaining a central landmark in the Birmingham Civil Rights District. In 1980, the 16th Street Baptist Church was added to the National Register of Historic Places, and in 2006 it was designated as a National Historic Landmark.

THE BLACK PANTHERS

They came down on us because we had a grass-roots, real people's revolution, complete with the programmes, complete with the unity, complete with the working coalitions, we were crossing racial lines.

BOBBY SEALE, 1996

After the death in 1965 of the Civil Rights activist Malcolm X, two men, Huey Newton and Bobby Seale, decided they wanted to form a party that would continue to fight for the rights of the African-American. In October 1966, in Oakland, California, together they founded the Black Panther Party, which was originally called the Black Panther Party for Self-Defence.

The initial aim of the organization was to promote armed resistance against society's oppression towards the African-American. However, as the party grew in size the views of some of its members became more extreme and started to clash with those of the original leaders. Although the initial aims of the party had been more focused on socialism and trying to alleviate poverty and hardship among their communities, the group's political goals were eventually overshadowed by their conflicting and often military-style tactics.

The Black Panthers were one of the first parties in the United States to use force to try to free the ethnic minority. They based their laws on those set out by the late Malcolm X, although his views on winning equality for the oppressed minorities were taken to new heights by the Black Panthers. They also turned to the works of Marx, Lenin and Mao for guidance on how to run their organization.

TEN POINT PLATFORM

The Party adopted a Ten Point Platform and Programme, which laid out the fundamental needs of the black majority in the United States, and addressed the longstanding grievances they had that alienated them from the rest of society. It was a manifesto that demanded that their needs be met and that oppression against the blacks be ended immediately, stressing that blacks had a constitutional right to bear arms and to use self-defence where deemed necessary.

1. We want freedom. We want power to determine the destiny of our black and oppressed communities.

2. We want full employment for our people.

3. We want an end to the robbery by the capitalists of our black and oppressed communities.

4. We want decent housing, fit for the shelter of human beings.

5. We want decent education for our people that exposes the true nature of this decadent American society. We want education that teaches us our true history and our role in the present-day society.

6. We want completely free health care for all black and oppressed people.

7. We want an immediate end to police brutality and murder of black people, other people of colour, all oppressed people in the United States.

8. We want an immediate end to all wars of aggression.

9. We want freedom for all black and oppressed people now held in the United States Federal, State, County, City and Military prisons and jails. We want trials by jury of peers for all persons charged with so-called crimes under the laws of this country.

10. We want land, bread, housing, education, clothing, justice, peace and people's community control of modern technology.

The first party's newsletter, *The Black Panther*, went into distribution on April 25, 1967, followed by a march to the California state capital. The marchers were all fully armed, and their protest was against the state that was trying to abolish the carrying of loaded weapons in public. One of the party's leaders, Bobby Seale, read out their statement of protest, but instead of being sympathetic to their cause the police responded by arresting him and his 30 armed followers. It was this act by the authorities that activated the new resistance movement within the United States, causing other minority black workers to obtain arms and set up offshoots of the Black Panther Party.

SPARKS FLY

The kindling fires of the Black Panthers were sparked into full flame when their Defence Minister, Huey Newton, was arrested in October 1967 for killing a white Oakland policeman. Already disillusioned by the horrors of the Vietnam War, young whites joined their fellow, urban blacks and raised their voices in unison to set Huey free. The Party soon expanded from being a once small urban set up into a fully fledged national organization. Support groups sprang up everywhere – Japan,

China, France, England, Germany, Sweden, Mozambique, South Africa, Zimbabwe, Uruguay and Israel – and even a group of senior citizens formed a party that became known as the Grey Panthers.

Back at the original party headquarters, the Panther movement formed a series of social programmes to provide services for the black and poor in their community. These were to become known as the Survival Programmes, of which there were 35 in total.

The first one to be set up was the Free Breakfast for Children Programme, which started in one catholic school in San Francisco and then spread to every major city in the United States. The programme meant that thousands of under-nourished children in the country would receive a free breakfast every day. This shed such a poor light on the government that it shamed them into setting up a similar programme for public schools, although the FBI said it was just a form of propaganda on the part of the Panthers. Even worse, the FBI described the Panthers as a group of communist troublemakers who were out to over-throw the government of the United States.

The Black Panther Party used funds from the sale of *Mao's Red Book* to buy arms, and realizing what valuable information was in the book, they decided to make it required reading for all their members. Meanwhile, fuelled by the information supplied to him by his men in the FBI, J. Edgar Hoover set out to try to eliminate the Black Panther Party. He called upon local police and authorities to help him eradicate them for good. By the end of the year, virtually every member of the Black Panthers had been aggressively beaten by members of the police or the FBI or had their property destroyed.

Seventeen-year-old Bobby Hutton was shot dead by Oakland police on April 6, 1968, in a 90-minute gun battle. Hutton himself was unarmed and after his house was set on fire he was forced to flee into a barrage of bullets. In August of the same year another 17-year-old member of the party was murdered, Tommy Lewis, together with Robert Lawrence and Steve Bartholomew. The FBI, with the co-operation of the police did everything in their power to intimidate and break the spirit of the Black Panther Party, resorting to many underhanded tactics, including the use of informants and agents provocateur. They destroyed Party property and tried their hardest to quell the programmes that had been set up to help the impoverished community.

One of the most remembered attacks by the FBI and the police was a raid on the home of the Panther organizer, Fred Hampton, in December 1969. The occupants of the house had been drugged by an informant working for the FBI and were asleep at the time of the raid. Hampton was killed along with his bodyguard, Mark Clark. The other people in the house were dragged out onto the street, beaten and subsequently charged with assault. These charges, however, did not hold up in court and they were later dropped.

Despite all the odds being stacked against them, the Black Panthers survived, strengthened and added to their Survival Programmes. They started to provide free medical clinics, gave groceries to the needy, distributed free clothes and shoes, provided education and transport and generally supported the community in any way they could.

UNDERHAND TACTICS

Realizing that their efforts to destroy the Black Panthers were not working, the FBI decided to employ even further underhanded tactics. In March 1970 they started to sew seeds of dissension among the members of the Black Panthers by sending forged letters to prominent members. One of their targets was a man named Eldridge Cleaver, who at the time was living in exile in Algiers. The letters contained false information about the party informing him that they were taking steps to remove Huey Newton from his position of power. Cleaver received many letters, asking for his assistance in getting rid of Newton so that he could take over control.

There was general unrest throughout the Black Panthers and the start of its downfall came when Cleaver was asked to do a television interview in which he expressed his complete contempt at what had happened to the party and its original standards. He criticised their Programmes as being reformist and demanded the immediate removal of their chief of staff, David Hilliard.

Following the derisory interview, Cleaver was forced to leave the party, and he set up his own Black Liberation Army. Bobby Seale ran for the post of mayor of Oakland in 1973, but having received only 40 per cent of the votes he was defeated.

Having struggled for years with factions and internal hatred, Huey Newton started to become more disillusioned and the party was starting to fall apart. By the start of the 1980s the party crumbled and many of the remaining members were either hunted down and killed, imprisoned on trumped-up charges, or forced to flee the United States.

On August 22, 1989, Huey Newton was shot dead on the streets of Oakland in a shoot-out over drugs, something to which he had become heavily dependent on over the years.

Cleaver came out of exile as a born-again Christian and in the later years of his life he adopted an attitude similar to his hero, Martin Luther King Jr, and became involved in different business ventures. He too became reliant on cocaine. Before his death he gave one last interview in which he said:

> *As it was the US government chopped off the head of the Black liberation movement and left the body there armed. That's why all these young bloods are out there now, they've got*

*the rhetoric but are without the political
direction . . . and they've got the guns.*

A band of people formed in Dallas in 1989,
calling themselves the New Black Panther Party. It
became an offshoot of the former Nation of Islam
members and members of the original Black
Panther Party say that it is not a legitimate organization and have denied any connection with the
newly formed party.

EL SALVADOR DEATH SQUADS

Much of the violence there – whether from the extreme right or left – is beyond the control of the government.

RONALD REAGAN

A 'death squad' differs from a regular terrorist group by the fact that violence is used to maintain the existing state of affairs rather than as a means to cause disruption. They are an armed group that will assassinate activists, dissidents, politicians or anyone in a position that would be a threat to the general political status quo.

El Salvador, a republic on the Pacific coast of Central America, has a reputation of violence that is carried out by neither the government nor the regular type of criminal. Violence has become a part of everyday life where land is limited but the population is ever expanding. It is a country fraught with political tensions, having a fractured society and an extremely weak system of justice.

The roots of the El Salvador death squads run deep and can be traced back to 1910 when the National Guard was formed to protect the interests of landowners. They became known as a 'local instrument of terror' and in 1932, with the support of the army and paramilitary groups, the National Guard carried out La Matanza massacre. Desperate to ensure their survival, the farmer-peasants started to organize anti-government groups. The government responded by rounding up the peasants, lining them up against a wall and shooting them down. This massacre, which took part in the western part of the country, is estimated to have killed over 30,000 peasants, with the sole purpose of quelling rural insurgence. The perpetrator of the 'Great Killing', or la Matanza, was General Martinez, and he defended his actions on religious grounds, saying:

It is more of a crime to kill an ant than a man because a man is born again at death, whereas an ant dies forever.

In 1963 the United States government offered to help General José Alberto Medrano by sending ten Special Forces personnel to set up a paramilitary death squad, which became known as the Organizacion Democratica Nacionalista. In co-ordination with the El Salvador military, this squad obtained privileged information and carried out political assassinations, and there is now proof that these type of activities have been going on for over 30 years.

Death squads have been known to massacre entire villages if they were suspected of hiding guerrillas, and this was especially prominent in Guatemala. Even today, death squads openly operate in Central America, going under the name of *Sombra Negra*. They consist of vigilantes who seek out suspected criminals and rival gang members.

MAJOR D'AUBUISSON

In 1979 Major Roberto D'Aubuisson formed a faction group because he felt that the Government Junta in El Salvador was 'infiltrated by Marxist officers'. He worried that if they failed to act then it could be fatal for the independence and freedom of El Salvador. He managed to obtain considerable support from wealthy businessmen who feared that their welfare could be at risk if the reforms intended by the Government Junta were not quashed. The richest landowners offered their homes, estates, cars and even bodyguards to help the death squads' cause. Before long they became a powerful source with enough finances to build up an arsenal of weapons. The attacks on civilians and any individual suspected of collaborating with the guerrilla movement began. With his contacts, D'Aubuisson was able to obtain important information that enabled him to infiltrate both the armed and political forces.

In March 1980 D'Aubuisson's squads assassinated Archbishop Óscar Romero because of his socialist activities, and in December of the same year, three American nuns and a lay worker were sexually assaulted and killed. The Major's influence and prestige grew until he was a powerful political force not to be messed with. Even though the Armed Forces were aware that information was being leaked out, nothing was ever done to control it, and this is possibly because there were several members of the Armed Forces who were active within D'Aubuisson's group.

DEATH SQUADS WORLDWIDE

Of course, looking further afield, death squads did not just exist in Central America. For example, in Vietnam, death squads trained, armed and directed by the CIA, murdered up to 50,000 people in 'Operation Phoenix'. In Indonesia in the 1960s, officers of the CIA put together 'death lists' for General Suharto during his seizure of power. In Brazil it is known that they have used death squads to kill poor, or homeless, people simply to get rid of 'undesirables' that did not contribute to society.

In 1993 in Haiti, death squads terrorized any person who was sympathetic to the cause of Jean-Bertrand Aristide, a former Roman Catholic priest and the President of Haiti. They used terror in the form of murder, massacres, public beatings, arson, even resorting to the removal of limbs with machetes, all in the aim of destroying support for the president. Aristide was very popular with the lower classes of Haiti, but although he had been elected by a landslide victory, his reign was short and after eight months was deposed in a military coup.

In Nicaragua a band of counter-revolutionaries known as the Contras could be described as death squads. They were armed opponents of Nicaragua's Sandinista Junta, and many of their attacks were targeted at civilians. The Contras received both financial and military support from the Argentine government and also the CIA in the United States. Their main targets were coffee plantations and farming co-operatives, and their methods were both brutal and indiscriminate.

For just a few days in October 1973, a self-styled army squad named the 'Caravan of Death' roamed the provincial cities in northern and southern Chile. They killed dozens of political opponents of Augusto Pinochet's coup, which had the backing of the CIA. They targeted members of Chile's Socialist Party, a group that included infantrymen and several army officers. Many of the Caravan's victims voluntarily turned themselves over to the military authorities, but the death squads travelled from prison to prison, taking the prisoners from their cells and executing them without the knowledge of either military or local authorities. The victims were buried in unmarked graves. It is assessed that more than 72 people died during this period and it will be remembered as one of the worst episodes of human rights abuse in the history of Chile's military rule.

Another band of militants that could be described as death squads are the United Self-Defence Forces of Colombia. It is an organization intended to consolidate the major local and regional paramilitary groups fighting against Colombia's Marxist guerillas. They claim to protect their sponsors, who are mainly wealthy businessmen and drug traffickers, from the left-wing guerilla groups. However, far from being merely a defensive organization, the AUC, as it is known, is notorious for attacking perceived supporters of the insurgents, often wiping out entire villages. They have gradually bought up large tracts of land in Colombia, possibly as much as 3.5 million hectares of agricultural land, not with the purpose of protecting the local population but solely to benefit their own interests.

When the Khmer Rouge took over Cambodia in 1975, they employed death squads to rid their country of noncommunists. After being rounded up, the victims were questioned and then taken out to killing fields, where they were either shot or beaten to death. More than 1.6 million Cambodians were massacred before the government was overthrown.

Death squads called the Interahamwe committed genocide in Rwanda in 1994, when they hunted down Tutsis and Hutus in surrounding towns and villages. The squads either shot their victims or chopped them down with machetes, aided very often by the Rwandan Hutu armed forces. The killings did not stop until the country was taken over by the Patriotic Front in July of that year, but the number of people massacred reached the startling figure of around 800,000.

To this day death squads operate in the cities of Iraq, in fact they are becoming part of everyday life in the Sunni neighbourhoods of Baghdad. Recently police found the bodies of yet another 19 Iraqi civilians who had been kidnapped and tortured by death squads that plague the capital city. Sunnis are terrorized daily, and the members of the death squads shoot randomly into their houses and back yards. They set fire to their houses giving the inhabitants only seconds to get out. For some reason no one seems to be able to stop the activities of these death squads, least of all the police. Sunnis now claim that they are more frightened of the terror attacks from the 'men in black' than they are from the daily air raids.

PART FOUR

1970–1989

AVIVIM SCHOOL BUS MASSACRE

Every year it's like it happened yesterday.
I knew everyone, and I still remember them.

SHALOM PERETZ

The Palestine Liberation Organization (PLO) was founded in 1964 by Egypt and the Arab League. It is a political and paramilitary group that is regarded as a legitimate representation of the Palestine people. The original aim of the organization was the dissolution of Israel, which it has been carrying out by means of armed forces. More recently, however, the PLO has been seen as a terrorist organization due to its conflict with Israeli military forces, but also because of its brutal attacks on innocent civilians.

Avivim, in Israel, is an agricultural community that was founded in 1963, and it is right on the border with Lebanon. The community was built up by Moroccan immigrants, and the greater part of the community was established by two principle families, the Peretz and the Biton.

Most of the families in the Avivim Moshav (a type of co-operative agricultural community of individual farms) belong to the Mizrachi (Modern Orthodox) form of Judaism, and they either work on the Moshav fruit farms, tend the chickens, or work outside of the community as teachers or members of the security services.

On the morning of May 8, 1970, the school bus arrived at Avivim to pick up the children who were aged between six and nine. As the children left the Moshav, bound for two separate schools, they waved goodbye to their families. About ten minutes after the bus left, shots could be heard in the Moshav and immediately the residents started to run down the road to reach the bus. The bus came from the local council and terrorists had obtained its schedule and were waiting in ambush. They fired on the bus killing all of the adults on board, with the exception of the bus driver himself. In an effort to get away from the terrorists the bus driver continued driving, until he too was shot. The bus crashed, injuring many of the children who were still on the bus. Some of the older children, aware of what was happening, had managed to get out of the coach windows and go into hiding.

By the time the residents of Avivim reached the wreckage of the bus, the majority of the children were already dead. By the time the army and the ambulance services arrived on the scene, even more had died from their injuries. The attack caused the death of nine children, three adults, and 19 others were left with crippling injuries.

One of the survivors, a seven-year-old boy by the name of Shalom Peretz, remembers:

> *I can still hear the shots. No one knew what was happening, but they knew it wasn't good. Everyone began to cry and run towards the bus.*

One little girl who had asked her mother if she could take flowers to her teacher, was found lying in the wreckage still clutching the posy. The entire community mourned for their lost children, and to this day they hold a memorial service every year for those who died in the attack.

Although the terrorists were never traced, they were believed to be members of the PLO, and members of the same group were responsible for another atrocity involving children which took place on May 15, 1974.

THE MA'ALOT MASSACRE

It was the 26th anniversary of Israeli independence and Palestinian terrorists, dressed as Israeli soldiers, stormed the Netiv Meir elementary school in Ma'alot, a community in northern Israel. Inside the school were a group of about 100 teenagers sleeping on the floor after a trekking outing. On entering the school the terrorists killed a security guard, one student and another adult. On waking and realizing what was happening, some of the students managed to escape out of the windows, but about 90 students and some of their teachers were held hostage.

Armed forces surrounded the school, unable to make a move for fear of anyone else getting hurt. The following morning the terrorists made their demands. They wanted the release of 23 Arab and three other political prisoners from Israeli prisons, and if their demands were not met they would start to kill the student hostages. They told the authorities they had until six o'clock that evening to comply with their demands.

The Knesset, or Israeli parliament, had an emergency meeting, and at around three o'clock they asked the terrorists if they were prepared to make a negotiation. However, the members of the PLO denied them extra time and at 5.45 p.m. a special unit of the elite Sayeret Maktal special forces stormed the school. Although they managed to eventually kill all of the hostage takers, they could not stop them using guns and explosives and 26 Israelies were killed and more than 60 people were wounded.

Since then terrorism has escalated in the hope of causing enough pandemonium to accomplish the PLO's lifelong goal of establishing a Palestinian state.

BLACK SEPTEMBER

This is your new captain speaking. This flight has been taken over by the Popular Front for the Liberation of Palestine.

VOICE OF A HIJACKER

September 1970 has become known as 'Black September' due to a number of terror attacks carried out by members of the Popular Front for the Liberation of Palestine (PFLP). In fact the world witnessed a series of serial hijacks that will never be forgotten. It was also the month when there was an attempt to overthrow the monarchy of King Hussein of Jordan, an attack which cost the lives of many Palestinians. The conflict lasted until July 1971 when the PLO and thousands of Palestinians were expelled to Lebanon.

Events started on September 1, 1970, when King Hussein received news that the PFLP were plotting to murder him and take control. Hussein was infuriated and decided to mobilize his forces in an all-out purge against the PFLP.

On September 6, acting on instructions from Dr Wadi' Haddad, better known as 'The Master', the PFLP started a series of hijackings that have become the most memorable in history. Their reason for the hijackings was to force the release of Palestinian prisoners held in Switzerland and West Germany.

Hijacking of aeroplanes was a recent development and airport security was still in its early stages. For example, there were no metal detectors to scan each passenger, and only random pieces of luggage were searched before being loaded onto the planes. In the case of these hijackers, they had managed to board the planes easily while carrying concealed weapons on their persons.

The sequence of events started with El Al Flight 219, a Boeing 707 that had taken off from Tel Aviv, Israel, and was heading for New York. On board were 148 passengers and 10 members of the crew. It stopped in Amsterdam to pick up more passengers, and it was here that two members of the Popular Front – Patrick Argüello, a Nicaraguan American, and Leila Khaled, a Palestinian – boarded the plane. They posed as a married couple and got on the plane, using less suspicious Honduran passports. They sat quietly in their seats until the plane approached the coast of Britain, when they took out their concealed guns and demanded entry into the cockpit. At first the captain refused to open the cockpit door, but a stewardess screamed, 'She has two hand grendades!' Captain Uri Bar Lev was determined not to give in to the hijackers and after announcing over the intercom to his passengers and crew that there was a hijacking in progress, he put the plane into a steep nose dive. This immediately threw the two terrorists off balance, but not before Argüello managed to throw one of his hand grenades down the aisle of the plane. Luckily it failed to explode and one quick-thinking passenger hit him over the head with a bottle of whisky before he managed to pull out his gun. Argüello responded by shooting one of the stewards, but he was shot by one of the sky marshalls before he could do any further damage. Khaled was held captive by both crew and passengers while the plane made an emergency landing at Heathrow Airport. The steward survived but Argüello died in the ambulance on his way to hospital. Khaled was subsequently arrested and held by the British government for questioning.

The original aim was to have had four hijackers on the plane, but two of the terrorists were prevented from boarding by security men at Amsterdam because they were travelling under Sengalese passports that suspiciously had consecutive numbers. Not to be foiled they purchased two first-class tickets for another flight and planned to hijack that plane instead.

The two terrorists were now on board Pan Am Flight 93, a Boeing 747, which carried 153 passengers and 17 crew members. The flight was going from Brussels to New York and the two men were determined to make this hijack work. They forced the plane to stop first in Beirut, where it refuelled and picked up several known associates of the two hijackers already on board. They also managed to smuggle on board enough explosives that would be capable to blowing up the entire plane. Realizing that the plane was too large to land at the arranged destination, Dawson's Field, they forced the pilot to land at Cairo. On arrival at Cairo the plane was blown up only seconds after the last person had stepped onto the runway.

Meanwhile two more planes had been hijacked. TWA Flight 74, a Boeing 707, took off from Frankfurt, carying 141 passengers and a crew of 10. Swissair Flight 100, a Douglas DC-8, carrying 143 passengers and 12 crew, took off from Zürich Airport and was bound for New York.

Both planes were forced to land at a remote desert airstrip in Jordan, 50 km (30 miles) from Amman, which was known as Dawson's Field, or Zerqa. The airfield was a base for the British Royal Air Force and it is nicknamed 'Revolutionary Airport' after the series of events that took place that September.

NEGOTIATIONS AT DAWSON'S FIELD

By September 7, 1970, several members of the press had made their way to Dawson's Field to interview the terrorists. The hostages, who had been asked about their religious beliefs, were divided up. The majority, around 310, were transferred to Amman and set free on September 11. Of the remainder, the hijackers segregated the flight crews and any Jewish passengers, keeping 56 people as hostages.

Standing on the sand in front of the media, several passengers and members of crew listened while the members of the PFLP made their demands. They told the press that their aim was:

> ... *to gain the release of all of our political prisoners jailed in Israel in exchange for the hostages.*

In the United States, the reaction of President Nixon was to bomb the PFLP positions in Jordon, but his Secretary of Defence did not think it was a viable option, and so the idea was dropped. Meanwhile the 82nd Airborne Division were put on standby, the Sixth Fleet took to the sea, and military aircraft flew to Turkey in preparation for a possible military assault.

Back in London, Prime Minister Edward Heath took a completely different view on the situation. He felt the best solution would be to negotiate with the hijackers, agreeing to release Khaled and other prisoners in exchange for the hostages held in Jordan.

The tension mounted between the two countries as they disagreed bitterly about the way to handle the crisis. Fighting had broken out in Amman at the Intercontinental Hotel between the PFLP and the

Jordanian forces. The PFLP were holding about 125 women and several children and it appeared inevitable that there was about to be a civil war.

On September 12, the aeroplanes held at Dawson's Field were blown up in front of the international media. The BBC World Service made an announcement in Arabic on September 13 on behalf of the government, stating that the United Kingdom would release Khaled in exchange for the hostages.

King Hussein complicated the situation even further by asking both Britain and the United States to request Israel to attack any Syrian troops that crossed the border into Jordan in support of the Palestinians. Hussein declared martial law on September 16, which was the start of the military conflict that later became known as the 'Black September Conflict'.

Jordan managed to gain quick control, however, and a deal was made on September 30, in which the remaining hostages held by the PFLP were released in exchange for the release of Khaled and three other PFLP members.

LOD AIRPORT MASSACRE

The Red Army fights not merely for the sake of fighting but in order to conduct propaganda among the masses, organize them, arm them and help them to establish revolutionary political power. Without these objectives, fighting loses its meaning and the Red Army loses the reason for its existence.

MAO TSE TUNG, DECEMBER 1929

Ben Gurion International Airport, which was once widely known as Lod Airport, is situated 15 km (9 miles) southeast of Tel Aviv. It is the largest international airport in Israel and is operated by the Israeli Airports Authority, a government-run corporation. Because of the high level of threat from terrorism, security at the airport is regularly scrutinized. However, despite their vigilance, in 1972 the airport was the subject of two terrorist attacks.

The first attack on Lod Airport came on May 9, 1972, when two men hijacked a Sabena Airlines passenger plane. The terrorists held 90 passengers and 10 members of the crew inside the plane for 23 hours, before 12 Israeli soldiers, who were disguised as maintenance workers, stormed the plane and managed to rescue the hostages.

The second attack, which became known as the Lod Airport Massacre, was a joint operation by the Popular Front for the Liberation of Palestine (PFLP) and the Japanese Red Army (JRA). The JRA is an international terrorist organization formed by a small section of extremists, which carried out revolutionary activities and felonious crimes in an effort to unify the world under the name of communism. It was through their contacts with the PFLP that the JRA managed to set up a base in the Middle East.

This attack, which occurred later the same month on May 30, was carried out by three members of the terrorist group, the JRA. Kozo Okamoto, Tsuyoshi Okudaira and Yasuyuki Yasuda had all been trained by the JRA at their base in Baalbek in Lebanon. They arrived at Lod Airport on board Air France Flight 132, a Boeing 707 jet. Dressed conservatively and carrying slim cases, the three men attracted little attention as they mingled with the remainder of the passengers leaving the plane. Security was always on the lookout for Palestinians, but they did not consider the Japanese as a major threat. Once inside the airport waiting area, the three terrorists grabbed automatic firearms from their carry-on luggage and opened fire on both airport staff and fellow passengers. The airport security staff acted quickly, but before they could get the situation under control 24 people had been killed and a further 78 injured. The majority of the victims were pilgrims who had been on a ten-day trip to the Holy Land. Yasuda was killed by the Israeli security guards. Okudaira, on the other hand, had moved from the airport building onto a landing strip and, after firing at passengers who were disembarking from an El Al aircraft, committed suicide by using a hand grenade. The third member of the JRA, Okamoto, was severely wounded but survived. He was tried by the Israelis and sentenced to life imprisonment.

Kozo Okamoto was released from prison in May 1985 with other prisoners in an exchange bargain with the PFLP. Okamoto quickly fled to Lebanon and lived in Beka'a Valley until he was re-arrested in 1997. In 2000 he was granted political refugee status in Lebanon and eventually disappeared, but he is rumoured to be living somewhere in North Korea.

Today Ben-Gurion Airport is heavily guarded and every passenger is not only thoroughly searched but has to go through vigorous questioning.

BLOODY FRIDAY

*At one time we were handling 21 bomb
scares, 20 of which turn out to be the real
thing . . . Manpower was stretched to the
limit. On the ground our men had difficulty
in controlling crowds of stampeding people in
the city centre as bomb after bomb exploded. It
was really a nightmare in the true sense of the
word.*

AN RUC OFFICER

In the early part of the 1970s Northern Ireland
experienced an explosion of political violence,
which peaked in the year 1972, when nearly 500
people lost their lives. One of the causes of this
violence was the formation of the Provisional IRA,
which was a detachment from the Irish Republican
Army (IRA), who were determined to fight against
British rule in Northern Ireland. The break-away
group soon became known as the 'Provos', and they
established themselves as a far more aggressive and
militant group in defence of their communities.
Despite the official IRA's aims to bring in reform,

the Provos continued to use force and the relationship between the Catholic community of Ireland and the British military weakened. The IRA demanded that Britain withdraw from Ireland before the beginning of 1975, but the British Secretary of State, William Whitelaw, did not give in to their demands, and talks broke down.

By 1972, the Provo's campaign was of such intensity that before the year ended they had killed over 100 soldiers, wounded 500 more and carried out 1,300 explosions. On July 21, 1972, the IRA planted a total of 22 bombs in and around Belfast, in an effort to cause major economic damage. In the resulting explosions, 9 people were killed and a further 130 people were seriously injured on the day that became known as 'Bloody Friday'.

SEQUENCE OF EVENTS

The events that occurred on 'Bloody Friday' were because of a decision made by the IRA to step up their campaign by attempting to disrupt the life of ordinary civilians. Talks had failed miserably between the IRA and the British army, and their temporary ceasefire had now come to an end.

At approximately 2.00 p.m. in Windsor Park, Belfast, a bomb – estimated to be about 14 kg (30 lb) – exploded on a footbridge that went over the top of the Dublin–Belfast railway line. There were no casualties in the resulting explosion.

Another explosion occurred at about 2.30 p.m. at

the Brookvale Hotel in north Belfast. The bomb had been planted in a suitcase and had been dumped in the foyer of the hotel by two men. Staff in the hotel were suspicious of the suitcase and evacuated the area, so consequently no one was hurt in the blast.

Every couple of minutes warnings were being issued about other explosive devices that had been planted in and around the city of Belfast.

Just ten minutes after the last explosion, a car bomb exploded outside a branch of the Ulster Bank in north Belfast, only a few hundred metres away from the site of the first explosion. This time the area had not been cleared and a local Catholic woman, who was walking past the car at the time, lost both of her legs. Passing motorists were also injured by the blast, and the result was total traffic chaos.

At around 2.52 p.m., outside the Botanic Railway Station in Belfast, another car bomb exploded. Although there was considerable damage to the building itself, miraculously no one was seriously hurt. One minute later, on the Queen Elizabeth Bridge, Belfast, a third car bomb was detonated and again, although there was minor damage to the structure of the bridge, no one was badly injured.

On Agnes Street, Belfast, at approximately 3.00 p.m. a fourth car bomb went off outside a group of Protestant houses. Although the inhabitants of the street had been given no warning, once again there were no serious casualties. Two minutes later a bomb exploded in the Liverpool Bar in Donegall Quay. Again there was no warning and there were a few casualties. At precisely the same time a bomb exploded on a bridge that crossed the M2 motorway in Bellvue, once again there were no casualties.

The explosions were now coming in quick succession, at only one minute intervals. At 3.03 p.m. a bomb exploded at York Street railway station, at 3.04 a car bomb exploded in Ormeau Avenue and another in Eastwoods Garage, Belfast.

The worst explosion occurred at 3.10 p.m. at the Oxford Street Bus Depot in Belfast, when a car bomb denoted right outside the depot. This one bomb caused the greatest loss of life and number of casualties than any of the other bombs that occurred on that day. Even though a warning had been issued and the area was being cleared, it was still remarkably busy when the Volkswagen car blew up. Two British soldiers were killed instantly along with four Protestant civilians who all worked for the Ulsterbus company.

At 3.15 p.m. a bomb that was believed to have been dumped on Stewartstown Road exploded, but caused no serious injuries.

Five minutes later a large car bomb, estimated to weigh around 23 kg (50 lbs), exploded outside a row of shops near the top end of Cavehill Road in Belfast. Yet again no one had received a warning that a bomb had been planted in the mixed Catholic-Protestant area of town. A Catholic mother of seven was killed in her car and her 11-

year-old daughter, who was in the car with her, was badly injured. A 65-year-old Catholic woman also died in the blast, as did a 14-year-old Protestant, and many others received serious injuries.

Two more bombs exploded at about 3.25 p.m., one on Crumlin Road at the Star Garage and the second on the railway line at Lisburn Road, but on these two occasions there were no casualties.

A landmine was detonated at 3.30 p.m. on the road that led to Nutts Corner, just as a bus carrying schoolchildren passed by. The driver managed to miss the worst of the blast by swerving at the last minute which avoided anyone getting seriously hurt. It is thought that the bus could possibly have been mistaken for a British military vehicle.

Another bomb exploded at 3.30 p.m. at the Northern Ireland Carriers depot but no one was hurt. And the final incident of the day was when the British Army successfully diffused a bomb that had been placed on the Sydenham flyover.

OPERATION MOTORMAN

The quick succession of bombs had a profound impact on the people of Northern Ireland and Britain alike. As a direct result of 'Bloody Friday' the British Government brought into action 'Operation Motorman', which entailed the British Army infiltrating the 'No-Go' areas of Belfast and Londonderry.

British troops began to make their move at 4.00 a.m. on July 31, 1972. They knew that this latest mission was dangerous and there was a possibility of heavy casualties if the IRA decided to fight back. It was important to keep the exact details of the operation a secret and the troops moved stealthily. Their aim was to hit the IRA hard, removing their barricades as quickly as possible. They wanted to take control of the area before the majority of the local population had woken up.

More than 21,000 British soldiers moved in successfully and built cordons around the 'No-Go' areas. In Londonderry, Royal Engineers had used bulldozers to gain entrance into Rossville and the Creggan Estate, with the support of infantry from four separate battalions. During the seizure one petrol bomber was shot dead, but apart from that there were no casualties and they had made the areas secure before 7.00 a.m.

In Belfast, however, the operation was a little more complicated. It involved 11 battalions, which took over Ligoniel, Ballymurphy, Whiterock, Andersonstown, the Ardoyne, New Lodge, City Centre and Markets, Beechmount and the Falls Road. Although not all of these areas were in the 'No-Go' section, the presence of such heavy military stopped any trouble from breaking out. In some of the areas local people even helped the Royal Engineers to dismantle the barricades erected by the IRA.

Operation Motorman was a total success and by the close of the day British security forces had reinstated their right to move freely anywhere within the province, and miraculously without any casualties.

The IRA had failed to respond to their actions, realizing that they were completely outnumbered and any action would be completely futile.

RESPONSE FROM THE IRA

People from all over Ireland were calling for peace. They had had enough of the constant fighting and the latest spate of terror attacks had done nothing to endure them to the IRA. In response to Bloody Friday, the IRA stated that it was the authorities that had caused the problems, not them, because they had given adequate warning of the intended bombs and that they did not intend any innocent civilians should get hurt.

The events of Bloody Friday, whichever way you look at it, had far-reaching and serious consequences. It made the members of the Unionist community realize that it was impossible to make any deals with the Catholics. It reinforced the position of the Protestant paramilitaries and once again made them a real force to contend with. It also convinced the British government that it was impossible to make any form of pact with the Republican movement.

UNCONDITIONAL CEASEFIRE

For over 25 years the IRA has fought against British imperialism, trying to drive out the British forces and bring Ireland into a state of unification. After years of bloodshed, with over 3,000 dead and nearly 37,000 people injured, it still seems that their ideals of a having united Ireland are far from being fulfilled. The IRA eventually declared an unconditional ceasefire, which became effective on July 20, 1997.

Following the ceasefire agreement, a political deal was set up aiming to settle the differences between the United Kingdom and the Republic of Ireland. The Belfast Agreement, also referred to as the Good Friday Agreement, because it was signed on Good Friday, April 10, 1998, was hailed as a major achievement. It held many controversial policies regarding the decommissioning of paramilitary weapons and the future policing of Northern Ireland, but it certainly was a rung in the very long ladder of peace between the two countries.

In July 2005 the IRA made an announcement that they wanted relinquish violence in an effort to settle their disputes and they instructed all of their members help develop the country through purely political and democratic means. They made a promise to give up all their weapons and their disarmament was overseen by an international mediator. The movements of the IRA are still heavily monitored but in general they seem to be moving along the right path towards peace in Ireland, but occasionally Republic paramilitaries still engage in violent acts.

MUNICH MASSACRE

*We have no choice but to strike at the terrorist
organizations wherever we can reach them.
That is our obligation to ourselves and to
peace. We shall fulfil the obligation
undauntingly.*

GOLDA MEIR, SEPTEMBER 1972

Even 30 years after the event, the massacre that
took place at the Munich Olympic Games is still
clearly remembered with horror. It was a prime
target for the terrorist group Black September,
because it had such an enormous impact as millions
of viewers watched the events unfold live in front of
their eyes on television.

WHO WERE 'BLACK SEPTEMBER'?

The massacre at Munich was ordered by Yasser
Arafat, Chairman of the Palestine Liberation Organization (PLO) until 2004. Arafat's faction Fatah, a
major Palestinian political party and the largest
organization in the Palestine Liberation Organiza-

tion, gave themselves the name 'Black September' in an effort to protect the image of the Fatah and the PLO. The chief commander of Black September and the mastermind behind the Munich Massacre was Abu Daoud, who was known to have had considerable help from the East Germans as well as Eastern European countries in his terrorist negotiations.

SEPTEMBER 5, 1972

Several of the Israeli athletes had been enjoying a night out on September 5, 1972, before returning to the Olympic village. At around 4.30 a.m., five Arab terrorists wearing tracksuits and carrying sports bags, scaled the 2m (6ft 6in) chain-link security fence surrounding the village, helped unwittingly by some American athletes who were also trying to sneak their way back into the grounds without being noticed. Once inside the compound, the terrorists met up with three associates who had managed to gain entrance earlier by using forged credentials. Their sports bags contained guns and grenades and a set of keys they had stolen to gain access to two apartments on 31 Connollystraße, which were occupied by the Israeli athletic team.

At about 5.00 a.m. Yossef Gutfreund, the Israeli wrestling referee, thought he could hear the sound of faint scratching coming from the door of his apartment. He went to investigate the noise, but as he got closer he noticed that the door was already partly open and that there were masked men carrying guns in the corridor outside. He yelled to his fellow team mates to come quickly and threw his quite considerable weight against the door to prevent the attackers from entering. It was this action by Gutfreund that allowed the weightlifting coach, Tuvia Sokolovsky and race walker, Dr Shaul Ladany, to escape from the apartment. Four other athletes, plus the two team doctors and head of the delegation, Shmuel Lalkin, managed to take cover.

As the kidnappers moved the remaining hostages to the second apartment, the bulky wrestling coach, Moshe Weinberg, attacked the men, which allowed one of his team, Gad Tsobari, to escape unhurt. The very muscular Weinberg succeeded in knocking one of the terrorists unconscious and stabbed another with a fruit knife, before being shot himself. Another of the weightlifters, Yossef Romano, was also brave enough to take on one of his attackers, wounding him quite badly, but unfortunately he also sacrificed his own life for the sake of his team members.

The Black September members were then left with eight Israeli hostages – weightlifter Seev Friedman, wrestler Eliezer Halfin, track coach Amitzur Shapira, shooting coach Kehat Shorr, wrestler Mark Slavin, fencing coach Andre Spitzer, weightlifting judge Yacov Springer, Yossef Gutfreund and one American-born weightlifter, David Berger.

It turned out to be a well-planned attack, as some

of the Black September members had been working in various jobs around the Olympic Village, finding out exactly where their intended targets would be staying. Even though two of the Palestinians had been spotted in the village just several hours before the hostages were taken, no one thought anything of it as they were recognized as village workers.

At about 9.30 a.m. the Palestinian terrorists announced exactly who they were and demanded the release of 234 Palestinians and non-Arabs who had been jailed in Israel, along with two members of the Red Army Faction, Andreas Baader and Ulrike Meinhof. The terrorists then demanded that they receive safe passage out of Germany.

The group of terrorists was led by Luttif Afif and his next in command was Yusuf Nazzal. The junior members of the team were Afif Ahmen Hamid, Khalid Jawad, Ahmed Chic Thaa, Mohammed Safady, Adnan Al-Gashey and finally his cousin Jamal Al-Gashey.

Many hours of tense negotiations followed, which were made worse by the fact the hostages were Jewish, and therefore it was rather an embarassment for the German authorities. Initially the Germans offered the Palestinians a large amount of money for the release of the athletes. They also offered to substitute the hostages with Germans of high rank, but the terrorists refused their terms of negotiation. The chief of Munich police, Manfred Schreiber and Ahmed Touni, head of the Egyptian Olympic team, tried to negotiate directly with the terrorists, repeating their initial offer. However, Luttif Afif simply replied:

> . . . *money means nothing to us; our lives mean nothing to us.*

Although their negotiations were unsuccessful, the police did manage to gain a number of extensions to the deadline, convincing the terrorists that they were considering their demands. Everywhere else in the Olympic Village athletes were carrying on as if everything was normal, seemingly totally unaware of the very delicate situation that was unfolding.

Dressed in Olympic-style tracksuits and carrying machine guns, a small squad of German police – totally untrained for such an occasion – infiltrated the village waiting for instructions. With no real plan, and no ban on the media, the German police were filmed and the images broadcast live on television. From the television in the apartment, the terrorists were able to watch the police as they took their positions ready to attack. In the end Luttif Afif threatened to kill two of the hostages, which forced the police to leave the village. Not quite knowing where to go from here, the negotiating team decided to try and speak to the hostages themselves, as they were not completely certain that they were all still alive.

The negotiators spoke again with the Palestinian leader, Luttif Afif, and demanded to speak to the

Israeli athletes before they would meet any of the terrorists' demands. The terrorists agreed reluctantly to this request and brought two of the hostages to the second-floor apartment window, while the terrorists held guns to their heads. However, it wasn't long before the terrorists became bored with the prolonged questioning, and realizing that these were further delaying tactics, the fencing coach Andre Spitzer was hit round the head with a gun before being taken away from the window.

RESCUE OPERATION

One-and-a-half days later, and after many hours of futile negotiations, the Palestinians demanded transportation to Cairo. The negotiators feigned agreement and arranged for them to be taken to a NATO airbase at Fürstenfeldbruck by helicopter, where they said a Boeing 727 would be waiting to transport them and their hostages to Cairo in Egypt. The terrorists believed that they were being taken to Reim international airport. When the bus arrived at the apartment to take the Palestinians and their hostages to the helicopter, they realized with horror that they had nine hostages and not the five they expected, which meant they had not assigned enough armed men to kill the terrorists when they arrived at the airbase. The German snipers, who had never received any special training for hostage situations, were positioned in prominent places at the airstrip.

On the runway was a Boeing 727, which contained a further five or six armed German police, all of whom were dressed as members of the flight crew. Their purpose was to overpower the terrorists as they inspected the plane, giving the other snipers a chance to kill the remaining terrorists back at the helicopter. However, at the very last minute the Germans inside the Boeing 727 decided to abandon their plan without informing the other members of the squad, which left only the five snipers to try and overcome a larger and more heavily armed band of terrorists as they stepped from the helicopter.

At about 10.30 p.m. the helicopters landed at the NATO airbase. The four helicopter pilots and six of the Palestinians emerged from the aircraft. While four of the kidnappers held the pilots at gunpoint, the other two walked over the tarmac to inspect the waiting jet. As soon as they found the Boeing was empty, they realized that they had been tricked and ran back towards the helicopters. At this point the German authorities gave the order for their snipers to open fire.

In the ensuing chaos, all of the nine hostages, five of the terrorists, one of the German policemen and a pilot were killed. The three surviving Palestinians feigned death by laying on the ground, but they were subsequently captured by the German police and by 12.30 a.m. the total fiasco came to an end.

The first reports published worldwide claimed that all the hostages were alive and all the terrorists had been shot dead, it was only later that a representative for the International Olympic Committee admitted that 'initial reports were overly optimistic'.

DISRUPTION TO THE OLYMPIC GAMES

For the first time in history the Olympic Games was suspended for one full day on September 5. The following day the Olympic Committee held a memorial service in the main stadium, which was attended by 80,000 spectators and 3,000 athletes. During this service the Olympic flag was flown at half-mast along with the flags of the majority of the other nations who were competing. Initially it was planned to abandon the remainder of the Games, but it was decided by the Israeli government, the chief of the Olympic Commission and the president of the Munich organizing committee that 'the Games must go on'.

The remainder of the Israeli team announced that they would be leaving the village on September 6, and any remaining Jewish sportsmen were put under heavy guard fearing that they might be future targets.

Two memorial plaques stand today to commemorate the loss of Israeli lives. One stands outside their former apartment at 31 Connollystraße and another was unveiled on October 15, 1999, outside the Sydney Olympic Stadium.

AFTER EFFECTS AND REVENGE

The bodies of the five Palestinians killed during the shoot-out at Fürstenfeldbruck were flown back to Libya, where they were buried with full military honours and deemed as heroes. The surviving three terrorists were imprisoned by the German authorities but were freed just a few weeks later as part of a deal following the hijacking of a Lufthansa plane by fellow Palestinians.

Even though Abu Daoud openly admitted in 1999 that he had planned the attack with the permission of Yasser Arafat, there has never been a thorough public inquiry into exactly what went wrong.

Israel decided to hit back on September 8 by sending their airforce to target ten PLO bases inside both Syria and Lebanon. The operation to rid the terrorists who perpetrated the Munich Massacre was started by the Israeli Prime Minister, Golda Meir, with the full backing of the Israeli Defence Committee in the autumn of 1972. It is possible that the revenge killings may have lasted for as long as 20 years, but the nature of the operation was carried out in such secrecy that the exact details of 'Operation Wrath of God', as it was to become known, are very difficult to report on. One thing is clear, though, that Operation Wrath of God was a mission to gain revenge for the families of those men killed in the Munich massacre. The operation was planned not only to punish the perpetrators of

Munich, but it was also intended to disrupt and try to deter any such future terrorist activities by assassinating as many known PLO suspects as possible.

Of the men who were believed to have planned the Munich massacre, it is only certain that one man survives today, Abu Daoud. He is believed to be hiding out somewhere in Africa or the Middle East. In 1981 he was shot 13 times by an assassin, but surprisingly survived the attack. Even today Abu Daoud says he has no regrets about his involvement in the dreadful events of September 5, which cost the lives of 11 innocent and talented men.

DIPLOMATIC
ASSASSINATIONS IN
KHARTOUM

*We are going to continue the Palestinian
revolution until the last martyr to create a
Palestinian state.*

YASSER ARAFAT

Once again members of the Palestinian Group
Black September caused havoc when they stormed
the Saudi Arabian embassy in Khartoum, the capital
of Sudan, on March 1, 1973.

There was a party being held at the embassy for
George Curtis Moore, the US ambassador's deputy,
and just before 7.00 p.m. on March 1, the reception
was starting to break up. The ambassadors were
relaxed and chatting as they got ready to go and
find their chauffeurs. However, just as the members
of the party were about to leave, eight masked gunmen stormed into the building, followed by a volley
of random gunfire. Those who were not quick

enough to escape were forced into the embassy's main reception room, where they were forced to sit down on the floor.

One by one the hostages were asked to reveal their identity to the terrorists and, with the exception of five men, one woman and four children, the majority of the party were free to leave. The diplomats that they kept hostage were:

US Ambassador Cleo Allen Noel, Jr
US Chargé d'Affaires George Curtis Moore
Saudi Ambassador Sheikh Abdullah al Malhouk, his wife and their four children
Belgian Chargé d'Affaires Guy Eid and his
Jordanian counterpart, Adli al Nasser

In the initial shootings both Mr Noel and Mr Moore were hurt and the sheikh, whose four children were still in the embassy, ordered that the terrorists send for a doctor. However, the members of the Black September group were not prepared to allow anyone else in the embassy until they had made their demands clear.

Heated negotiations took place for over 26 hours, in which time the gunmen sent out a note stating that they would hold the diplomats hostage until such time as any Palestinian militants held in Jordan were freed along with Abu Daoud, the perpetrator of the Munich massacre. They also wanted Sirhan Sirhan released who was being held in jail in California for the murder of Robert Kennedy.

Finally, they wanted the freeing of all 'Palestinian women in prison in Israel' along with members of the Baader-Meinhof gang held in West Germany. They also requested for a plane to take them and their hostages to the United States, but this was rejected by both the American and Sudanese authorities. President Richard Nixon said that although he would do everything in his power to negotiate the release of the hostages, there was no way that he would succumb to blackmail.

On the evening of March 2 a message came over the radio from the Beirut headquarters of the PLO ordering the execution of all the hostages.

> *Why are you waiting? The people's blood in the Cold River cries for vengeance!'*

The message was in code and personally delivered by the chairman of the PLO, Yasser Arafat. Strangely, there appeared to be no police or security guards on duty in the embassy on the night of the party, but Sudanese troops and armoured cars were placed around the building while the government was involved in emergency talks on how best to handle the delicate situation.

Shortly after receiving the recording the gunmen took the two Americans and the Belgian, tied their hands behind their backs and lined them up against a basement wall. All eight of the gunmen opened fire, killing all three of the hostages, whom the terrorists claimed were enemies of the Palestinian cause.

The eight gunmen sent messages out to the administrators to say that they were quite prepared to kill themselves and the remaining hostages if any of their troops attempted to enter the embassy building. However, the Sudanese government refused to bargain with the members of Black September, and 60 hours after the siege started, the remaining hostages were released and the eight gunmen gave themselves over to the authorities.

They were tried by a court in Sudan on June 24, 1974, and all eight of the killers were sentenced to life imprisonment. The United States demanded that they receive the death penalty, but instead of complying to this request, the Sudanese president reduced their sentences to seven years and then proceeded to have them deported to Cairo in Egypt. In protest, the United States withdrew its ambassador to Sudan and froze any economic assistance to the country. However, this was only a temporary measure as the ambassador returned before the year was out and financial aid resumed in 1976.

Three of the terrorists disappeared, while the other five did actually serve out their sentence before finally being released back into society.

DUBLIN-MONAGHAN BOMBS

I do not know which evil men did this but everyone who has practised violence or preached violence or condoned violence must bear his share of responsiblility. It will bring home to us what the people of Northern Ireland have been suffering for five long years.

IRISH PRIME MINISTER, LIAM COSGRAVE

May 17, 1974, saw the biggest mass murder occurrence in the history of violence in Northern Ireland. Without any warning whatsoever, three car bombs exploded within minutes of one another right in the heart of Dublin during the Friday evening rush hour, when the crowds were at their height, thus ensuring maximum casualties. The three explosions killed 26 people, including an unborn baby, and injured hundreds more. There was a fourth car bomb, which exploded 90 minutes later in Monaghan town, killing a further seven people.

The three cars used in the Dublin bombings had all been stolen in Belfast on the same day. The first of the three cars, a metallic olive-green Hillman Avenger, had been taken from outside its owner's home that morning at about 10.00 a.m. by three men wearing masks. The owner of the car was held by two of the men until about 4.00 p.m., at which time he was released and immediately reported the incident to the police. This car, packed with explosives, was detonated at 5.28 p.m. in Parnell Street, Dublin. Eleven people died.

The second car, a blue Ford Escort, was hijacked on the morning of May 17 from outside the warehouse belonging to a firm of haulage contractors. This car belonged to a man who worked at the haulage company, and was stolen between 8.00 and 10.00 a.m. After the explosion in Talbot Street, Dublin, at approximately 5.30 p.m., several bodies lay in the road for half an hour as ambulances struggled to get through the build-up of traffic. A witness who was walking into a hotel on Talbot Street when the bomb exploded, explained:

> *There were hundreds of people in the street who were running and screaming aimlessly. A newspaper stand was blown into the air right past me and the newsboy next to it just disappeared in front of my eyes!*

The majority of the number plate on the Ford Escort had been destroyed by the blast, making this car much harder for the Garda to trace. Fourteen people died as a result of this explosion.

The third car was a Lagoon blue Austin 1800 taxi stolen from an area off the Shankill Road at 9.00 a.m. Again the owner of the car was held hostage for a while before being released unharmed at 2.00 p.m. He was told to go home and to report his car missing in about one hour's time to the police at Tennent Street RUC station. The man did as his hijackers had asked and reported the car missing at about 3.20 p.m. It exploded just two hours later in South Leinster Street, causing a further two deaths.

The fourth explosion happened in Monaghan in the province of Ulster at approximately 6.58 p.m. The green Hillman Minx had been stolen from a car park in Portadown while its owner was shopping. On discovering the car missing, the owner reported that it had been stolen to the Portadown RUC station at about 4.20 p.m. This, the last car bomb, killed five people instantly and a further two died in hospital in the following weeks.

All the bombings had been timed to coincide with the strike of the loyalist Ulster Workers' Council (UWC). The strike was a general strike that took place between Wednesday May 15 to Tuesday May 28, 1974, called in protest of both the security and political situation in Northern Ireland. It was also opposed to the proposals put forward in the Sunningdale Agreement, which meant that the governing body of the Republic of Ireland would have been in direct control of the running of the area. The strike was successful in bringing about the downfall of the power-sharing Northern Ireland Executive, and as a result the responsibility then lay with the British Parliament under the arrangements laid out for 'Direct Rule'. So whoever planned the car bombs knew it would have a maximum impact in a time when Ireland was undergoing great political instability.

THE AFTERMATH

Both the Ulster Defence Association (UDA) and the Ulster Volunteer Force (UVF) denied responsibility for the bombs and the Provisional IRA issued a statement that called the explosions 'vile murder'. The investigations by the Garda seemed to grind to a halt after a few weeks, despite the fact that they had the names of several known suspects. Over the years the families of the victims and those injured in the blasts came to question the actions of those people in authority in Northern Ireland.

Yorkshire Television, more than 20 years later, made a documentary – *Hidden Hand: The Forgotten Massacre* – about the car bombs in Dublin and Monaghan with the cooperation of retired members of the Irish Garda. Using information supplied to them, the television programme claimed that the atrocities were the responsibility of the UVF, which were a loyalist paramilitary organization. However, the documentary went on to say that the UVF did not have the knowledge to build bombs of such a sophisticated nature and felt that they must have had outside assistance, and it alleged that British intelligence had provided the bombers with military assistance. Previous bombs that had been assembled by the UVF had been simple, primitive devices, yet when forensics studied the remains of the Dublin and Monaghan bombs, they were found to be relatively sophisticated requiring quite a high degree of knowledge regarding explosives.

The relatives of the people killed in the explosions believed that there were just too many questions left unanswered, and in 1996 they formed an organization called the Justice For The Forgotten. Since their formation, the group has continued to put pressure on the Irish government to carry out a public enquiry in an effort to find the truth. Eventually, their efforts paid off and a private inquiry into the bombings was set up in 2003 by Henry Barron, a former Irish Supreme Court judge. The British authorities were not willing to cooperate with Barron or provide him with the necessary files and information he requested. The Barron Report was a long and detailed document, which consisted of some 448 pages, and it gave a close insight into the lack of investigation by the Garda. It makes many claims and accusations but does not really draw any final conclusions that could be supported by circumstantial evidence.

It is still incomprehensible that possibly the most lethal crime in the history of Northern Ireland on any one day has not been pursued in any depth.

After all the bloodshed and loss of lives, which appalled the nation, not one person within the central government wanted to pursue the case with the Garda. Those at the higher levels insisted that the investigation did not produce any conclusive evidence, and over the years the enthusiasm grew less and less, possibly proving even further that this was some sort of government cover-up.

GUILDFORD AND WOOLWICH PUB BOMBINGS

The day will dawn when all the people
of Ireland will have the desire for freedom
to show. It is then we'll see the rising of
the moon.

BOBBY SANDS

The Guildford and Woolwich pub bombings were
part of a campaign mounted in the 1970s by the
Provisional Republican Army (IRA) to strike fear
into the inhabitants of the British mainland. Five
people were killed and over 40 injured when a bomb
exploded in the Horse and Groom pub, Guildford,
on the evening of October 5, 1974; half an hour later,
another bomb went off in the Seven Stars nearby,
but this time the landlord was able to evacuate the
pub and there were no casualties. Just over a month
after these atrocities, a further bombing took place in
Woolwich, at the King's Arms pub, in which two

men were killed and another disabled for life. All of the targets were places where army personnel were known to gather, and most of the victims were British soldiers.

PRESSURE MOUNTS

Throughout 1974, the attacks continued, including two horrifying bombings of pubs in Birmingham that killed a total of 21 people and injured many more. Naturally, as the IRA's campaign of terror continued, the pressure was on from the government, the media and the public for the police to find the culprits and bring them to justice.

By the end of the year, the police had arrested three men and a woman: Gerry Conlon, Paul Hill, Patrick Armstrong and Carole Richardson, who later became known as the Guildford Four. When their cases came to trial, all were convicted of murder, as well as other charges. However, the Guildford Four constantly maintained that they were innocent, and after many years of campaigning, were found to have been entirely unconnected with the murders. Their convictions were overturned. In the same way, those convicted of the crimes in Birmingham, who were known as the Birmingham Six, were freed after years of protesting their innocence.

SIX POUNDS OF GELIGNITE

On the evening of October 5, 1974, British army soldiers and their friends met up in Guildford, Surrey, to drink in the Horse and Groom pub. Unbeknownst to them, that afternoon, a bomb containing 2.7 kg (6 lb) of gelignite had been placed under some seats by the bar. As the evening wore on, the pub became more crowded, until at 8.30 p.m., the bomb suddenly went off. There were no warnings.

Those who died that night were Paul Craig, a plasterer, and four teenage soldiers from the Scots Guard Regiment and the Women's Royal Army Corps. They were Guardsman William Forsyth, aged 18, Guardsman John Hunter, 17, Private Caroline Slater, 18, and Private Ann Hamilton, 19. As well as killing these young people as they began their adult lives, the bomb also injured around 50, and caused widespread panic – as it had been calculated to do.

After hearing the blast that went off in the Horse and Groom, the landlord of the Seven Stars pub nearby wisely evacuated all his customers. Another bomb containing 2.7 kg (6 lb) of gelignite then detonated in his pub at 9.00 p.m., but thankfully, this time no one was hurt.

LEG BLOWN OFF

The bombings were widely condemned by politicians and the media, who swore to bring the culprits to justice. However, although the police suspected that an IRA active service unit had planted the bombs, the terrorists had covered their traces well, and there were few leads to follow up. Meanwhile, as other attacks on army and establishment targets continued, including kidnappings and shootings, an atmosphere of fear and anxiety, particularly in and around London, began to build up.

On November 6, 1974, the IRA struck again with the bombing of a pub in Woolwich. This time, the pub was the King's Arms, situated opposite the Royal Artillery Depot of the British army – another popular watering hole for soldiers and their friends. The bomb used was similar to those planted in the pubs at Guildford, only as well as the gelignite, it was packed with shrapnel. And instead of hiding it under a seat, the bombers threw it through the pub window, killing a civilian, Alan Horsley, and a soldier, Gunner Richard Dunne. Another victim narrowly escaped death when he had his leg blown off by the blast.

MASS MURDER

Later the same month, two bombs exploded in pubs in Birmingham, the Tavern in the Town and the Mulberry Bush. In these attacks, 21 people died and more than 50 were injured. Next, there was a spate of bombs placed in pillar boxes, followed by shootings, a car bomb, and an attempt on the life of the British Prime Minister, Edward Heath. At

Christmas, the Provisional IRA called an 11-day truce, but it was not long before the campaign of terror began again the following year.

In this atmosphere of brutality and intimidation, it is not surprising that the police were desperate to find suspects for the attacks, especially for the pub bombings that had wreaked so much devastation. However, the four people they eventually picked up for the murders at Guildford and Woolwich had had nothing to do with the bombings, a fact that did not emerge until over a decade later, by which time they had spent many years in jail being punished for crimes that they never committed.

TORTURED BY POLICE

The Guildford Four – Gerry Conlon, Paul Hill, Patrick Armstrong, and Carole Richardson (an Englishwoman) – turned out to have little or no connection to the Provisional IRA at all. Conlon had grown up in Belfast, and in 1974 he had moved to London to work there for a few months before returning once more to his home city. In November that year he was arrested and flown to Guildford, where he was interrogated for several days until he signed a confession. In his statement, which was later shown to have been altered by police, he implicated his friends Hill, Armstrong, and Richardson, who were arrested and also signed false confessions. Conlon's father Guiseppe travelled to England to help his son and was also arrested, along with other members of the family, who later became known as the Maguire Seven.

At the trial the Guildford Four protested that they had been tortured by police to sign confessions. No evidence could be brought to bear that any of the four had links with the Provisional wing of the IRA, but nevertheless they were convicted on 33 charges of murder and conspiracy. They were each given prison sentences of 30 to 35 years. In 1977, their appeal was turned down. Three years later, Guiseppe Conlon died while under police guard in Hammersmith Hospital, where he had been sent from Wormwood Scrubs Prison due to illness.

MISLEADING EVIDENCE

The campaign to free the Guildford Four continued unabated, and the prisoners became the subject of several television documentaries. Finally, on October 19, 1989, came a breakthrough. A detective looking through notes on the case had found that the police had tampered with statements made by Patrick Armstrong when he was under interrogation. There were many deletions and additions, and all the notes had been rearranged. It was thought that hand-written notes presented at the trial had been made after the interview took place, implying that the police had altered the evidence to fit in with the picture they wanted to present in court. A new right to appeal was granted, and at this trial, the Lord Chief Justice, Lord Lane, ruled that the police had lied and that the evidence was misleading.

The Guildford Four's convictions were over-turned and they were released, after serving 15 years in prison. In addition, Paul Hill's conviction for the murder of a British soldier named Brian Shaw, based on a so-called confession that he had while being interrogated by the Surrey police force, was found to be unsafe.

SIX-DAY SIEGE

However, it was not until 2005 that the Guildford Four received an official apology for their many years of wrongful imprisonment from the British Prime Minister, Tony Blair, who stated that he was 'very sorry that they were subject to such an ordeal and injustice'. He added that the Four 'deserved to be completely and publicly exonerated'. Conlon expressed delight at the apology, although some felt that it did not go far enough, and that the announcement should have been made in Parliament.

Back in 1977, the authorities had had their chance to free the Guildford Four. During the trial of a group of IRA operatives known as the Balcombe Street Gang, the men accused instructed their lawyers to draw attention to the fact that four totally innocent people were serving massive sentences for crimes that they had not committed:

the bombings in Guildford and Woolwich. The members of the gang, Martin O'Connell, Eddie Butler, Harry Duggan and Hugh Doherty, had taken a couple hostage in Balcombe Street, London, and had surrendered after a six-day siege. As well as murdering Ross McWhirter, who had advertised a £50,000 reward for the capture of the terrorists, they had also launched bomb attacks on military and establishment targets in and around London. The gang all received life sentences for their part in these crimes, but the lead on the Guildford and Woolwich pub bombings was not followed up, and it never became clear whether or not they were guilty of these attacks as well. Thus, to this day, no one has been convicted of these heinous crimes.

THE LAJU INCIDENT

*Singapore condemns in the strongest terms
these attacks and all other forms of terrorism.
The perpetrators of these terrible crimes cannot
go unpunished. They must be brought to
justice. Others must be deterred from
contemplating similar horrific acts.*

AMBASSADOR KISHORE MAHBUBANI

The small island of Pulau Bukom is situated just a
few kilometres to the south of Singapore and is
currently the site of the Shell oil refinery. The
company's association with the island dates back to
1891 when Shell used the island as a store for
kerosene. The tranquil island was the scene of a
terror attack on January 31, 1974, when a group of
four terrorists attempted to blow up the refinery.

THEIR PLANS GO AWRY

The group of four terrorists comprised of two men
from the Japanese Red Army (JRA), or 'Sekigun',
and two Arabs from the Popular Front for the

Liberation of Palestine (PFLP). The JRA has had a long-term relationship with the PFLP, possibly due to the fact that their centre and training camp was based in the Bekaa valley in Lebanon. They had carried out other terror attacks together, the most notable one being the massacre of 26 people at Israel's Lod Airport in May 1972. The mission of these four men was to blow up three oil storage tanks belonging to the Shell Eastern Petroleum Company, situated on the island of Pulau Bukom, with the aim of disrupting the oil supply from Singapore to other countries, especially South Vietnam.

To reach the island, the four men had commandeered a small boat, but their mission hit problems right from the beginning. As they tried to steer their craft towards Pulau Bukom, they felt something hit the underneath of their vessel. Looking into the water, they realized that they had run aground on some coral reef. Unsure of what to do next, the four men waited until they managed to trick an unsuspecting boatmen to tow them to the shore of the island.

Once on dry land, the four men – carrying submachine guns and explosives – climbed over the sea wall and ran towards the gates of the Shell refinery. The terrorists fired at a tanker as it tried to enter the gates but failed to stop the driver. They also fired at an engineer who was working on the island, but he too managed to escape unharmed. There was only one guard at the security post and, although he was taken by surprise, he managed to escape and raised the alarm.

Out of the 12 explosive devices the terrorists were carrying, they only managed to actually detonate three of them, and these caused little damage. Realizing that their mission had been a complete failure, the four men had to think quickly about how best to escape the island. Seeing the *Laju* ferry at the Bukom jetty, they decided they would hijack the vessel and take the five crew members hostage. The ferry headed out to sea, quickly pursued by marine police boats. When they reached the Eastern Anchorage, the small boat was intercepted and was blocked in by 15 marine police boats, custom launches and three Singapore Maritime Command gunboats.

Using the five crew members as bait, the terrorists started to make their demands. The negotiations went on for several days, in which time two of the hostages managed to escape by jumping overboard. Later after many hours of intense bargaining, the terrorists agreed to release the remaining three hostages in return for a selection of 'guarantors', which included four commandos from the Singapore Armed Forces and eight government officials. The group of 'guarantors' was led by MINDEF's Director of Security & Intelligence, Sellapan Ramanathan (also known as S. R. Nathan), who later became the President of Singapore.

The plan was to move the terrorists from the *Laju* on the night of February 7 and transfer them to the Marine Police Headquarters, and from there a minibus would pick them up and take them to the airport. Before they left the boat, the three terrorists covered their faces with hoots and tied the three remaining hostages, securing their hands behind their backs. Determined not to let anything else go wrong, the terrorists held the hostages at gunpoint during the entire 30-minute journey to the Marine Police jetty.

On arriving at the airport, the terrorists, true to their word, immediately freed their hostages and surrendered all their weapons. They left Singapore for Kuwait on February 8, along with the members of S. R. Nathan's team, subsequently ending a very delicate situation.

ROLE OF THE GUARANTOR

The 'Laju' incident, as it has become known, shows the skill with which the Singapore Armed Forces Commandos handled their role as 'guarantor'. They formed in 1969 as an elite branch of the Singapore Armed Forces with the aim of specializing in neutralizing delicate situations in enemy territories. The term 'guarantor' was not really used until 1997, and was a term for a mediator who would take part in the negotiations between disputing parties. Due to the vigilance of their Internal Security Department, the Singapore government was able to foil the attempts of people who wanted to harm their country.

Therefore, the steps we have taken over the years have been to ensure that Singapore is safe and secure.

MINISTER WONG

IRA COACH BOMB

We've come to terms with it, but we'll never ever forgive, and never ever forget. It will be with me to the day I die, that morning.

ANNE MORRISON

The bombing of a coach carrying British army soldiers and their families from Manchester to an army base in Catterick, North Yorkshire, was just one atrocity in a long campaign of bombings mounted by the terrorist Irish Republican Army (IRA) on mainland Britain during the 1970s. Eleven people died in the coach bomb blast, including two young children; 12 more were seriously injured. Later in the same year, the IRA began to plant bombs in pubs, in Guildford and Birmingham, killing 26 people and injuring many more. In all these cases, the wrong people were jailed for the murders, in a series of high-level miscarriages of justice that did little to enhance the reputation of the police and judiciary in Britain. In the case of the coach bomb, the woman jailed for the crime was Judith Ward, a woman with a history of mental illness who served 18 years in prison before eventually being released. During the investigation, it became clear that police had cobbled together a story from the garbled evidence she gave, so that they could secure a conviction for the crime. Thus, the M62 coach bombing, and the attacks that followed it, were not only disasters for the victims involved, and for the security of the British public in general; in the aftermath of the events, the way they were handled in the courts also turned out to be indictments of the British justice system.

TWISTED METAL

In the early hours of Monday, February 4, 1974, a coach was travelling up the M62 motorway between Gomersal and Birkenshaw. It had come from Manchester, and was on its way to a British army base at Catterick, in North Yorkshire, and to an RAF base near Darlington. The coach was full of soldiers and their families, who had been taking a weekend break together. Normally, soldiers with 48-hour passes would have taken trains, but at the time, there was widespread industrial unrest, and many railway workers were on strike, so the trains were not running properly. Thus the soldiers had come to rely on the coach rather than the rail services to get them back to their stations on time, and special coaches had been commissioned to take soldiers out on their weekend leave and run them back again to their bases on Sunday night.

As the coach sped along the motorway south of Leeds, near Bradford and Drightlington, there was a massive explosion. It was just past midnight. The sound of the blast was carried for several kilometres, and the blast itself left the coach a tangle of twisted metal. Bodies were strewn along the motorway, in some cases blasted 228 metres (250 yards) away. Police and army bomb disposal experts were immediately called to the scene, but in the pitch-black darkness, it was difficult initially to work out what exactly had happened. In their first public statements, West Yorkshire police only commented: 'We are treating this with an open mind. It could have been the work of terrorists.'

YOUNG FAMILY DEAD

As daylight dawned, it became clear what had happened. Out of a coach load of more than 50 people, 11 people were dead. Tragically, in one instance an entire young family had lost their lives: Lance Corporal Clifford Houghton, his wife Linda, both aged only 23, and their two sons Lee and Robert, aged five and three. In addition, 12 people had been taken to hospital with serious injuries, including a six-year-old boy who had suffered severe burns. Many more of the passengers had sustained minor injuries.

A memorial service for the victims was held shortly after the bombing, led by the chaplain of the

First Battalion King's Regiment. Linda Houghton's sister, Anne Morrison, spoke of her loss, saying, 'We've come to terms with it, but we'll never ever forgive, and never ever forget. It will be with me to the day I die, that morning.'

MISCARRIAGE OF JUSTICE

When news of the atrocity was reported, with horrifying pictures showing the extent of the damage, the public were outraged. The attack was condemned by all the major political parties, and the government vowed to bring the perpetrators to justice as soon as possible. Naturally enough, given this pressure, the police were extremely keen to make an arrest, but in their haste to find a culprit for the atrocity, they initiated a terrible miscarriage of justice that later came back to haunt them.

Judith Ward, a 25-year-old woman from Stockport, voluntarily confessed to the crime, and to two other IRA bombings: the bombing of Euston station, London, in September 1973; and the bombing of the National Defence College in Buckinghamshire on February 12, 1974. What the court was not told was that Ward had changed her 'confession' repeatedly, and that parts of it were so confused that the police and the prosecution had to select sections from it so that it made sense.

Moreover, the forensic evidence that was available for the case was faulty.

FALSE FORENSIC EVIDENCE

Ward had apparently been found to have traces of nitroglycerine on her hands, on her bag and in the caravan where she was living. These traces had been picked up using tests, such as the Greiss test, which have since been discredited. The Greiss test is a chemical analysis that shows whether organic nitrites are present on the surface of an item. However, since it also shows the presence of nitrates that are found in ordinary household cleaners, it often gives false positive results. In addition, the forensic scientists working on the case did not give impartial evidence, exaggerating some features of their findings, and they withheld information about other aspects of the case.

In retrospect, Judith Ward appears to have been used as a convenient scapegoat for IRA crimes that the police were unable to solve. Her history revealed her to be a woman who suffered from mental illness and who had led an unstable life. As a young adult, she had worked as a horse-riding instructor in Dundalk, Ireland, and she had then joined the Women's Royal Army Corps. However, she went absent without leave from the army, and she was later discharged after claiming that the IRA had tried to recruit her. She then broke into the British army headquarters in Northern Ireland, but was not charged. In the years leading up to the bombing, she had had a variety of jobs, including working as a chambermaid in London and travelling with Chipperfield Circus. While in custody for the bombings, she made a suicide attempt, which was not reported to the court.

IMPROBABLE CONFESSION

The prosecution barrister in the case, John Cobb QC, alleged that Ward had joined the army under instructions from the IRA, so that she could pass information to them that would help them select targets for their bombings. This information had led to several attacks, and to the deaths of at least six people. For the defence, Ward's solicitor Andrew Rankin QC said that there were many anomalies in her confession, and that much of it seemed highly improbable. Ward's family maintained that she was innocent and had never been a member of the IRA. According to her brother Tommy, much of the testimony she gave, such as the information that she had been married to an IRA Provo and had borne a child by another IRA man, was 'romancing'.

Nevertheless, Judith Ward was jailed for life at Wakefield Crown Court in 1974, and went on to serve 18 years of her sentence. Then, on May 11, 1992, her conviction was declared unsafe by a Court of Appeal. The three Appeal Court judges in the case stated that there had been a 'grave miscarriage of justice': the jury in the trial should have been told of Ward's history of mental illness. Moreover, forensic scientists had withheld evidence in the case that could have led to a different outcome. The judges declared that Ward's conviction had been 'secured by ambush', and went on to free her.

After her release, Ward wrote an autobiography entitled *Ambushed*, which was published in 1992. She also began to study criminology and campaigned for prisoners' rights.

ANTITERROR LAWS

As well as the M62 coach bomb case, there were other important miscarriages of justice that took place in the 1970s as a result of the police and judiciary's haste to find scapegoats for what were, of course, appalling terror attacks. In 1974, the IRA mounted a series of horrific pub bombings, resulting in the deaths of five people in Guildford and 21 in Birmingham. Four people were convicted for the Guildford atrocity, and six for the Birmingham attack. After a long campaign, all the convictions in both cases were overturned by the Court of Appeal: the Guildford Four, as they became known, were released in 1989, followed two years later by the release of the Birmingham Six.

As well as leading to these miscarriages of justice, the bombings also prompted the government to introduce new antiterrorist laws in Britain. The police gained powers to allow them to hold suspected terrorists for seven days without charge, while the authorities also gained the right to expel individuals from mainland Britain to Northern

Ireland or the Republic of Ireland. However, despite these and other measures, the IRA campaign of bombings on the British mainland continued for two more decades, before a lasting ceasefire was declared.

CAMBODIA GENOCIDE

I did not join the resistance movement to kill people, to kill the nation. Look at me now. Am I a savage person? My conscience is clear.

POL POT

Cambodia is a country in Southeast Asia that was once the centre of the ancient kingdom of Khmer. Its present day capital is Phnom Penh, and in 1953, it gained independence after nearly 100 years of French rule. In April 1975, the Communist forces of the Khmer Rouge, led by Pol Pot, began a brutal four-year regime in Cambodia, which resulted in the deaths of 25 per cent of the country's population.

Cambodia was no stranger to violence; in 1964 the USA entered the Vietnam war, and Cambodia became part of the battlefield. During the following four years, Cambodia lost almost 750,000 civilians when B-52 bombers used napalm and dart cluster-bombs in an effort to destroy suspected North Vietnamese supply lines.

POL POT AND THE KHMER ROUGE

The Khmer Rouge were fanatical communists that were determined to create the most perfect form of communism in the world. They were a small guerilla movement, which started in 1970, under the leadership of Pol Pot.

Pol Pot was born in 1925 and, at the age of 20, travelled to Paris to study electronics. During this time he became obsessed with Marxism and started to neglect his studies. He failed to gain a scholarship and returned to Cambodia in 1953, immediately joining an underground communist movement.

Shortly after his return, Cambodia gained independence from France and came under the rule of a royal monarch, Prince Sihanouk. By 1962, Pol Pot had become leader of the communist move-ment and, in order to avoid the wrath of Sihanouk, who did not agree with his politics, he fled into the jungle. Pol Pot formed a new communist move-ment, which he called the Khmer Rouge (Red Cambodians), and waged a war against the govern-ment of Sihanouk. Under the rule of Sihanouk, Cambodia had managed to maintain neutrality in the Vietnamese war by offering favours to both sides, but his prime minister, Lon Nol, did not have the same views as the prince and planned to take over his sovereignty.

THE MILITARY COUP

In 1970, Prince Sihanouk was deposed in a military coup that was organized by Lon Nol and the then acting prime minister, Prince Sirik Matak. In early March, Lon Nol organized anti-Vietnam demonstrations across Cambodia and ordered the Vietnamese to leave immediately or they would face an attack. On March 12, thousands of people marched into Phnom Penh, raiding the North Vietnamese and Viet Cong embassies. The next day, Matak cancelled the secret smuggling deals that Sihanouk had set up via the port of Sihanoukville.

At the time Sihanouk was away in France. When he heard the news he was furious, threatening to have his two ministers arrested. However, instead of returning to Cambodia to sort out the mess, Sihanouk travelled to Moscow and ignored the further actions of the two men. Lon Nol and Sirik Matak managed to convince the National Assembly to remove Sihanouk from power, which had the effect of ending Cambodia's neutrality. Both the USA and Vietnam were delighted by the change of government and felt that Lon Nol would be a far better man to deal with than his predecessor.

Sihanouk, however, was not prepared to leave quietly, and he retaliated by joining forces with his former enemy, Pol Pot and the Khmer Rouge. They set about opposing Cambodia's new military government. In the same year, the USA invaded Cambodia to drive the North Vietnamese out of their border camps. However, their mission failed because, rather than drive them out of Cambodia, they drove them deeper into the country where they allied themselves with the Khmer Rouge.

SUPPORT FOR POL POT

Cambodia became the target for US bombing raids from 1969 until 1973, killing more than 150,000 peasants. The peasants fled in panic from the countryside and settled in the capital of Phnom Penh, which resulted in both economic and military destabilization. This was good news for Pol Pot, who was now receiving a lot of support, and by 1975 he had an estimated force of over 700,000 men.

The USA withdrew their troops from Vietnam in 1975 and Cambodia, which was now plagued by a corrupt government, also lost its American support. Pol Pot and his army took advantage of the situation and marched into Phnom Penh on April 17 and took control of the capital, and effectively the whole of Cambodia. With military victory over the Lon Nol government and absolute power in their hands, the Khmer Rouge wasted no time in building their 'utopia'.

THE GENOCIDE

Within days of overthrowing the government, Pol Pot started a radical campaign to reconstruct Cambodia, modelling it on Mao Tse-Tung's Cultural

Revolution, which he had witnessed first-hand during a previous visit to China. He declared that he was about to 'purify' Cambodian society and banished any Western culture, city life, religion and any form of foreign influences. Embassies were closed and foreigners were forced to leave; Newspaper offices and television stations were shut down; radios and bicycles were confiscated; the use of the telephone and mail were curtailed; money was forbidden; and health care was eliminated – in fact Cambodia was completely shut off from the remainder of the world. Pol Pot's intention was to create an extreme form of peasant communism, in which the population would all work together as labourers in a huge coalition of collective farmers.

Giving them little time to gather their belongings, and under the threat of death, the inhabitants of the towns and cities were forced to leave their homes. Regardless of their physical condition and age, every member of the population was press-ganged into leaving – not one single person was exempt from the mass exodus. Those who did not obey were murdered, and children not old enough to work were taken away from their parents and placed in separate labour camps. Factories, schools, hospitals and universities were all closed and professional people in any field – lawyers, doctors, teachers, engineers, scientists alike – were all murdered along with any members of their families.

Any form of religion was banned. Buddist monks were killed and their temples were destroyed. The slaughter of the population was so severe that even minor disabilities such as wearing glasses, was considered a weakness and the punishment was death. The main slogan for the Khmer Rouge was, *To spare you is no profit, to destroy you is no loss.*

Those who escaped the massacre were forced into labour camps, where they worked for no money and the minimum of rations. They were housed in despicable conditions and forced to work exceptionally long hours. Any form of personal relationship was discouraged, along with any signs of affection. Before long people became weak and sick from overwork and lack of nourishment, and as there was no medical assistance, most died a sad and lonely death.

Pol Pot's new regime also targeted the minority groups, which included Chinese, Vietnamese, Thai and anyone with ethnic ancestry. Almost half of the Chum Muslim population were killed, along with 8,000 Christians. There was no end to the extremes that Pol Pot and his murderous communist party would go to, and even some of the party's own leaders lived in fear. The Khmer Rouge frequently interrogated their own members if they were suspected of even the slightest thought of treachery of sabotage, often ending in imprisonment and execution. It is estimated that the death toll during Pol Pot's reign was as many as two million people.

KHMER ROUGE IN RETREAT

On December 25, 1978, Vietnam launched a full-scale assault on Cambodia with the sole purpose of wiping out the Khmer Rouge and their evil leader. By January 7, 1979, Phnom Penh fell and Pol Pot was deposed. The remaining members of the Khmer Rouge, along with Pol Pot, retreated into Thailand.

The Vietnamese, now free to control, formed a puppet government (basically, one formed from foreign power), which included many members who had managed to defect from the Khmer Rouge. Pol Pot's strict regimes had left Cambodia in a poor economic state, and with no foreign aid and no professional people left alive, they struggled to bring the country into any sort of order.

The Khmer Rouge continued to oppose the new socialist government, but their organization was starting to crumble. Many of them had already defected to the new government, and many offered pleas to try to escape execution. The government did everything in their power to bring the leaders of the communist organization to justice and made plans for an international tribunal.

Pol Pot, who had managed to obtain assistance from US relief agencies, had amassed 20,000–40,000 guerillas and waged a war against the succession of Cambodian governments, which was to last for over 17 years. The recovery of Cambodia and its people was a long, hard struggle. Pol Pol eventually lost control of the Khmer Rouge in the 1990s, and was arrested. However, before they were able to bring him to trial under an international tribunal, Pol Pot died of a heart attack in April 1998, at the age of 73.

AFTER THE GENOCIDE

From 1995 onwards mass graves were uncovered revealing just how extensive the atrocious massacre had been. The bones and skulls uncovered from the graves were preserved to create a potent memorial of what had happened, and the area became known as the 'killing fields'. In Phnom Penh, the place where Pol Pot and his leaders carried out their acts of torture and murder, it is not only the skulls that are displayed, but also photographs of the victims are pinned to the walls.

The exceptional terror that the population of Cambodia had to endure was brought about by the atrocities of war. Because it was the war that equipped them with weapons and gave them the will to use them, turning them into an enormous army of bullies. It appears that as long as war is regarded as permissible, there will be an ongoing problem with regard to the act of genocide. It teaches people intolerance, bullying, violence, prejudice, hatred, victimization, fantacism and extremism, and on top of all this a hunger for power.

Cambodia has to rely on the strength of its people to overcome the evils of Pol Pot's regime and now, over three decades later, it seems likely that at least some of the people responsible for the genocide will be brought to trial. Nine years have passed since Cambodia and the United Nations agreed to work together on the trials, and yet international prosecutors only started work at the beginning of July 2006. With the court proceedings themselves still many months away, the question which nows hangs in the balance is whether any of the remaining Khmer Rouge members, who are all elderly and many in ill health, will ever see the inside of a court room.

Apart from one of the leaders, Ta Mok, who recently died while in detention, most of the former members have been living freely in Cambodia, and campaigners are still fighting to make the authorities act before the culprits simply die off one by one, without having to pay for their crimes. Their are now many sceptics among the Cambodian people as to whether the eventual trials will prove to be a meaningful event, because it is so long after the event.

THE OPEC HOSTAGES

Tell them I'm from Venezuela and my name is Carlos. Tell them I am the famous Carlos, they know me.

ILICH RAMIREZ SANCHEZ

In the 1970s, the public became aware of an enigmatic figure who by many was regarded as a freedom fighter. The man's name was Ilich Ramirez Sánchez, who was born in Venezuela on October 12, 1949. He was the son of a rich attorney, a strong believer in Communism, and was fed with his father's beliefs throughout his childhood. Heavily influenced by figures such as Che Guevara, the young Sanchez became involved with revolutionary groups in Venezuela. His talents in sabotage methods and other radical techniques were obvious, and before long he attracted the attention of the KGB. In July 1970, Sanchez met the recruiting officer for the Popular Front for the Liberation of Palestine (PFLP), who believed that global terrorism was the best way of achieving the group's objectives. He soon became a shrewd and bold assassin and assumed the name 'Carlos the Jackal', and to this day he is really only known by that title.

The Jackal's career in crime spans over three decades, and he has been accused of several brutal bomb attacks that took place in Paris. He has also been blamed for the shooting of Edward Sieff, the president of Marks and Spencer, and for a grenade attack on the English headquarters of an Israeli bank. Perhaps, more notably, he was thought to be the 'godfather' behind the Munich Massacre, where a number of Israeli athletes were murdered at the 1972 Olympic Games.

His name and reputation truly came to the fore when he planned the seizure of 70 hostages at the headquarters of OPEC (Organization of Petroleum Exporting Countries) in Vienna.

MAKING PLANS

Acting in the name of the PFLP, and with the guidance of Wadie Haddad, who had organized his early terrorist training, Carlos started to implement his plan by selecting a team of men to assist him in his new mission. The attack was aimed at a group of oil ministers at the headquarters of OPEC in Vienna, Austria. His chosen team members were from West Germany, Wilfred Bose and Joachim Klein, who were both unsure of their roles when they learned what the mission was to be. They felt that it was not only a highly ambitious attack, but also that it could be an extremely dangerous attack. Carlos managed to talk them round by saying that it would certainly be very advantageous for the Palestinian cause, and he went on to explain how he planned to carry out the terror attack.

The aim, he explained, was to take over the Conference, which was to take place in December 1975, and hold all the government ministers hostage to extort a large ransom. Carlos also explained that two men who would be present at the Conference, Sheikh Yamani from Arabia and Jamshid Amouzegar from Iran, were not to be taken hostage but were to be executed when they raided the building.

Realizing that the success of the mission depended on more recruitments, Carlos decided on another four members to join them. One was a German woman by the name of Gabrielle Krocher-Tiedemann, who already had a criminal record for shooting a policeman. The remaining three were two Palestinians and a man from Lebanon, who used the codes names Joseph, Yussef and Khalid. Carlos briefed his team and organized the necessary equipment for the operation and he then flew to Aden to receive final instructions from his mentor Haddad.

Meanwhile, the other members of his team rented an apartment just outside Vienna and started to keep a vigilant watch on the activities at the OPEC headquarters. On December 19, Carlos had a secret meeting with one of his contacts, and when he returned to the apartment he was in possession of several rifles, pistols and revolvers and a large amount of explosives. The team spent the evening cleaning and checking the weapons and decided that they were now ready to carry out their mission.

On Sunday morning, December 21, the team, with the exception of Bose, left the apartment and caught the local tram to the OPEC headquarters, armed with two sports bags, which were used to carry all the weapons and explosives.

Carlos was the first man to enter the lobby of the OPEC building and, after asking a group of journalists if the conference was still taking place, he beckoned for his team to follow him upstairs to the first floor. Reaching the top of the stairs, the terrorists removed their weapons, ran to the doors of the conference room and started shouting to the occupants inside. The only security on that floor were two policemen, who were standing guard outside the doors. Carlos had sent Klein off to destroy the reception switchboard so that no one could raise the alarm, however, the receptionist had acted quickly and managed to get a call through to the police station before Klein managed to disable the phones. He did this by shooting the entire contents of his gun into the apparatus.

The remainder of the team had managed to easily overpower the two policemen standing guard outside the conference room, one of whom was shot in the neck, while the other was locked in an empty office. Unbeknown to his assailants, the second policeman had managed to find a phone and contact his headquarters to ask for assistance as the OPEC building was under siege.

Carlos and his men stormed into the conference room firing off a volley of bullets. The occupants of the room cowered and tried to take cover. Initially, they were all forced to sit on the floor, and while the team were questioning the men, a detachment of police who had been summoned by the guard locked in the office arrived at the building. Armed with machine guns, the members of Vienna's Special Command made their way up the stairs only to be greeted by bullets from both Klein and Joseph, who were on guard outside. Klein told the police to retreat or he would use a hand grenade and the hostages would be killed. With these threats the police withdrew to the ground floor, but not before shooting Klein in the abdomen.

Back inside the conference room, Carlos had started to divide the hostages into three groups which he categorized as:

Liberals and semi-liberals – which consisted of ministers from Algeria, Libya, Iraq and Kuwait
Criminals – from United Arab Emirates, Saudi Arabia, Iran and Qatar
Neutrals – from Venezuela, Indonesia, Gabon, Ecuador and Nigeria.

The group called the 'Liberals' were told to stand

up at the windows that faced the street, and next to them were placed the explosives to which had been connected timers. The 'Neutral' group were told to stand on the other side of the room, while the final group of 'Criminals' was told to stand in a line in front of Carlos.

MAKING NEGOTIATIONS

Carlos spoke clearly to the group of men in Arabic, informing them that he was the leader of a group of Palestinian commandos and that he did not intend to harm them as long as everyone cooperated. He then forced a British secretary, Griselda Carey, to write a note to the Austrian authorities, which he dictated. Carlos informed them that he was holding various hostages and that he wanted a report to go out via television every two hours. He requested they send a bus to the OPEC headquarters, with the windows blacked out, so that his team and their hostages could be taken to Vienna airport, where a DC9 with a full crew was to be waiting on the runway. He pointed out that they would have no other option than to shoot the hostages if their demands were not met.

After the secretary had finished writing the ransom note, Carlos told her to take the letter to the rightful authorities and at the same time help the injured policeman out of the building.

After the Austrians had read the note and heard the secretary's report about the division of the hostages and the large amount of explosives that had been set to detonate, they knew that they had to start serious negotiations with the terrorists.

Klein's condition had deteriorated considerably, and Carlos told one of the other secretaries to help him out of the building and to call for medical help.

The intense negotiations began, with the Iraqi Charge, Riyadh Al-Azzawi, acting as mediator. Again Carlos told him what he required, and this time he added to the list a radio, a length of rope and five pairs of scissors. He also said that if Klein was well enough, he wanted him released from hospital so that he could make the trip with the rest of the group. However, when Carlos was informed that his companion Klein was on a life-support machine in hospital, he replied that he didn't care what condition he was in, and that if Klein was going to die he might as well die with his friends while supporting their cause.

At about 6.00 p.m. that evening the Austrian broadcasting company started to televise the events of the siege at two-hourly intervals as they had been instructed. In view of the fact that there were so many hostages and the risk that they might lose their lives, the Austrian chancellor decided to comply with the wishes of Carlos the Jackal.

The following morning, just before 7.00 p.m., a bus arrived with curtains across the windows. The terrorists led the hostages out of a back entrance and into the bus and, accompanied by two police cars, it wound its way through the morning traffic to the airport. Klein, who was being transported in an ambulance with a doctor who had agreed to accompany him, followed the convoy.

Once at the airport Carlos oversaw the loading of the hostages onto the Austrian Airlines DC9 and once again separated them into their three 'groups'. He placed explosives under the seats of Yamani and Amouzegar and also their deputies.

Their first stop was at El Beida airport in Algiers, where Carlos was warmly greeted by the Algiers Foreign Minister as he stepped off the plane. While Carlos enjoyed refreshments in the VIP lounge, his companion Klein was taken off the plane and taken by ambulance to a nearby hospital.

Despite the fact that Carlos had requested a second plane to continue their journey, the Algerian authorities had denied his request and so after re-fuelling they took off in the original DC9 and headed off towards Tripoli, Libya. When they landed at Tripoli the welcome was anything but warm, and the authorities refused to help Carlos unless he released his hostages. He was becoming exceptionally tired through lack of sleep and agitated, and the situation on board the plane was becoming volatile. Eventually, after hours of negotiation and Carlos threatening to shoot his hostages, he relented and released all of the Libyan hostages and five other delegates.

Carlos tried to negotiate for a larger plane with the Saudi Arabian government. However, it also denied any help all the time that he held Sheikh

Yamani as a hostage. Realizing that his demands were futile, Carlos again arranged for the plane to be refuelled and deciding that Algiers was a far more neutral ground, he ordered the crew to return to El Beida airport.

Carlos had now been without sleep for more than 48 hours and was rapidly losing control of the situation. This time the Foreign Minister in Algiers was less than impressed that his country was once again having to handle a delicate situation and did not greet Carlos with such kindness. By now the hostages were all convinced that their lives would shortly come to an end, and their was a distinct atmosphere of restlessness and apprehension on board the plane.

Carlos spent many hours trying to negotiate with the Algerian authorities but made no headway. Eventually, he returned to the plane in a sombre mood and informed the hostages that they were all free to leave. They were no longer in any danger.

Carlos left the airport in a convoy of official black cars and once again he had escaped unharmed from a tense political situation.

Estimated at having been responsible for more than 80 deaths, Ilich Ramirez Sánchez was finally arrested in 1997, and in December of that year he was found guilty of murder with aggravating circumstances. He was sentenced to life imprisonment and has been held in the maximum-security wing of Le Santé prison in France.

ASSASSINATION OF ALDO MORO

Kidnapping should be considered as one form of terrorism.

PRESIDENT SALEH OF THE YEMEN

The use of kidnapping and the taking of hostages usually attracts a lot of media interest, which in the eye of the terrorist means that he is in a better position for bargaining. Although it is harder to plan the kidnap of someone in a prominent position due to the amount of security surrounding that person, if the kidnap is successful the terrorist group can demand money, release of imprisoned comrades and publicity for their cause for a long period of time. The main aim of the terrorist in a kidnapping is not the hostage himself, but the audience that it attracts.

THE RED BRIGADES

The Red Brigades are a militant Communist group based in Italy, who formed in 1970 and advocated violence in the pursuit of class warfare. It has been recorded that throughout the 1970s the leftist group committed more than 14,000 acts of violence.

In 1978, the Red Brigade's target was Aldo Moro, a major political figure, and the five-times prime minister of Italy. Moro was a great political mediator and an important leader of the then all-powerful Christian Democrats (*Democrazia Christiana*). Moro had a very powerful influence on Italian politics even though he held no public office, and he was one of the men who helped in forming Italy's government of national solidarity.

THE KIDNAP

Aldo Moro was kidnapped on March 16, 1978, on his way to parliament in his blue Fiat 130. He was a man of routine, and his established pattern of going to church at the same time every morning made it easy for his kidnappers to know where he would be at a certain time. Inside the car were also Moro's bodyguard and chauffer, and they were followed by another car carrying three police bodyguards. As the two cars approached a road junction, a car showing diplomatic licence plates pulled in front of the Fiat and stopped abruptly. Moro's chauffeur had to jam on his brakes so sharply, the security car behind went into the back of the Fiat. Both the driver and passenger of the car that had stopped in front of them climbed out as if to check for damage. The two men approached Moro's car from both sides, and as they came in line with the windows they pulled out pistols and shot the driver and the security guard sitting in the front seat. Both men died instantly.

Four men dressed in Air Alitalia uniforms were standing at the junction. As they heard the shooting they crossed over the road to the cars, pulled automatic rifles out of their flight bags, and shot at the security guards in the follow-up car. Two of the guards died straight away, while the third one rolled out of the car onto the street. He bravely managed to fire three shots before being killed by a fatal shot from a sniper positioned on a roof overlooking the street.

Aldo Moro was driven away and taken to a secret location. Then one of the members of the Red Brigades made a telephone call to a newspaper office based in Rome, informing them that they had kidnapped the 61-year-old Christian Democratic leader. His words were:

We kidnapped Aldo Moro. He is only our first victim. We shall hit at the heart of the state.

Following the shock of the kidnap of such a prominent figure, the Italian security forces made literally hundreds of raids in the cities of Rome, Milan and Turin, but nothing turned up. For the entire two months that Moro was missing, the kidnappers kept him locked in a hidden closet in an apartment. While the entire country was out looking for this man, it appeared he was being held in an apartment in Rome, not far from where he lived.

As soon as the news spread of his kidnap, leaders of the trade unions called a 24-hour general strike, which left many of the shops and offices in Rome closed. Meanwhile the Italian police and army continued to scour the country looking in every possible nook and cranny where Moro could be imprisoned. Still they did not come up with any solid clues.

NEGOTIATIONS

The members of the Red Brigades used Moro as their lever for the freedom of imprisoned terrorists, but the Italian government took a hard rule in the negotiations, stating that they were not prepared to bend at all on the terrorists' requests. The government claimed that if they gave in to their demands it would not only undermine the state it could also throw Italy into an immediate state of chaos.

During his period of captivity Moro wrote letters to the principal leaders of the Christian Democrats and also to Pope Paul VI apparently pleading with them to negotiate with his captors. He made it clear that their prime intention should be the saving of lives, but still the government refused to budge.

The government arranged secret talks with the Red Brigades, but the talks led them nowhere. The government were simply not prepared to release the 13 members of the Red Brigades who were held in Turin in exchange for Moro's life.

On May 7, Moro was allowed to send a final letter to his wife saying,

> *They have told me that they are going to kill me in a little while, I kiss you for the last time.*

BRUTAL ASSASSINATION

On May 9, the Red Brigades, frustrated with their lack of success in negotiating with the Italian government, decided to kill Moro. Telling him that they had decided to take him to another location, the terrorists bundled him into a car and told him to hide underneath a blanket on the back seat. As soon as Moro had covered himself they opened fire, emptying as many as ten rounds into his crumpled body.

The *Polizia di Stato* discovered Moro's bullet-riddled body in the boot of a car in the Via Caetani, which is a site in between the Christian Democratic Party and the Communist Party headquarters.

Mario Moretti, the man who actually shot Moro, made a statement to an Italian newspaper regarding the murder that it 'was the ultimate expression of Marxist-Lennon revolutionary action'.

Although no one was immediately arrested for the murder of Aldo Moro, over the next ten years, many Red Brigade leaders and members were arrested which considerably weakened their organization. With very limited funds and few members to carry out terror attacks, the group today is almost inoperable.

Just as in the John F. Kennedy assassination, the Moro case became shrouded with conspiracy theories, none of which have ever been proven. People are still asking today why, out of the many terrorist crimes in Italy, was no effort ever made to rescue Maldo either by force or negotiation? The case still haunts Italy today and over the years powerful evidence of official misdeeds and cover-up have emerged. There have even been suggestions that we need look no further than Italy itself for the motive behind his murder. At the time Italian politics was in a state of turmoil and some of the reforms that Moro was proposing could have easily upset the political balance of ruling authorities, especially the Christian Democratic Party.

AIREY NEAVE
BOMBING

He was one of freedom's warriors. Courageous, staunch, true. He lived for his beliefs and now he has died for them.

MARGARET THATCHER

Airey Neave was a prominent British Conservative MP who helped to mastermind the rise of Prime Minister Margaret Thatcher. On March 30, 1979, he was murdered when a car bomb that had been fixed to his car detonated as he drove away from the Houses of Parliament. Afterwards, the Irish National Liberation Army (INLA, a paramilitary organization that had split from the official Irish Republican Army (IRA), claimed responsibility for the killing. It was the group's first major terror attack.

ESCAPE FROM COLDITZ

However, after the assassination, there was some controversy as to whether the INLA was actually behind it. Various politicians claimed that Neave had been on the verge of shaking up the security services for alleged corruption, and that he had been murdered by MI6 agents. Others alleged that Neave had himself been planning to bring down, even murder, Labour opposition politicians. Whether or not these allegations were true, no one was ever convicted of his murder, a circumstance that has continued to foster rumours about why he was assassinated, and by whom.

Airey Neave was born into a privileged family background in 1916. He attended the prestigious Eton College before going on to study law at Merton College, Oxford. During World War II, he became a prisoner of war and made several daring escapes, including one from the notorious Colditz Castle. In August 1941, he made the first attempt, but he was caught because his home-made Nazi uniform was spotted. (According to his auto-biography, he had dyed the fabric green himself, but because he was colour blind, it was too bright.) The following year, he made another attempt, accompanied by a Dutch officer, and this time managed to escape through a trap door under a stage while a play was in progress. The pair walked all the way to Switzerland and then made their way through France, Spain and Gibraltar, finally returning to England. This made Neave the first British army officer to make an escape from Colditz and return all the way home unharmed. He became a well-known national figure, writing several books about his adventures during the war, and also participated in the Nuremberg Krupp trial, in which German industrialists were accused of helping the Nazis to themselves for war, and of using slave labour – including prisoners of war – in their factories.

CHARRED BODY

During the 1950s, Neave became involved in politics, but his career stalled because of ill health: he had a heart attack in 1959 which meant that he had to pace his workload. Even so, by the 1970s he had risen to a prominent position in the British Conservative Party, and had become a champion of Margaret Thatcher, who 1975 appointed him campaign manager in her bid for party leadership. He was very close to Thatcher, who appointed him shadow Secretary of State for Northern Ireland. However, just before the 1979 election that swept Thatcher to power, and which would have made him a member of the Cabinet in the new government, he was brutally murdered.

On March 30, 1979, Airey Neave got into his car and drove out of New Palace Yard in the Palace of Westminster (Houses of Parliament). At 2.58 p.m., there was a huge explosion and onlookers saw a car with smoke pouring out of it, standing on a ramp between the MPs' car park and the courtyard below Big Ben. The blast was heard in the House of Commons, where Parliament was just about to be closed before the upcoming General Election. MPs, journalists and police rushed to the scene to find the car burning, its windows broken, with a charred body behind the steering wheel. Both of the driver's legs had been blown off. Incredibly, he was still breathing, but unconscious. He was rushed to hospital, but he died eight minutes after arrival.

VIOLENT THUGS

The victim, who was wearing the formal dress of black coat and striped trousers favoured by Tory MPs, was soon identified as Airey Neave, one of Mrs Thatcher's most devoted aides. There was a national outcry, and members of all the political parties denounced the crime. Mrs Thatcher paid an emotional tribute to her former friend and ally, calling him 'one of freedom's warriors' and describing him 'a gentle, brave and unassuming man'. She added: 'He lived for his beliefs, and now he has died for them.'

The Irish National Liberation Army (INLA) claimed responsibility for the murder. The INLA was a relatively new terror group, formed in December 1974 as the military wing of the Irish Republican Socialist Party (IRSP). The IRSP had split from the official IRA after the IRA had declared a cease-fire, and the IRSP had committed themselves to the continuation of terror attacks on British military and political targets.

There was a great deal of in-fighting between the different wings of the IRA during this time, and several leading figures in the movement were assassinated, prompting an image of the group as a bunch of disorganized thugs dedicated to violence and brutality rather than to political change. According to some sources, their reputation was so bad that INLA slogans painted on walls in Northern Ireland were often changed to read 'I Never Leave Anything', while IRSP ones became 'I Rob Shops and Post Offices'.

AN INSIDE JOB?

What was remarkable about Neave's assassination was that no one was prosecuted for it – even though he was such a prominent member of the Tory party who, had he lived, would have held high office in Thatcher's new administration. There was much speculation as to the reason for this. Some believed that the police had simply failed to track down the INLA operatives who had planted the bomb. The IRA and its splinter groups had become adept at covering their tracks, and it may have been that there were simply no leads for police to follow in this instance. However, there were those who suspected otherwise, and they believed that Neave had not been killed by the INLA or any Republican group, but that he was the victim of an 'inside job'.

Early on in Neave's career, he had been recruited as an intelligence agent for the British security services. It was thought that in the early 1970s, when his assassination took place, he may have involved in a right-wing plot by British security services against the Labour government of Harold Wilson. (At that time, the security services feared a change of policy under the Labour administration and were politically committed to the continuation of cold-war tactics against the USSR.) Later, after Neave's death, journalist Duncan Campbell alleged, in an article in the New Statesman magazine in 1981, that Neave had planned to have Labour politician Tony Benn assassinated were he to become Prime Minister. Both these claims suggested that Neave's relation to the security services was a complex one, whether or not it had something to do with his eventual demise.

HIGH-LEVEL CORRUPTION

Another allegation, made by Irish journalist, Kevin Cahill, maintained that MI6 had killed Neave because he had threatened to prosecute senior members of the service for corruption. Ulster Unionist MP Enoch Powell, known for his controversial views on racial segregation, had a different view: he believed that Neave had been killed by American agents, because the USA disagreed with his policy on Northern Ireland. According to Powell, the Americans had worked in tandem with MI6 to assassinate Neave, so as to ensure a policy in Ireland that would be acceptable to them.

Whatever the truth of the matter, although Prime Minster James Callaghan announced directly after

Neave's assassination that 'no effort would be spared to bring his murderers to justice' no one was ever charged with the crime. This prompted further speculation, which still continues to this day. In recent times, a new theory has emerged, that the killing was perpetrated by the INLA helped by a left-wing informant, possibly working within the Houses of Parliament.

A SOLDIER'S DEATH

It is always the case that a leading politician has many enemies, and thus that, when he or she is assassinated, many will be suspected of the crime. But what is puzzling in the Neave case is why the authorities have failed to prosecute anyone for the murder, especially as the INLA publicly claimed responsibility for it. Their failure to do so has prompted speculation that the establishment has something to hide; and that, if the culprits were brought to justice, there might be a story to tell that would reflect badly on the politicians at Westminster, on government intelligence agencies or possibly on Neave himself.

In the meantime, the story behind the assassination remains something of a mystery. Even Neave's daughter, Marigold, believes that not all the facts have yet emerged. She has, she claims, found it difficult to get any information out of the authorities regarding her father's assassination. 'They only say, "He died a soldier's death",' she recently told a journalist. 'I think there was a cover-up.' But whether or not this is the case we shall never know, unless the assassins are brought to book.

IRANIAN EMBASSY SIEGE

They then took the two terrorists, pushed them against the wall and shot them. They wanted to finish their story. That was their job.
A HOSTAGE (TALKING ABOUT THE SAS)

The siege of the Iranian Embassy in London, which lasted for six days, was one of the most dramatic terror attacks ever to take place in the UK. It was also one of the first such attacks to be covered from beginning to end by the world's media, heightening the sense of tension as fears for the hostages held captive in the building grew day by day. Not only this, but the siege attracted public attention, for the first time, to the British army's counter-terrorist team, the SAS (Special Air Service). The team were brought in as a last resort after the Iranian terrorists brutally murdered one of the hostages, and in a final shoot-out, which was filmed live on television on a bank holiday Monday, the soldiers stormed the embassy, killing all but one of the terrorists. Within only 15 minutes, the SAS had brought the siege to an end, to the immense relief of the hostages, their families and the world at large – but the political fall-out from the incident had only just begun.

THE NIGHTMARE BEGINS

The morning of Wednesday, April 30, 1980, started out as a morning like any other at the Iranian Embassy in Prince's Gate, Kensington. Standing outside the building was PC Trevor Lock of the Metropolitan Police. Despite the air of quiet calm in the street, British security forces were aware that the embassy needed constant surveillance: this was a period of intense political conflict in Iran, following Islamic revolution there the previous year. In the wake of the Shah's overthrow, many radical political and religious groups in Iran were now vying for power, and the embassy in London, a symbol of the country's links with the West, was likely to be a focus for this struggle.

The security forces were right to be vigilant, and perhaps they should have been more so. On that fateful morning, PC Lock left his post outside the building for a few minutes and nipped inside for a coffee with the concierge. As the men were chatting, a face suddenly appeared at the window. PC Lock was about to come forward to let the person in, when a hail of bullets were fired at the door, shattering the glass panel. Within seconds, six terrorists rushed in, quickly overpowering the policeman. Then, waving their guns at the terrified embassy workers and visitors in the lobby, they took 25 more hostages. They forced them all, at gunpoint, to sit on the floor, and put PC Lock on a chair in the middle. The nightmare had just begun.

STANDOFF

Initially, it appeared that the gunmen were members of a radical group called the Democratic Revolutionary Movement for the Liberation of Arabistan, and they wanted to gain political sovreignty for the region in southern Iran known as Khuzestan. Both Iran and Iraq had for many years struggled for control of this region, which is rich in oil. However, the terrorists then went on to demand the release of 91 political prisoners held in jail by the Ayatollah Khomeini after the Islamic revolution. Later, once the siege was over, it transpired that the terrorists had been trained in Iraq, prompting speculation that the whole incident had been masterminded by Saddam Hussein, in an attempt to undermine the Iranian government prior to the outbreak of the Iran-Iraq war.

When news of the attack came in to Whitehall, the security services immediately sprang into action. Terrorism was an issue at the top of Prime Minister Margaret Thatcher's agenda, especially after the assassinations of Lord Mountbatten and Conservative MP Airey Neave the previous year. While the SAS set up a base in a building next door to the embassy, military officials and government ministers gathered in the cabinet office briefing room, otherwise known as Cobra. When the terrorists' demand for the release of the prisoners came in, the Iranian government flatly refused to comply. It was clearly going to be down to the British to resolve the situation.

THREATS TO KILL

Over the next six days, the world watched as the siege continued. Police officers outside the embassy negotiated with the terrorists, offering them food and cigarettes in return for leaving the hostages unharmed. Inside the embassy, as the hostages' mental and physical condition deteriorated, PC Lock struggled to find a way out of the crisis. He had a gun hidden away in his clothing, but he could not think of a way of using it without running the risk of a blood bath. So instead, he waited, consumed with guilt at having left his post outside the embassy at the crucial moment when the gunmen first appeared.

To begin with, the terrorists were reasonably humane, releasing five of the hostages as the siege progressed. Concessions were made, and there was even talk of offering the terrorists a safe passage home if they kept the hostages safe. However, as the siege wore on, it became clear that no such offer was on the table: whatever the outcome of the attack, they would be captured and tried as criminals. As the terrorists became more desperate, they began to make threats to kill one of the hostages unless their demands were met.

Abbass Lavasani, the embassy's press attaché, became the first victim of the siege. Lavasani was an idealistic young man who was fervently attached to the Ayatollah Khomeini's brand of Islamic fundamentalism. He saw this as his chance to become a martyr for his country, and he apparently offered himself as a sacrifice to the cause. According to PC Lock, Lavasani said, while chained to a banister and waiting to be executed, that he was not afraid to die. Lavasani was shot three times, and his body was thrown out of the front door of the embassy onto the pavement.

OPERATION NIMROD

It was this horrific act that prompted the authorities to finally declare a state of emergency and send the SAS troops into the embassy. By all reports, the soldiers themselves, far from being afraid to undertake such a risky operation, were only too keen to start the attack. They had been in training for such an event for many years, were armed to the teeth with extremely powerful shotguns, and had never had the opportunity to practise their skills. In fact, by the time they went in, they were hoping that the terrorists would not surrender, so that they could finish the job as they had been trained to do.

Six days after the siege began, the SAS tore into

the building, guns blazing. Television programmes were interrupted – including the snooker championship, which thousands of viewers were watching – to watch the extraordinary sight of a wild-west style shoot-out in the heart of central London. When the smoke cleared 11 minutes later, it emerged that the SAS had been victorious. All the hostages except one, who was shot dead by a terrorist, had been rescued. Five of the terrorists lay dead, and the sixth had been captured. The siege that had lasted for six days had finally ended – in only a matter of minutes.

Operation Nimrod, as the exercise was called, had in military terms been an unqualified success. Afterwards, Mrs Thatcher went in person to congratulate the team, who had shown such tremendous bravery and skill. However, in the days and months after the siege, when the political implications of the event began to become clear, some of their actions, and those of the British government, began to be questioned.

POLITICAL CONTROVERSY

The main criticism to be levelled at the SAS was that, instead of bringing out the terrorists alive, they had shot at least two of them in cold blood. In some cases, the soldiers could claim self-defence; but in others, it was claimed that the terrorists would have surrendered had they been given the chance. Indeed, commentators pointed out that the surviving terrorist, Fowzi Nejad, was only allowed to live because he pretended to be a hostage and was brought outside with the others on the pavement. At his trial, witnesses recounted how soldiers had been on the point of dragging him back inside the building to shoot him, but they had been stopped by officials.

The SAS responded by claiming that the government had unofficially instructed them to shoot all the terrorists dead. They claimed that the Prime Minister herself had commented before the attack that she did not want an 'ongoing problem' of terrorists in the country, and that the soldiers had taken this to mean that they should shoot the perpetrators.

Whatever the truth of the matter, few people had much sympathy with the Iranian terrorists, who had subjected the hostages to a nightmare ordeal for nearly a week, brutally murdering one of them in the process. Not surprisingly, the surviving terrorist Fowzi Nejad was charged, brought to trial, convicted and sentenced to life imprisonment for his part in the atrocities.

Today, the siege of the Iranian Embassy continues to be discussed as one of the most fascinating – and disturbing – terror attacks in mainland Britain. As one of the first high-profile events of its kind, it raises many questions for our times: about the role of the media in portraying violent attacks as they take place; about the role of the British army, especially the SAS, in combating terrorism; about diplomacy and negotiation in such times of crisis; and finally, about the limits of government and military secrecy within a democracy.

THE BOLOGNA MASSACRE

It was with shock and horror that I learned of the tragic loss of life following the explosion at Bologna railway station . . . Following as it does our discussions in Venice, this deplorable incident only confirms the need to pursue unrelentingly the common struggle against terrorism in all its forms.

LETTER FROM MARGARET THATCHER TO
FRANCESCO COSSIGA, ITALIAN PRIME
MINISTER, AUGUST 5, 1980

The bombing of the Central Station at Bologna in 1980 killed and wounded so many people that it has become known in Italy as the *Strage di Bologna:* 'The Bologna Massacre'. In a terror attack that has gone down as one of the worst in the history of the Italian nation, a total of 85 people lost their lives and hundreds more were injured. The atrocity took place when a home-made bomb hidden in a waiting room ripped through the station building, also hitting a train full of passengers.

The incident was just one in a string of Italian terror attacks during the 1970s and 1980s that many ascribe to neo-fascist groups, working to create a 'strategy of tension'. According to this theory, extreme neo-fascist groups in Italy, such as the Fronte Nazionale, Ordine Nuovo and Avanguardia Nazionale, were committing these atrocities and blaming them on the extreme left, so as to influence public opinion against communism. Some believe that right-wing government intelligence agencies were also involved. Whatever the truth of the matter, successive Italian governments have seemed unable – or unwilling – to confront and resolve the internal political problems that have led to such attacks over the decades since the 1960s.

A SCENE OF CARNAGE

The morning of the August 2, 1980, was a beautiful, sunny one in the town of Bologna, Italy. Tourists crowded into the busy station, as they did every summer, to catch their trains for destinations all over Italy and the rest of Europe. It was a hot morning, and the heat in the station had become unbearable, so many travellers had taken refuge in the air-conditioned waiting room, trying to get away from the heat of the sun and the bustling crowds on the platforms. As it turned out, they could not have chosen a worse place to take a quiet break.

At 10.25 a.m., a home-made TNT bomb that had been hidden in a suitcase left unattended in the waiting room suddenly detonated. The explosion not only ripped the room itself apart, but shattered most of the station building and also hit a train waiting at one of the platforms. The deafening blast of the bomb could be heard right across the city, and within minutes people came running to the station to find out what had happened.

The scene they found was one of devastation. People were screaming in panic as they tried to help the dying and injured in the waiting room, many of whom were bleeding profusely. The emergency services were immediately called in, but the local ambulances could not cope with carnage on this scale, so buses and taxis were commandeered to take victims to hospital. Meanwhile, workers sifted through the wreckage, freeing the dead and injured trapped beneath it, and beginning the long work of clearing up the debris.

GOVERNMENT INCOMPETENCE

As the chaos subsided, it became clear what the extent of the damage was. Eighty-five people were dead, and a further 200 were injured. The train station was completely wrecked. Someone was to blame for this terrible crime perpetrated against the people of Bologna – but who?

At first the government and the police announced that they believed the blast to be accidental, possibly

ABOVE: *Franz Ferdinand, archduke of Austria, and his wife Sophie riding in an open carriage during a visit to Sarajevo shortly before their assassination.*

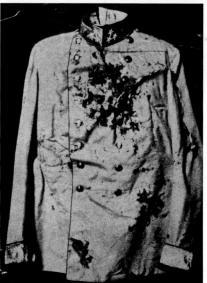

LEFT: *The jacket worn by Archduke Franz Ferdinand when he was assassinated in Sarajevo on June 28, 1914.*

ABOVE: *Coffin being loaded into hearse among the crowd at the funeral for the victims of 16th Street Baptist Church bombing.*

BELOW: *Members of the Ku Klux Klan participate in a membership ritual, swearing not to reveal any of the group's secrets.*

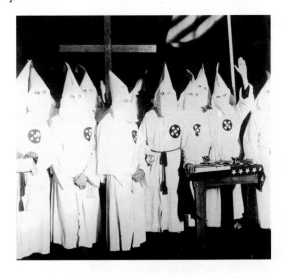

RIGHT: *Italian politician Aldo Moro, (1916–1978).*

BELOW: *The body of the former Italian Prime Minister and Christian Democrat leader Aldo Moro is found in the back of a van parked in a street in Rome. Moro was kidnapped by Red Brigade terrorists and held for 54 days before he was killed.*

LEFT: *Specially-trained Army commandos are about to enter the Iranian embassy after a bomb exploded and fire broke out on the first floor. Shortly after the explosion the six-day siege, which took place in April 1980, came to an end and the hostages stumbled out.*

BELOW: *Sim Harris (left) the BBC-TV hostage jumps across the balcony of the Iranian embassy, covered by an army commando, after a bomb exploded and fire broke out on the first floor.*

BELOW: *Emergency services in action after the IRA bombing of the Grand Hotel in Brighton, during the Conservative Party Conference in October 1984.*

ABOVE: *Smoke billows from the World Trade Center's twin towers after it was struck by a commercial airliner in a terror attack on September 11, 2001 in New York City.*

ABOVE: *On July 7, 2005 London was hit by a series of coordinated bomb blasts that struck London's public transport system during the morning rush hour. The picture above shows a number 30 double-decker bus in Tavistock Square in central London, after it was hit by one of the blasts. The bombings came while the UK was hosting the first full day of the 31st G8 summit, and a day after London was chosen to host the 2012 Summer Olympic Games.*

ABOVE: *A woman mourns the death of her husband who was killed in one of the bomb blasts on trains in the Indian financial capital of Mumbai on July 11, 2006.*

triggered by an electrical fault. However, when evidence of the improvised TNT bomb hidden in a suitcase emerged, they had to revise their initial theory. They then put the blame on the left-wing, militant group The Red Brigade, despite having very little evidence to show its involvement in this particular incident. And, as the police investigation got underway, it became clear that there were political factions, both inside and outside the government, who were making it their business to disrupt the process in every way possible.

After the bombing, there was considerable social unrest in Bologna and throughout Italy. The Italian people were understandably angered by a government who appeared unable to control the situation, and moreover who seemed to have their own political agenda to pursue, at the expense of public safety. There were a series of strikes, most notably in Bologna, where workers took action only two hours after the bomb exploded. The handling of the massacre itself, and the bungled investigation that took place afterwards, seemed to point to government and police incompetence to a greater degree than ever before, and Italy was once more plunged into political crisis.

A 'STRATEGY OF TENSION'

But worse was to come. A number of political analysts then made the shocking claim that the government itself – or agencies close to it – were in fact responsible for the massacre. According to this theory, the authorities were in league with violent radical groups from the far right, working to create a 'strategy of tension'. These groups would conduct terror attacks, and the government would then blame left-wing factions for the atrocities. The ultimate aim of these 'false flag' operations, as they were known, was to discredit the Communist Party in Italy, who had for many years played an important role in the country's political life.

This allegation may seem extraordinary, but in the context of the cold-war political landscape of the time, it was perhaps not so far-fetched as one might think. The Italian government, like many European governments, feared that a strong communist presence in their country might make them vulnerable to attack from the Soviet Union, which at that time was still a massive world superpower, and whose record on democracy and human rights was abysmal. It was argued – and still is, in some quarters – that Western governments were right to use any means necessary to ensure their sovereignty as free, democratic countries – even if that meant mounting 'false flag' terror attacks to discredit Soviet sympathizers in the West.

OPERATION GLADIO

Whether or not the Italian government were in any way connected to the Bologna Massacre remains unclear, but it has certainly been well documented that, during the Cold War years, US and European governments were involved in many kinds of covert, anti-Communist operations. In Italy, one of these was the CIA- and NATO-sponsored group known as 'Operation Gladio', whose purpose was to counter communist influence in Italy after World War II. (Many 'stay-behind' operations, as they were called, also existed in other Western European countries.) It has since been shown that Gladio had links with neo-fascist Italian groups, and it had begun to operate in a maverick, independent way after the Cold War years. Since the most likely suspects for the Bologna bombing were the neo-fascists, and Gladio was in league with them, it follows that the Italian government, through their sponsorship of Gladio as an intelligence agency, may have been indirectly connected to the attack.

PROPAGANDA DUE

Not surprisingly, given the shady political dealings going on behind the scenes, the investigation into the bombing was a long and tortuous one. Frustrated by the constant delays in bringing the perpetrators to justice, relatives of the victims formed an association to try to keep up pressure on the authorities, but it was not until 15 years later that the Italian Supreme Court finally convicted two neo-fascist terrorists, Valerio Fioravanti and Francesca Mambro, of the bombing. The pair had pleaded innocent throughout their trial.

In addition, the court sentenced a number of individuals for the crime of obstructing the investigation: officers Giuseppe Belmonte and Pietro Musumeci of the Italian security service SISMI (Servizio per le Informazioni e la Sicurezza Militare); Francesco Pazienza, a consultant to the service, who was deeply involved with CIA operations in Italy and worldwide; and Licio Gelli, the head of the Italian Masonic lodge Propaganda Due (P2), which boasted many powerful figures among its members. An associate of Gelli's, Stefano Delle Chiaie, who was also a member of a revolutionary wing of the neo-fascist group Ordine Nuovo, was also named as an instigator of the attack.

It was well known that, ever since the mid-1960s, P2 had attempted to control the political situation not only in Italy, but also in South America, via the influence of its high-profile members, in a covert, entirely undemocratic fashion. Gelli himself was a neo-fascist who had been involved with a number of far-right political organizations, including the CIA-sponsored group Gladio. He was also thought to be a player in several major political scandals, including the murder of Italian Prime Minister Aldo Moro in 1978.

HONOURING THE DEAD

Today, the victims of the attack are commemorated with a concert in Bologna's central square, which takes place on August 2 each year. The station has been rebuilt, but some cracks in the pavement and walls remain, and the clock still stands at 10.25 a.m., as a reminder of the devastation that was wrought there on that fateful day in 1980. The town council and the family members' association have done their best to ensure that the victims of the attack are remembered by all who visit the city. However, the fact remains that, to this day, the full story of the Bologna Massacre is still not known; and until it is, the victims who lost their lives in the attack will never be properly honoured.

HYDE PARK AND REGENT'S PARK BOMBINGS

The Irish people have sovereign and national rights, which no task or occupational force can put down.

IRA

The Provisional Irish Republic Army got just what they wanted when they bombed military targets in London in July 1982 – sensational media coverage. It was one of the most serious terror attacks by the IRA since the Balcombe Street siege eight years earlier, and a lot of what happened that day was caught on camera and replayed around the world. People watched in horror as scenes of horrendous carnage were unveiled before their eyes.

HYDE PARK

The Changing of the Guard in London is one of the oldest and most familiar ceremonies associated with

Buckingham Palace. The actual ceremony involves a new guard exchanging duty with the old guard, and both guards are drawn from one of the regiments of foot guards. A band accompanies the new guard from the Wellington or Chelsea barracks to the forecourt of Buckingham palace, and when the ceremony is over, leads the old guard back to his barracks.

The attack at Hyde Park took place along the route used by the household cavalry during the changing of the guard ceremony, on July 20, 1982. The plumed members of the Blues and Royal were a magnificent sight as they rode proudly on their shiny, black horses through London's Hyde Park. Unaware of any danger, the cavalrymen rode past a parked car. Little did they know that it contained a hidden nail bomb. As the car exploded, windows shattered in nearby buildings, flames burst high into the sky and nails, which were wrapped around the bomb, shot out like bullets. Horses fell, writhing in agony, with their riders lying on the ground bleeding, their uniforms in tatters.

Three members of the Blues and Royals were killed instantly and another died three days later from his injuries. The Blues and Royals were formed in 1969 from an amalgamation of the Royal Horse Guards (the Blues) and the Royal Dragoons (the Royals) and, not surprisingly, they have served in Northern Ireland.

The remainder of the soldiers were badly wounded, and members of the public watching the parade were also injured by the flying shrapnel and nails. Added to the horror was the fact that seven of the regiment's beautiful horses also died, either as a direct result of the blast or from being put down due to the severity of their injuries.

The IRA admitted carrying out the attack, which they had timed perfectly to coincide with the passing of the household cavalry. They claimed the attack was a result of the words of self-determination said by Margaret Thatcher when she announced that Britain was to enter the Falklands War: ' . . . people have sovereign and national rights, which no task or occupational force can put down', a phrase that the IRA claimed they could totally identify with.

REGENT'S PARK

Regent's Park in London is a magnificent open space situated in the heart of the city. It offers a large boating lake, an open-air theatre, a rose garden, a large sports area and the world-famous London Zoo. In the heart of the park is a picturesque bandstand that offers lunchtime and evening concerts, where people can sit and relax.

On July 20, 1982, the band of the Royal Green Jackets was playing music from *Oliver* to a crowd of 120 spectators. It was the first concert of a season of lunchtime venues for tourists and local office workers. People were enjoying the music in the warm sunshine.

Unaware that a bomb had exploded just a couple of hours earlier in Hyde Park, people were simply unprepared when a second device was detonated beneath the bandstand. The blast was powerful and literally blew the bandsmen off the bandstand, one of them becoming impaled on iron railings over 27 metres (30 yards) away.

Nearby spectators and workers from shops and hotels in the vicinity rushed to help the wounded. The police were worried that their might be a second device and tried their hardest to clear the area while they searched for further bombs.

One member of the audience later said, 'Everything seemed to come up from the bottom of the bandstand and flew right into the air, the bodies, the instruments, everything. A leg came within five feet of me.'

Seven members of the band were killed instantly and once again there were many injuries from the flying nails and shrapnel. The wounded were treated at the Westminster Hospital where, workers that were supposed striking, returned to work and helped handle the large number of casualties.

In one day the IRA had brought their war with the English to England and wrought havoc. The blast at Hyde Park killed four cavalrymen and injured 22 guards and civilians. It also took the lives of seven of the treasured cavalry horses. In Regent's Park, six bandsmen died and 24 musicians and 4 civilians were injured.

WELL-PLANNED ATTACK

The bombing of Hyde Park and Regent's Park were two well-planned attacks. The terrorists had parked a blue Morris sedan car on Carriage Road, about 549 metres (600 yards) along the cavalry's regular route. Hidden inside the car was a 4.5-kg (10-lb) piece of gelignite wrapped with literally hundreds of 10- and 15-cm (4- and 6-in) nails. As the cavalry passed by, a member of the IRA, possibly hidden among the trees of Hyde Park, pushed the remote-controlled detonator exactly at the right moment.

The bomb in Regent's Park was probably planted some weeks before the explosion. It was similar to the earlier bomb, but was probably equipped with a timer that was set to go off at the time and day of the well-advertised concert.

DANNY MCNAMEE

On August 16, 1986, members of the Scot's Guard broke down the door of an apartment owned by an electronics engineer named Danny McNamee. He was arrested and flown to London to face conspiracy charges regarding the explosions in Hyde Park and Regent's Park. He was accused of making the bombs for the IRA that were used in the London bombings in 1982. McNamee denied having any sympathy with the IRA, and no evidence was ever presented at his trial that he had paramilitary links.

Despite this, McNamee was found guilty at the Old Bailey of bombing offences and was sentenced to 25 years in prison. He was convicted on the evidence that his fingerprint was found on an electronic circuit board, which was linked to the Hyde Park bombing. He explained that he had handled many circuit boards when working for a previous employer, but had no idea that they had IRA connections.

In 1998, he was released under the terms of the Good Friday Agreement and a year later his case went to the Court of Appeal.

At his second trial in 1998 his conviction was overturned because they found more prominent fingerprints on the original circuit board that belonged to a known IRA bomb maker by the name of Desmond Ellis. This evidence was not disclosed in the first trial. His sentence was quashed on the ruling that the verdict was unsafe because there had been a failure to disclose relevant evidence.

When McNamee was asked how he felt about the 1982 Hyde Park and Regent's Park bombing, he said, 'I thought the same as everybody. It was a terrible atrocity and a sad loss for the families.'

RANGOON BOMBING

It was the most sickening thing I have ever seen – dead, wounded and bloody monks, women and children piled up on gurneys and on the floor of a third world hospital.

VISITOR TO RANGOON GENERAL HOSPITAL

The Rangoon Bombing, as it is known, took place in the city of Yangon (formerly Rangoon), Burma. It was timed to coincide with an official visit to the city mausoleum by the President of South Korea, Chun Doo Hwan. However, by a extraordinary twist of fate, the President arrived a few minutes late, just after the bomb had detonated. He was lucky to escape with his life, but others in the crowd that had gathered were not so fortunate: the death toll numbered 21 in total, and 46 more people were injured.

'THE LAST POST'

October 9, 1983, was the day that President Chun Doo Hwan of South Korea was planning to lay a wreath at the tomb of Thankin Aung Sang, as a mark of respect to the former leader of Burma who had been brutally assassinated in 1947. Aung Sang was much respected in Burma, and around the world, as the leader who had negotiated the country's independence from their colonial masters; today, his daughter Aung Sang Suu Kyi has bravely continued this tradition, following a path of nonviolent resistance to the current oppressive regime in the country.

Before the President arrived at the mausoleum, his aides began to gather there. Many of them were top-ranking officials in the South Korean government, and there were also security personnel, journalists and advisers present. Unbeknown to them, three bombs were hidden in the roof above them. Meanwhile, President Chun was running late for his appointment, his car held up in the city's busy traffic.

The small crowd waited for the President to arrive, and eventually, his car appeared on the driveway. As it did, a trumpet player struck up *The Last Post*, practising the tune before the ceremony took place. It was a stroke of good fortune for President Chun that he did, because the bombers, who were watching from a safe distance, took this as a sign that he had arrived in the building, and accordingly, detonated the bombs by remote control.

A LEGACY OF HATRED

In the event, only one of the bombs went off, but it was enough to do an enormous amount of damage. Some of the most important people in the South Korean government were killed: the Deputy Prime Minister, Suh Suk Joo, the Foreign Minister, Lee Bum Suk; and the Minister for Industry and Commerce, Kim Dong Whie. In addition, 18 others lay dead, and many more sustained serious injuries. Not only this, but the building was ripped apart by the explosion.

The fact that President Chun had escaped was lucky for him, but it was also a relief in terms of the political dynamics of the region. Many commentators speculated that if he had been killed in the blast, war might once again have broken out between North and South Korea, as had happened in the 1950s with the Korean War. The Korean War, which had been one of the central conflicts of the Cold War, had become a battle for control of the peninsula between the Western Allies, who backed South Korea, and the Soviet Communists, who backed North Korea. It had led to over one million casualties on each side, decimated the populations of both countries, destroyed their infrastructure and economy, and left a legacy of hatred and distrust between the two sides. From that time on, the peninsula had been divided: an extremely repressive Communist regime ruled in the North, while a dictatorial, pro-US government ruled in the South.

Between them lay one of the most heavily guarded borders in the world.

SUICIDE BY HAND GRENADE

When the Rangoon bombing took place, suspicion immediately fell on Kim II Sung, leader of North Korea. Since the partition, North Korea had repeatedly been involved in acts of terrorism against South Korea, and this seemed to be another episode in the continuing hostilities between the two nations. President Chun immediately issued a statement linking the North Koreans to the attack. The North Korean Central News Agency retaliated by calling this a 'preposterous and ridiculous act'. Nevertheless, Chun remained convinced that the bomb was the work of Kim II Sung, and he showed his disgust by deciding to start again a ballistic missile programme, an action that did not bode well for stable relations between the two states.

Initially, there was no direct evidence to link Kim II Sung to the attack. However, two days later, a North Korean suspect was picked up, who tried to blow himself up with a hand grenade. On the same day, Burmese villagers reported the presence of two foreigners in their rural area, and when these men were arrested, they too were found to be North Koreans. They also attempted to blow themselves up with hand grenades, and one of them managed to do so, committing suicide in this way. The two remaining men were taken into custody and confessed that they had been sent as envoys from the North Korean government to carry out the assassination of President Chun.

SHOOT-OUT IN THE CABINET

To this day, however, the real story behind the Rangoon Bombing has never been fully uncovered. Although it seems likely that the attack was the work of the North Korean government, it was also the case that President Chun had enemies within South Korea, who conceivably could have been responsible for the atrocity.

President Chun Doo Hwan had lived a turbulent life and was no stranger to violence and political intrigue. Born in 1931, he had made his way up through the military, and had set in motion the events leading up to the assassination of his predecessor, Park Chung Hee, who had died in a shoot-out at a secret government meeting. Chun had effected a military coup in 1979, imposed martial law on the country, and dissolved the country's National Assembly, arresting many political leaders opposed to his views. His government had been responsible for brutally suppressing protests and demonstrations against the regime, notably at Gwangju, in what became known as the Gwangju Massacre.

Despite the bloody way in which he had come to power, President Chun had gone on to rule South Korea in a less autocratic way than had his predecessor Park, and the economy had continued to prosper under his leadership. However, in the mid-1980s, dissent was beginning to grow once more as a new wave of student protests took place, demanding political rights and freedoms. These protests were supported by large sections of the population, especially those who were now earning high incomes and had begun to demand the kind of democratic rights that they saw in the West.

CORRUPTION CHARGES

Prompted by the US government, Chun wisely accepted that reforms would have to be made, but his political career remained in jeopardy and eventually he was forced to resign. In 1996, he and his successor Roh were charged, as former presidents, with corruption, and they were also found guilty of treason in connection with the way they had taken over power. Chun was sentenced to death, but this was later changed to life imprisonment, and in the end he was pardoned.

Given Chun's turbulent career, it was clear that he had plenty of enemies. At the time of the Rangoon Bombing, there could have been any number of factions plotting to kill him within South Korea: from supporters of the previous president, to former opposition leaders, to all kinds of political activists. However, the consensus today is that it was the North Korean government, not dissident elements in the South, that was responsible for the murder.

CULT OF THE PERSONALITY

The communist regime of Kim II Sung in North Korea had been a constant source of threat to the South Koreans ever since the partition of the peninsula at the end of the World War II. Kim II Sung had distinguished himself during his military career, and he was an undoubtedly a courageous and charismatic man, but as leader of South Korea he presided over one of the most repressive regimes in the world, in which all opposition to the government was brutally quelled. He also instigated a bizarre cult of the personality, in which his subjects were required to call him 'Eternal Leader', and which encouraged the belief that he had supernatural powers. Under his regime, North Korea became extremely poor, in contrast to the prosperity of its neighbour in the South, which during the same period experienced a booming economy. By 1994, when Kim II Sung died, North Korea had become almost completely isolated from the rest of the world, so much so that its population were almost entirely unaware of their own backwardness compared to the rapid advances of their neighbours in the South.

STATE TERROR

As Kim II Sung's regime continued, he became less dependent on support from the Soviet Union and North Korea began to operate more and more as a maverick state. Not only were the North Koreans suspected of involvement in the Rangoon Bombing of October 1983, they were also thought to be behind the bombing of the Korean passenger plane, Flight 858, in November 1987. In this incident, which took place over the Andaman Sea, the entire crew and passengers of the plane lost their lives, totalling 115 deaths. It was thought that the attack was mounted to frighten away visitors to the 1988 Olympics in Seoul, and it was also a protest at the fact that the North Koreans had not been invited to co-host the Olympics.

It is not clear whether Kim Il Sung himself was personally involved in these acts of state terror, but given his autocratic style of government, it seems likely. Sadly, the situation has not greatly improved in North Korea since his successor, his son Kim Jong-il took over the country in 1994. Today, North Korea continues to be an international pariah, with an appalling record on human rights, nuclear weapons proliferation and many other issues – not the least of which is state terror, as the Rangoon Bombing incident continues to remind us.

THE SABRA AND SHATILA MASSACRE

*Our entry into West Beirut was in order to
make war against the infrastructure left by
the terrorists.*

ARIEL SHARON

The brutal massacre of hundreds, possibly thousands,
of innocent victims at the Sabra and Shatila Massacre
in 1982 was one of the worst atrocities to take place
during the course of war in Lebanon. For many, it
continues to rankle, partly because the perpetrators
were never brought to justice. After the event, the
commander of the massacre, Elie Hobeka, became
a minister in the Lebanese government; he was later
assassinated. A court case was mounted against the
Israeli Defence Minister, Ariel Sharon, when he
became Prime Minister in 2001, in the hopes that
his indirect involvement in the incident would also
be recognized; however, the case was dismissed,
much to the anger of the many families whose
loved ones had been killed.

Today, there remains a great deal of controversy surrounding the incident, especially with the regard to the number of victims. Many argue that the massacre was a deeply shameful episode in the civil war, and that it was a crime against the refugees of Sabra and Shatila that has never been properly recognized by the international community. Others point to the atrocities committed by Palestinian sympathizers that provoked it. But whatever the human cost of the massacre, it seems that it will continue to be a source of bitter dispute between opposing factions in the Middle East for the foreseeable future.

CHAOS AND VIOLENCE

The massacre took place against a complex political and military backdrop of conflict in Lebanon and surrounding countries, which had been going on for decades. The central issue was that of the presence of Palestinian refugees in the country, many of whom had fled from Israel, but who were resented by nationalist elements in Lebanon, especially Christian religious groups. From 1975, fighting had broken out between Lebanese Christian militias and the Palestine Liberation Organization (PLO), led by Yasser Arafat. It was not long before neighbouring countries, such as Syria, were pulled into the conflict, supporting the Lebanese militias against the Palestinians, who were forced out of Beirut into the South. In 1978, Israel itself had invaded

Lebanon, but they had been ordered out by the United Nations.

Hostilities then escalated as the PLO began to attack Israel's border from its base in Southern Lebanon, until in 1982 Israel once more invaded the country, with the purpose of evicting the Palestinians. This was the point when the Sabra and Shatila Massacre took place, in an atmosphere of such general chaos, violence and lawlessness that it has been difficult for historians and other commentators to agree on exactly what happened.

REVENGE KILLINGS

According to reliable reports, the massacre took place at the command of Elie Hobeika, the commander of the Lebanese Phalange party's militia force. In 1976, Hobeika's fiancée and some members of his family had been killed in a PLO terror attack at Damour, so he had plenty of reason to want revenge. When the Israeli army invaded in 1982, the opportunity came for the Phalange militia to move into the Palestinian refugee camps of Sabra and Shatilia, ostensibly to deal with PLO terrorists. Instead, they raped, murdered and brutalized the civilian inhabitants of the camps over a period of three days.

Later, radio workers reported that the militia soldiers had been given the order to do so by Hobeika himself. They alleged that when a militia leader asked Hobeika how to treat Palestinian women and children who had been taken prisoner, he said, 'This is the last time you ask me a question like that. You know exactly what to do.' However, Hobeika later claimed that he had been forced into ordering the massacre by Israeli Defence Minister Ariel Sharon.

RAPED, TERRORIZED AND SHOT

Whatever the truth of the matter, there is no doubt that defenceless men, women and children, who had already been displaced as a result of war, were killed at Sabra and Shatila. Sabra is a run-down suburb of Beirut, while Shatila had been set up by the United Nations as a Palestinian refugee camp in 1949, and it had grown larger as refugees continued to flee there over the years. These powerless victims of war, who lived in poverty and squalor, were now subjected to vicious assaults by the Lebanese militia: women were raped, children terrorized, and whole families shot in front of horrified onlookers. While the militia soldiers performed their gruesome crimes, the Israeli forces patrolled the borders of the camps, making sure they could continue their dirty work. Tellingly, the ostensible reason for the raids – to seek out PLO terrorists – was forgotten: no PLO activists were handed over to the authorities, although a large amount of ammunition was apparently confiscated.

Eyewitnesses to the attacks report that on September 15, 1982, the Israeli military circled the camps, setting up observation points around the periphery. They then fired flares into the area, lighting up the sky so that the soldiers could see what was happening in the camp. The following evening, Elie Hobeika and his Phalangist militiamen stormed the camps, attacking entire families in an orgy of violence. Meanwhile, the Israeli army continued to fire illumination flares into the sky, and they blocked the exits of the camps so that the refugees could not find a way to escape. It also provided the militia troops with food and water, and made sure they had enough ammunition. The militia soldiers reported many of the killings to the Israelis, who allowed the massacre to carry on, turning a blind eye to the atrocities they knew were being perpetrated against the refugees.

THE UNKNOWN DEAD

Eventually, after three days, the Israelis ordered the militia out of the camps, but by this time the soldiers were in no mood to listen to orders. Instead, they frogmarched the remaining victims out of the area and herded them into a stadium to be questioned, killing many of them at random on the way.

By September 18, the massacre was over. According to reports by journalists and international relief agencies such as the Red Cross, who were the first to arrive at the scene of carnage, there were hundreds of mutilated bodies lying dead in the streets. Later, a great deal of controversy arose as to the exact number of victims. Estimates varied from 700 (based on Israeli intelligence figures) to 3,000 (as alleged by Israeli journalist Amnon Kapeliouk). Tragically, because of the chaotic, random way in which the murders took place, many bodies were left uncounted and unburied, so to this day the real number of victims remains unknown.

BITTER AFTERMATH

Not surprisingly, the aftermath of the massacre was a bitter one. The United Nations General Assembly responded by declaring the massacre to be an act of genocide. Initially, the Israeli government tried to defend itself by denying the massacre had taken place, but as evidence to the contrary grew, it realized this position was untenable. Under pressure from the international community, as well as their own people, who held large demonstrations in the capital Tel Aviv, the Israeli government set up a commission to look into their army's part in the massacre. It eventually reported, a year after the massacre took place, that the Israeli army had not been 'directly' involved in the killings; however, it held Defence Minister Ariel Sharon, among others, to be 'indirectly responsible'. The commission recommended that Sharon, along with several other powerful figures, be dismissed. Sharon accordingly stepped down. The commission also recommended that he should not hold public office in Israel again. Despite this, he became prime minister in 2001.

There were attempts to bring Sharon to justice, but they failed. After he became prime minister, relatives of the massacre victims attempted to mount a case against him in Belgium; however, the case was thrown out of court. A number of other human rights cases were also being put forward in the Belgian courts, against such figures as Fidel Castro, Yasser Arafat, George Bush, Colin Powell and Augusto Pinochet. Faced with the enormous complications of these proceedings, and under pressure from the US and NATO (who threatened to move their headquarters from the country), the Belgian courts decided that only crimes against Belgian citizens could be considered within their legal system. To the dismay of many international commentators, Sharon escaped trial and continued to hold office as prime minister until he became ill and was forced to retire in 2006.

Elie Hobeika, commander of the militia forces who had perpetrated the attack, also went on to become a powerful political figure in his country, as a minister in the Lebanese government. However, he met a violent end when in January 2002, when he became the victim of a car bomb. At the time, he had been about to give evidence against Sharon in the upcoming Belgian trial; this, of course, prompted a great deal of speculation as to who was behind the assassination. Hobeika had no shortage of enemies, and there were several suspected parties: the PLO and other Palestinian organizations, the Syrians, the Israelis and the CIA. No one was ever brought to trial for the assassination, but the consensus is that, for complex political reasons, the Syrians were probably behind it.

Today, with continuing conflict in the Middle East between the Israelis and the Palestinians, there seems little likelihood that the perpetrators of the Sabra and Shatila massacre will ever be brought to justice. Sadly, when BBC journalist Martin Asser visited the area 20 years after the event, all that he found to mark the graves of the many victims who lost their lives there was a pile of breeze blocks – a telling sign of the continuing poverty and power-lessness of a persecuted refugee community.

GULF AIR
FLIGHT 771

Don't be alarmed, there's nothing wrong with this plane. But, we do have a rather unusual circumstance here.

CAPTAIN GORDON VETTE

The bombing of Gulf Air Flight 771 was the only terrorist attack ever to have taken place on this airline, but it was a fatal one, killing the entire crew and passengers outright. In a matter of minutes, as the bomb detonated and the plane plummeted out of the sky into the desert, six crew members and 111 passengers were dead. After the tragedy, it was suspected that the attack was the work of the notorious Abu Nidal organization, which was also behind many other atrocities during the 1970s and 1980s. However, it was not until Abu Nidal himself died in 2002 that the organization claimed direct responsibility for the attack.

On September 23, 1983, Gulf Air Flight 771 took off from Abu Dhabi airport in the United Arab Emirates to fly to Karachi, Pakistan. There was no sign that anything was amiss. The aeroplane was a modern Boeing 737, and the airline was a well-established one. Gulf Air had been in existence since the 1940s, set up by a British pilot named Freddie Bosworth, who had operated a small commuter service between neighbouring Arab countries. Since that time it had become a highly successful airline, at first supported by the British aviation industry, and then sold to the governments of Bahrain, Qatar, the Emirate of Abu Dhabi, and Oman, to create a national carrier for the gulf states. By the 1980s, as air travel had increased, so Gulf Air had expanded, boasting a fleet of up-to-date aircraft that reflected the wealth of its owners and becoming one of the major carriers for flights out of Abu Dhabi to a variety of destinations around the world. It also held a completely clean record for safety in the air: up until that fateful day, there had been no major accidents or incidents on Gulf planes. All that was to change – within seconds.

DESERT DISASTER

Unknown to the crew and passengers of the aircraft, a bomb was hidden in the baggage compartment, and at 3.30 p.m. it exploded. The pilot immediately sent out a distress message and attempted an emergency landing in the desert. But it was too late:

the aeroplane caught fire and was unable to land safely, crashing on its descent and killing everyone on board.

At first it was unclear what had caused the crash, but as security services sifted through the wreckage in the desert, it became clear that there had been a bomb on board the aeroplane. But who had planted it, and why?

Over the following weeks, as the relatives of the crash victims began to mourn their dead, there was a great deal of speculation as to the perpetrators of this latest atrocity. Eventually, it became clear that the most likely culprit behind the bombing was the infamous Abu Nidal and his organization.

REIGN OF TERROR

Nidal was a Palestinian revolutionary who had started out with clear political aims, but who appeared, over his career, to have become entirely callous and opportunistic in his attacks, to the point of becoming a mercenary: 'a gun for hire', as some commentators put it. There were also those who claimed that Nidal was, or had become, a psychopath: as well as the random cruelty of his terror attacks, he showed a paranoid distrust of members of his own organization, and his sadistic treatment of them was legendary.

By the 1980s, there was ample evidence to show that Nidal's reign of terror had left him isolated from other revolutionary groups, and that he had few supporters left. There were also few countries willing to offer a home to such a dangerous, unruly subject, and he was running out of places to live – not to mention ways of making a living. Accordingly, he was starting to blackmail the governments of countries such as Saudi Arabia, Kuwait and the United Arab Emirates, threatening to mount terror attacks on their territory unless they paid him large amounts of money. And, for a while, his protection racket seems to have worked: soon after the attack on Gulf Air Flight 771, Kuwait and the United Arab Emirates paid Nidal a substantial sum. This was not, of course, made public. However, it is now common knowledge that in the 1970s and 1980s a number of Arab state leaders offered protection of different kinds to international terrorists, whether because they shared political and spiritual beliefs, or simply because they wanted immunity from terrorist acts on their soil.

MERCENARY OR REVOLUTIONARY?

So who was Abu Nidal, this shadowy figure, who managed to do business with heads of state while at the same time blowing up their aeroplanes and terrorizing their people? Abu Nidal or 'father of struggle', as he dubbed himself, was born Sabri Khalil al-Banna in 1937 in Jaffa, a town on the coast of what was then known as the British Mandate of Palestine. His childhood was one of extreme disturbance and disruption, both emotional and social. His father, Khalil, was the wealthy owner of one of Jaffa's largest orange groves. Khalil was married with 11 children, but then took another wife, a 16-year-old maid, who gave birth to Sabri, the future terrorist. When Khalil died, the family threw his mother out of the house; seven-year-old Sabri was allowed to stay, but grew up neglected and unloved. The family then lost their orange groves, as a result of the partition of the area after the World War II, and fled to refugee camps in Gaza and the West Bank.

Not surprisingly, as a young man Nidal became a lifelong Palestinian nationalist, moving around the Arab world and setting up revolutionary terrorist groups. He also became a highly successful business-man, with companies that acted as fronts for his political activities. He then severed his links with the Palestine Liberation Organization (PLO), publicly criticizing Yasser Arafat, and mounted his first terror attacks. Ostensibly, there were political differences between the PLO and Nidal's organiza-tion; but it soon became clear that, by this time, Nidal was acting to save his own skin and line his own pocket, rather than to pursue any clear political objective. The PLO came to regard Nidal as a mercenary rather than a revolutionary; and as his career progressed, other radical leaders came to the same conclusion, eventually leaving him and his followers completely isolated.

BIZARRE TORTURES

Over the years, rumours began to circulate that Nidal was losing his mind. Ex-members of his organization, now called the Fatah-Revolutionary Council (FRC) and operating in Syria, told lurid stories of how Nidal had begun to hold his own followers captive, accusing them of being spies and torturing them. He routinely forced members to write out their life histories, again and again, and if they got any detail wrong, subjected them to bizarre tortures: they were forced to sleep standing up, fed through tubes, or had boiling oil poured over their genitals. Horrifyingly, there were also reports of purges, in which hundreds of followers had been shot and buried in mass graves.

Amazingly enough, throughout all this, Nidal was running an extremely successful business operation. The FRC's companies – under a variety of different names – were making huge amounts of money by selling arms from European and American companies to the Middle East and laundering money through respected international banks such as BCCI. Nidal was also hobnobbing with powerful Arab heads of state such as Colonel Gaddafi of Libya. He is thought to have mounted several appalling atrocities on behalf of Gaddafi, the worst being the Lockerbie air disaster of 1988. The FRC was also suspected of masterminding over 100 other attacks during the 1980s, which killed and wounded a total of 900 people in 20 countries around the world.

NOWHERE TO RUN

By the new millennium, however, Nidal's reign of terror was beginning to crumble. His opportunistic, mercenary tactics had, not surprisingly, left him with few friends. In 1999, hoping to renew diplomatic relations with the West, Gaddafi expelled Nidal from Libya. Nidal went to live in Baghdad, apparently under the protection of the Iraqi government, even though he was wanted for murder in Jordan for his part in a terror attack there. On August 19, 2002, he was reported to have died of gunshot wounds, in a house in a rich district of Baghdad owned by the Mukhabarat, the Iraqi Secret Service. The Iraqis claimed he had committed suicide during a raid on the house; Palestinian and other sources suggested that Saddam Hussein had ordered the killing.

After Nidal's death, one of his former aides, Atef Abu Baqr, confirmed what had long been suspected, that the Gulf Air bombing had been personally ordered by Abu Nidal, as a punishment for the United Arab Emirates' refusal to pay protection money to the FRC. Baqr suggested that this action had 'displeased' the Iraqis, and it was for this reason that they had changed their attitude towards Nidal.

The story behind the Gulf Air Flight 771 disaster is, on the one hand, the story of a violent terrorist with a warped mind, bent on destroying the civilized world. On the other hand, it is the story of how elements of that world colluded with him, in a complex power game of political intrigue and financial double dealing that ultimately led to the deaths of many innocent victims.

HARRODS
BOMB BLAST

*The public's reaction to the Harrod's bomb
has been the same as the government's –
that the fight against terrorism must go on
and be won.*

MARGARET THATCHER

At 1.00 p.m. on December 17, 1983, a large
explosion rocked the district of Knightsbridge
located in the heart of London. It is an area of
luxurious apartments, mews houses and exclusive
shops, and where the famous Harrods department
store is situated. The founder of Harrods was a man
named Charles Henry Harrod and, from the day it
opened in 1849, the store always prided itself on a
reputation for excellence. In 1883, the store burnt to
the ground at the beginning of December, but
Harrod's son, Charles Digby, not only succeeded in
fulfilling all of his Christmas deliveries, but also
made a new record profit for the store. A new
building rose out of the ashes, and for the first time

it could boast about legendary customers such as Oscar Wilde, Lilly Langtry and Ellen Terry.

The current owner of Harrods is Mohammad Al Fayed, an Egyptian-born, Swiss-based businessman who has had a tempestuous relationship with the British authorities over the years, constantly being turned down for British citizenship. He has also become famous in more recent years for his conspiracy claims against the Royal Family in regards to the death of his son Dodi Fayed and Princess Diana in a Paris car crash.

THE BLAST

The famous shopping district of Knightsbridge was busy with Christmas shoppers and everyone was jostling in and out of the shops buying their seasonal gifts. Suddenly a huge blast ripped through the throng of people, sending out a mass of thick black smoke, rubble and shards of broken glass. A large plume of smoke rose above Harrods, coming from the Hans Crescent end of the store. The scene was one of utter devastation and people stood dazed, not quite sure what had happened.

A bomb had apparently exploded in a car in one of the side streets outside the famous department store. Many people were walking round wounded, while others lay unable to move.

Immediately after the blast there was a strange silence, but when it sank in exactly what had occurred, there were screams, shouts and crying. People who weren't too badly hurt, stopped to help those who were more seriously injured until the emergency services arrived at the scene. The pavement was like a sea of glass, tainted red by all the blood.

People sat or lay numbly, waiting to be helped, surrounded by the distinctive olive and gold shopping bags from the Harrods store. Brightly wrapped gifts lay in the streets among the grim remnants of the explosive-laden car.

Sirens could be heard wailing their way through the busy streets of London and amid all the chaos somebody said, 'They've bombed Harrods!'

Four hospitals were put on emergency alert, ready to receive the people who could not be treated at the scene. The toll at the end of the day was six people dead, including three policemen and one American, and 90 injured.

Inside Harrods the reaction was shocked horror as some of the people witnessed the force of the explosion as several windows were blown in. A mother clutched her two children in complete terror at the top of the stairs, too scared to move. The employees, who tried their best to remain calm, started to lead people out by a side entrance. It wasn't until they got outside that they realized the full gravity of the situation.

These were the days before mobile phones, and it was hard for people to get word to their families that they were unhurt in the explosion. A large queue formed outside a phone box in the vicinity.

Lying in the gutter was a severely injured policeman and his dog, the man pleading for help. In the middle of the road, was another policeman who was in an even worse state, he was severely traumatized and unable to speak or move. Lying beside him was his walkie-talkie, which he was probably using to warn of a suspicious looking car, just before it exploded. The scene was horrific and for the rest of the day many people were wandering around London stunned and in tears.

WARNINGS

The police were given a coded warning at 12.45 p.m., saying that there was a bomb in a car outside the Harrods store in Knightsbridge. As officers cordoned off the area and began a detailed search to make sure there were no more hidden explosives, a second warning call was made. This call warned of a bomb in the heart of the shopping district of London, Oxford Street.

Police hurriedly tried to clear the crowded area, but the warning of a bomb which was claimed to be outside the C&A store, turned out to be a false alarm.

The following day the Irish Republican Army (IRA) claimed responsibility for the explosion, saying that it was part of a pre-Christmas bombing campaign they had planned for London. The police moved hundreds of extra police, including plain clothes officers and mobile bomb squads, into the city, in an effort to protect the public from any further attacks.

HARRODS REOPENS

Harrods reopened for business three days later under tight security, saying the store would not be defeated by acts of terrorism. The police introduced new anti-terrorist measures to prevent a repetition of the car bomb. Although many Londoners who had been interviewed by the media claimed they would not be put off by Irish terrorists, Christmas shopping the following week got off to a slow start.

On December 20, detectives made a series of early raids and arrested four suspected sympathizers of the IRA, but no official charges were ever made.

Terrorism is one of the greatest scourges that the world faces today, especially when the target is innocent people – for example, people simply doing their Christmas shopping. The terrorist activities of the IRA have been going on for more than two decades and have been an evil inspiration to terrorists worldwide. The success of bombs, such as the one at Harrods, only heightens our awareness of their presence, which is exactly what they want.

There are currently more than 60 paramilitary fighters who are sought in connection with terrorist-related crimes that took place before 1998. These people could benefit from a new Northern Ireland Offences Bill, which is currently being discussed in the House of Commons. Under this new legislation, many terrorist suspects could be released and would be free to return to Northern Ireland.

THE BRIGHTON BOMB

*My failure to kill former Prime Minister
Margaret Thatcher made it possible for future
peace talks to take place.*

PATRICK MAGEE

The bombing of the Conservative Party Conference at Brighton in 1984 sent shock waves through Britain. This was the first time a terrorist attack aimed at assassinating the entire British government cabinet had taken place on the mainland. On October 12, in the early hours of the morning, a huge explosion ripped through the Grand Hotel, where senior party members were staying. Such was the force of the blast that a huge section of façade of the building was blown off, several interior floors collapsed, and a fog of thick dust hung in the air for hours afterwards. Incredibly, all the members of the cabinet, including Prime Minister Margaret Thatcher, escaped with their lives. However, five people were killed, and 34 were injured, including

Mary Tebbit, the wife of cabinet minister Norman Tebbit, who was left permanently disabled. After the attack, the Provisional Irish Republican Army claimed responsibility, issuing a chilling warning: 'Today we were unlucky, but remember we only have to be lucky once. You have to be lucky always.'

BOMB IN THE BATHROOM

That year, Conservative party members had gathered from all over the country for their annual conference in Brighton. Top MPs and officials stayed at the Grand Hotel, an impressive, old-fashioned Victorian hotel on Brighton's promenade. There were also party members and media crews staying next door, at the Metropole Hotel and at other hotels in the area. As always, there was something of a festive air at the conference, with crowds gathering to cheer politicians' speeches and celebrating afterwards, staying up drinking and talking until the small hours. The fact that the prime minister was celebrating her 59th birthday during the conference added to the general excitement that year.

The night before the bomb went off, Prime Minister Thatcher was working late at her desk, preparing her speech for the next day. She was well known for her ability to function on as little as four hours' sleep a night, and it was this trait that saved her. Had she been in her bedroom, she would almost certainly have died, since a bomb had been secretly placed in a bathroom nearby. As it was, the part of the hotel where she was working escaped the worst of the blast.

A SMOKING RUIN

After the bomb detonated, there was initial confusion. Firefighters at the local station received an emergency signal from the hotel, and at first thought the alarm had been accidentally set off by a drunk, which had often happened in the past. However, as they reached the hotel, it became clear that this was no false alarm: the hotel was a smoking ruin, its front blasted off and a pall of dust hanging in the air around it. As the emergency services began work on clearing the wreckage and leading the survivors to safety, camera crews arrived to film the event. Thus it was that viewers were able to see the prime minister's immediate reaction to the event, as she walked out of the debris and calmly greeted the emergency workers with a polite, 'Good morning. Thank you for coming.'

Thatcher's ruthless determination as a political leader, and her right-wing social and economic policies, which many felt to be hardhearted and unsympathetic to all but the most able in society, had earned her the nickname 'the Iron Lady': in this instance, however, her stoicism in the face of disaster showed that the name had its positive aspect, too.

END OF AN ERA

As the dust – literally – began to settle, the damage that the bomb had done began to emerge. Five people were dead: Sir Anthony Berry MP, Regional Chairman Eric Taylor, and three wives of Conservative politicians (Jeanne Shattock, Roberta Wakeman and Muriel Maclean). In addition, Mary Tebbit, the wife of Cabinet Minister Norman Tebbit, had been seriously injured. She survived, but she was left disabled for the rest of her life. Scores of people were taken to hospital with lesser injuries. Considering the force of the blast, there were remarkably few casualties: however, the damage to the morale of the Conservative Party, and to the way of life of the British nation, was immense.

Up until the Brighton bombing, political rallies in Britain took place in a relatively relaxed atmosphere; often, even high-profile figures were able to move freely among the public without a great deal of supervision. However, from the day of the Brighton bombing, that changed dramatically: security was stepped up to the maximum degree, and events such as party conferences became tense, tightly controlled affairs in which the general public were kept well away from politicians and officials. Sadly, this made the events less enjoyable for everyone, politicians and public alike; but with the threat of terror attacks hanging over any major political gathering, there seemed to be no alternative.

A CAMPAIGN OF TERROR

The immediate suspects for the bombing were the Provisional IRA, who had openly pledged a campaign of terror attacks against the British government unless it withdrew troops from Northern Ireland. Later, they released a statement claiming responsibility for the attack and issuing a warning that such attacks would continue indefinitely until their objective was met.

Despite this, Prime Minister Thatcher went on to give her speech as planned that day, much to the admiration of her followers. During her speech, she took the opportunity to reiterate her stand against terrorism, declaring, 'This attack has failed. All attempts to destroy democracy by terrorism will fail'. She continued: 'This government will not weaken; this nation will meet the challenge; democracy will prevail.' The prime minister received a standing ovation for her address, and it became clear that the IRA's action, far from undermining confidence in the government, had in fact increased the nation's sympathy towards them.

SUSPECT HUNTED DOWN

It was clear who the culprits behind the bomb attack were: but how had they managed to plant a large explosive device in the hotel and detonate it during the conference? Forensic investigation revealed that the bomb had been hidden in the bathroom of Room 629 of the hotel, a full three weeks before the explosion. A large amount of Semtex had been attached to a long-delay fuse and hidden behind a bath panel. When the hotel records were checked, it was found that a man had checked into the room at that time using a false name. A fingerprint on his hotel registration card was found, which was matched against a fingerprint found at the Rubens Hotel, London, where a similar bomb had been planted, but which had been defused before it could detonate. The two fingerprints were identical. Clearly, the same bomber was at work in both attacks.

The police also had in their possession the fingerprint of Patrick McGee, a leading member of the IRA who was known to have committed bombing offences. This imprint had been taken when McGee had been stopped as a teenager for a driving offence, decades before. The two sets of the hotel bomber's fingerprints were now matched with this one, and they were found to be exactly the same.

THE AFTERMATH

Now the police had a suspect: their next step was to find him. Since McGee was a known IRA bomber, police had conducted surveillance on him for some time, so it was not long before he was tracked down and arrested in Glasgow. Soon afterwards, he was brought to trial, convicted, and was sentenced to life imprisonment – eight times over. However, in 1999, he was freed, after serving only 14 years of his sentence. His reprieve came as part of the Good Friday Agreement, a political initiative that aimed to address issues of conflict and national identity in Ireland for the first time. As such, the agreement was an important step in negotiations for peace in Northern Ireland: however, there were many who felt that McGee did not deserve to be released as part of this process.

In prison, McGee followed an Open University course, gaining both a BA and a PhD. However, he remained unrepentant about the bombing. He then began to correspond and meet with victims of the bombing and their relatives, most notably Jo Berry, the daughter of murdered Conservative MP Sir Anthony Berry.

In a further strange twist, 20 years later, the apartment that McGee had rented during the Brighton bombing was also occupied by Abu al-Hindi who was suspected of being a top operative for Osama Bin Laden's terrorist group al-Qaeda, and it was subsequently raided by police.

So what is the legacy of the Brighton bombing? In hindsight, it remains debatable whether the British government did, in fact, as Thatcher claimed, stand firm on the issue of terrorism. A year after the attack, the Prime Minister signed the Anglo-Irish Agreement, conceding for the first time that the Republic of Ireland had a role to play in the future of Northern Ireland, and setting in motion the negotiations that eventually led to the Good

Friday Agreement. Whether or not the Brighton bombing was a factor in prompting the process is difficult to say, but it is certainly the case that the IRA's extended campaign of violence focussed attention on the need for both the British and the Irish to bring the situation to a peaceful conclusion as quickly as possible.

TWA FLIGHT 847

He has pulled a hand-grenade pin and is
ready to blow up the aircraft if he has to.
We must, I repeat, we must land at Beirut.
We must land at Beirut. No alternative.

CAPTAIN, FLIGHT 847

The hijacking of TWA Flight 847 in 1985 was one
of the most chaotic and terrifying in the history of
terror attacks. What should have been a short hop
between Athens and Rome ended up as an epic
three-day nightmare journey when two hijackers
boarded the plane and forced the pilot to fly
backwards and forwards between Beirut and
Algiers, issuing death threats, picking up gunmen
and terrorizing hostages, all the while making
political demands. The crazed behaviour of the
gunmen, who claimed to be suicide bombers,
created an atmosphere of sheer panic, not only on
the aeroplane but among airport landing staff, as the
hijackers threatened to blow the plane up or crash

into control towers. When an American passenger, US Navy diver Robert Stethem was murdered and his body thrown out on the tarmac at one of the plane's stops, it became clear that the threats were for real; but eventually, after their horrifying ordeal, all the other hostages were returned to safety. However, the hijackers, who belonged to the Lebanese Hezbollah militant group, were never caught and currently remain on the US's Most Wanted Terrorists list.

HAND GRENADES AND GUNS

On the morning of Friday, June 15, 1985, Flight TWA 847 landed at Athens airport. It had come from Cairo and was headed for Rome, stopping in Athens to take on extra passengers. Many of them were American Roman Catholics, who were on a tour of the Holy Land. Three others were also among the crowd: smartly dressed young Arab men carrying shoulder bags. Only two of them got on the plane; the other had an argument with TWA staff and was not allowed to board.

Shortly after the plane took off, the two young Arabs took guns and hand grenades out of their bags and ran down to the cockpit, waving their weapons and shouting. Once there, they held up the pilot, Captain John Testrake, and ordered him to fly directly to Beirut. However, once they arrived in Beirut airspace, they found that the air controllers were refusing permission for the plane to land. The airport also blocked the runway, using buses and other vehicles. It was only when the pilot began to plead with the staff, describing the terrorists as beating passengers and about to detonate their hand grenades, that the control tower relented and let the plane land.

The hijackers then demanded that the airport staff refuel the engine, which was done. At this point, they issued their demands, which centred around the presence of Israeli forces in the Lebanon. They demanded the release of all Shi'ite Muslim prisoners captured by Israel in Lebanon and international condemnation of the Israeli presence there. They also wanted condemnation of CIA activity in the region, especially in regard to a car bombing that had recently taken place in the Beirut suburb of Bir al Abed and was rumoured to be the work of the CIA operatives. (The bomb had killed 80 people.) The hijackers wanted to speak with a spokesperson from Amal, a mainstream political group supporting the Shi'ite Muslims; Amal, however, refused to get involved with the negotiations.

SUICIDE BOMBERS

The hijackers then released 19 women and children from the aeroplane, pushing them down an emergency escape slide. Once released, the freed hostages reported that many of the remaining passengers inside the plane were hysterical and that the hostages had shot a man in the neck. However, there was nothing security services could do to help – the risks of storming the plane were too high, and no one wanted to provoke a blood bath. Thus airport staff stood helplessly by as the hijackers demanded that the pilot take off once more. This time, the destination was Algiers.

On arrival in Algerian airspace, the pilot once again had difficulty in getting permission to touch down. Naturally enough, airport staff were extremely unwilling to endanger themselves and their passengers by allowing a hijacked aeroplane to land on their runway. Officials on the ground responded to the pilot's request to land by closing the airport.

It seemed that the hijackers and the controllers had reached stalemate, much to the anxiety of the hostages, who were now having to contemplate circling the airport until the plane ran out of fuel. However, at this stage President Reagan himself intervened, asking the Algerian government to consider the safety of the passengers and allow the plane to land. The Algerian authorities eventually relented and permission was granted, and the plane duly touched down at Algiers airport. This time, the aeroplane spent several hours on the runway, and the hijackers released 20 more passengers.

But the ordeal was not yet over. The exhausted pilot was then commanded to fly back to Beirut, and once more had to persuade air controllers there to allow him to land. He described how the plane was running out of fuel, but it was not until one of the hijackers shouted out that they were suicide bombers and would crash the tower – or the presidential palace nearby – that the Beirut airport staff wearily agreed to allow the plane to land.

BRUTAL MURDER

Back in Beirut airport, the hijackers once more demanded a spokesperson from Amal, the official Shi'ite political group; and once again, Amal declined. What happened next was horrifying: the hijackers killed an American passenger, a young man from the US Navy named Robert Stethem, beating him and then shooting him in the head. Once he was dead, his body was unceremoniously bundled out of the aeroplane onto the tarmac. The hijackers then threatened to kill another passenger, so an Amal official was immediately dispatched to the plane, along with a bodyguard.

The negotiations lasted several hours, during which time the hijackers asked for all the lights in the airport to be switched off. This request was complied with, and later the reason for it became clear: while the lights were out, the hijackers smuggled on more gunmen, and also offloaded several passengers with Israeli-sounding names. The hijackers went on to order large quantities of food, water and fuel, confirming the hostages' worst fears that the ordeal was to continue. Then the Amal official left, and the plane took off again – back to Algiers.

Meanwhile in Athens, the third would-be

hijacker, Ali Atwa, who had been prevented from boarding the plane in the first place, was by now in police custody. The hijackers demanded that he be released and flown to Algiers, threatening to kill the Greek passengers on the plane (including the well-known Greek singer Demis Roussos, who happened to be among them) if the authorities did not let him go. The terrorists' wishes were complied with. In Algiers, the hijackers released 61 more hostages, after negotiations with Algerian officials.

By now, the crew and the remaining hostages were desperate, and the aeroplane itself was in need of maintenance, but the terrorists seemed not to care – or, frighteningly, to know what to do next. They announced that if their demands were not met this time, they would fly to an unknown destination and blow up the plane with its remaining passengers. However, in the end, they forced the pilot to fly back to Beirut again, which he did. Once on the ground, they demanded more fuel and food, along with newspapers and videos, and issued further threats.

This time, a senior Amal official, Nabih Berri, conducted negotiations with the hijackers. Berri was a politically moderate Shi'ite and a member of the Lebanese government, which at the time was in a state of disarray because of the civil war in the country. By the afternoon of Monday, June 17, the crisis showed signs of coming to an end: the hostages were taken off the plane and taken under Berri's protection. For two further weeks, they remained captive before being driven to the Syrian border and released.

WANTED: FOR MURDER

After the hijacking, the Israelis did actually release many Shi'ite Muslims from their prisons, though they claimed that this was unconnected to the hijacking. Moreover, the four major players in the hijacking, Hassan Izz-Al-Din, Imad Mugnivah, Mohammed Ali Hammadi, and Ali Atwa, all escaped and are at large today. One of them, Hammadi, was actually caught in 1987 as he tried to smuggle explosives into Germany. As well as being tried for the smuggling, he was charged with the murder of Robert Stethem in the hijacking incident two years earlier. He was convicted of the murder and sentenced to life imprisonment. However, Hammadi was released on parole in 2005 and allowed to return to Lebanon. The US government has since demanded that he be extradited.

In the aftermath of 9/11, the four hijackers were added to the FBI's Most Wanted Terrorists list, with rewards of five million dollars offered for information leading to their arrest and conviction. The political group, Hezbollah, which they claimed allegiance to, has categorically denied any involvement in the TWA Flight 847 incident. Hezbollah, which was formed in 1982 in response to the civil war in Lebanon, claims that it is an Islamic resistance group, working to improve conditions for the poor; however, the US government, along with many other Western nations, considers it to be a terrorist organization, responsible for the nightmare hijacking of TWA Flight 847, as well as for many other attacks.

AIR INDIA
FLIGHT 182

*They have betrayed us, mother, they have
betrayed us*

SHIPRA ARORA, FLIGHT ATTENDANT

One of the worst terror attacks in aviation history
was the bombing of Air India Flight 182, which
took place in 1985. It killed everyone on board: a
total of 329 people, 82 of them children. Prior to the
bombings of 9/11 in 2001, this was the biggest air
attack ever to have taken place. Afterwards, two
men were brought to trial, but they were both
acquitted, after an extremely long and expensive
court case. The Canadian authorities were severely
criticized for the incompetent handling of the case,
which took nearly 20 years to reach a conclusion,
and which yielded little in the way of results.
Eventually, one man, Inderjit Singh Reyat, was
charged with manslaughter for his part in making
the bomb used on the flight. He pleaded guilty and
was convicted, but the judge went on to give him a

sentence of only five years in prison. The difficulties in bringing the perpetrators of the attack to justice have led to accusations of government corruption and conspiracy; and the issue has continued, in the new millennium, to be a source of controversy in Canada.

BOMB BLAST

On June 23, Air India Flight 182 had set off from Montréal-Mirabel Airport in Canada and was flying towards Heathrow Airport, London, when a bomb exploded on board. It was 7.15 a.m. and the aeroplane was nearing its destination, flying over Ireland. Air traffic controllers at Shannon airport later reported that a crackling sound had been heard on their radio at the time of the explosion.

The plane landed in deep water out at sea near County Cork, and everyone who was on it perished. As the emergency services began the dismal task of sifting through the wreckage, a picture of what had happened began to emerge. Piecing together the evidence, investigators found that a bomb had been placed in the cargo towards the front of the plane, which had caused rapid decompression, so that the plane broke up while it was flying along. Amazingly, some of the passengers had survived the break-up of the aircraft, only to drown once they fell into the freezing waters of the Atlantic Ocean, almost 325 km (200 miles) offshore.

This was a tragedy on a grand scale, and the

Canadian government duly set about bringing the perpetrators of the crime to justice. It was thought that the bombing was the work of a Sikh separatist group called the Babbar Khalsa, who wanted to create a state for Sikhs in the Punjab. They called this state 'Khalistan', meaning 'Land of the Pure'. Most of the members of this organization lived outside India, in Canada and Britain, and were suspected of mounting numerous terror attacks during the 1970s and 80s. Indeed, shortly before the bombing of Air India Flight 182, a bomb had exploded in Narita Airport, Japan, killing two baggage handlers. The bomb was in a suitcase destined for Air India Flight 310 bound for Bangkok. Thankfully for the 177 crew members and passengers on board that flight, the bomb detonated before it reached the aeroplane.

DOUBLE DEALING

As the investigation ground on, it became clear that this was going to be a long-winded enquiry. This was partly because of the complex nature of the evidence and the extreme bureaucracy of the legal system; but there were also those who believed that some double dealing between the Canadian authorities and the terrorists was going on behind the scenes.

Initially, four men were suspected of involvement in the bombings: Talwinder Singh Parmar, Inderjit Singh Reyat, Ajaib Singh Bagri and Ripudaman

Singh Malik. Parmar was the prime suspect, as Canadian leader of the Babbar Khalsa sect. He had grown up in Punjab, India and had emigrated to Canada in 1970, living in Burnaby, B.C., with his family. A devout Sikh, he joined the Babbar Khalsa sect and became committed to the establishment of a Sikh homeland in his native Punjab. Like others in the sect, he believed that Khalistan, as the homeland was to be called, must be established by violent overthrow of the status quo in India.

Two years before the Air India bombing, Parmar had been arrested in Germany, suspected of murdering two policemen while he was in India. He spent nearly a year in prison before being released and returning to Canada. The Indian authorities requested that he be extradited to face trial in India, but they were turned down – with tragic consequences, as it turned out.

Because of his terrorist links, Parmar was under constant surveillance from the Canadian police. Not long before the Air India bombing, they had followed Parmar and an associate, Inderjit Singh Reyat, on a trip into woods on Vancouver Island, where the pair were thought to be testing an explosive of some kind. Although a loud bang was heard, when the police later searched the area, they found nothing to incriminate the pair. They then raided Parmar and Reyat's homes and arrested them, charging them with possession of weapons and explosives, and with conspiracy. However, the charges were later dropped due to lack of evidence.

THE BOMB MAKER

Next on the list of suspects was Inderjit Reyat, who had grown up in India and emigrated, this time to England. Interestingly, it was not until his move to England, aged 13, that he became a practising Sikh, joining Akhand Kirtani, a religious devotional group. He trained as a mechanic and married before moving to Canada, where he lived and worked in Duncan, B.C. On the face of it, he seemed a model citizen, working hard, attending the local Sikh temple regularly, and living quietly with his family.

However, the security services had their eye on him as an associate of Parmar and suspected him of harbouring weapons. In 1985, he was arrested and fined for his activities. Afterwards, he moved back to England with his family – out of harm's way, as he hoped. But the British police were keeping a close watch on him too. In 1988, he was arrested by British police on charges of manufacturing the bomb that had exploded at Narita Airport in Japan. He was then extradited to Canada to face his trial. Two years later, after a trial lasting eight months, he was convicted of the crime and received a ten-year prison sentence.

Reyat was also suspected of involvement with the Air India Flight 182 bombing and was charged accordingly. At his trial, he pleaded guilty, and he was charged with manslaughter rather than murder. He was convicted but only received a five-year sentence. This caused a great deal of controversy in

Canada at the time, and outraged the family and friends of the victims. Rumour had it that the murder charges were dropped because he had struck a deal with the prosecution whereby he had agreed to give evidence against two co-conspirators, Bagri and Malik. The press and public were further outraged when Reyat took the witness box and claimed that he could remember nothing about the two men charged with the attack.

THE PREACHER AND THE MILLIONAIRE

So far, the leader of a known terrorist group (Parmar) and a bomb maker (Reyat) had, quite literally, got away with murder. But there was worse to come. Two other suspects, Ajaib Singh Bagri, a militant Sikh who had publicly called for the death of 50,000 Hindus, and Ripudaman Singh Malik, who was thought to have bankrolled the operation, were both acquitted, after facing eight counts each of first-degree murder.

Like Parmar and Reyat, Bagri was an immigrant to Canada and was a devout Sikh, well-known as a speaker among the local religious community where he lived, in Kamloops, B.C. He worked as a forklift truck driver in a sawmill by day, but much of his spare time was devoted to his work as a Sikh preacher. At a packed political rally in Madison Square Garden, New York, he made a rabble-rousing speech in which he vowed to kill 50,000 Hindus. This was in response to the notorious attack on the Sikh Golden Temple at Amritsar by Indian troops in 1984. Because of his violent rhetoric, he was immediately suspected of being behind the bombing of Air India Flight 182, but he did not face trial until many years later.

The other suspect, Ripudaman Singh Malik, was also a Canadian immigrant, where he had forged a successful career as a businessman, importing Indian clothing. By the time of the bombing, he was a multi-millionaire, but he was also a devout Sikh and devoted much of his income to good works within the Sikh community, including setting up a bank, a school and various charities.

CONTINUING SCANDAL

Unbelievably, despite the fact that each of these men was charged with first-degree murder eight times over, the court did not manage to gain a single conviction for them, despite many years of costly court proceedings. Thus today, the perpetrators of one of the major terror attacks of our time have, for the most part, gone unpunished – a scandal that, to this day, continues to haunt Canada's political leaders. In May 2006, a public enquiry was set up to find out how such a situation could have occurred; but the architects of the investigation have left an 'open time frame' for the questions to be answered.

EGYPT AIR FLIGHT 648

*Over the years, I have had to adapt to
the effects of being shot in the head and
the resulting brain injury, which includes
impaired vision and a loss of short-term
memory.*

SURVIVOR, JACKIE PFLUG

The hijacking of Egypt Air Flight 648, and the
commando raid that ended it, caused the deaths of
58 passengers out of a total of 90 on the aeroplane.
The high death toll of this horrible attack, which
took place in 1985, has given it a place in history as
one of the most tragic incidents of its kind: not only
because the hijackers were so brutal, shooting passengers in cold blood at point-blank range, but also
because the authorities handled the situation so
badly, leading to further deaths, which many felt
could have been avoided.

ARMED TERRORISTS

On the evening of November 23, 1985, passengers waited at Athens airport to board their flight to Cairo. Security was high, as only a few months before there had been a major hijacking incident on a flight out of the airport to Rome, in which gunmen had commandeered a plane for days, and one passenger had lost his life (TWA flight 847, see page 337). Athens security services were apparently checking baggage on all outgoing flights thoroughly (later, they insisted that they had conducted five checks on the flight to Cairo). Nevertheless, three Palestinian terrorists somehow managed to escape detection, even though they were heavily armed with hand grenades and pistols. How this happened was never satisfactorily explained by officials at Athens airport.

Entirely unaware of the terrifying ordeal awaiting them, the passengers boarded the Boeing 737 for their flight to Cairo. The crew, led by pilot Hani Galal, prepared for take off, and Egypt Air Flight 648 soared into the air at 9.00 p.m. All went well until ten minutes into the flight, when the three terrorists suddenly leapt up, brandishing their weapons and announcing themselves as 'The Egypt Revolution'. In a bizarre parody of official bureaucracy, they began their reign of terror on the aeroplane by checking all the passengers' passports. Naturally enough, the passengers complied with the gunmens' wishes, realizing that they were in mortal danger.

SHOOT-OUT IN THE AIR

There was one passenger, however, who chose to resist. He was an armed undercover police officer, or 'sky marshal'. He took out a gun and shot at the hijackers, managing to kill one of them. However, even though one of the gunmen was dead, the situation was now worse, in several ways: the other two hijackers, not surprisingly, became even more aggressive; other passengers were caught in the crossfire and seriously wounded; and, most frightening of all, one of the bullets made a hole in the aeroplane's fuselage. This caused major decompression in the aeroplane, and the pilot had to fly as low as possible to avoid disaster.

The two remaining gunmen now ordered the terrified crew to fly to Libya, but there was not enough fuel to complete such a long flight, so they decided that Malta was a better destination. However, they were wrong, as it turned out; when they came into airspace over Malta, the officials at Luqa Airport refused to allow the aeroplane to land. The pilot made it known that there were wounded passengers on board, that the plane had been badly damaged, causing low air pressure inside the cabin, and – as if that were not enough – that their fuel was running out. But the Maltese authorities could not be persuaded, and threatened to turn off the airport lights if the aeroplane tried to land.

HOSTAGES MURDERED

With great skill and courage, Galal managed to bring the plane down safely, despite the fact that it was damaged and he could not see where he was going. Once on the ground, the Maltese Prime Minister Carmelo Mifsud decided to take over negotiations. Unfortunately he and his aides were not very experienced in this kind of situation, and the government were later heavily criticized about the way they handled the crisis. Immediately after the plane landed, it was surrounded by armed Maltese troops (though it later transpired that they did not have any bullets in their guns). Communicating from the airport control tower via an interpreter, Prime Minister Mifsud took a stern line and refused to allow the plane to be refuelled until all the hostages were released. He also refused to withdraw the soldiers surrounding the aircraft.

Initially, two crew members who had been wounded in the fighting on board were allowed to leave the aircraft. Next, 11 passengers were released. But as the Prime Minister and the hijackers reached stalemate on the issue of refuelling and hostage release, the crisis escalated. The hijackers began to shoot passengers at random, beginning with an Israeli woman named Tamar Artzi. Their leader, Omar Mohammed Ali Resaq, then threatened to kill another passenger every quarter of an hour unless the authorities conceded to their demands. Tragically, he was not bluffing: he went on to shoot

Nitzal Mendelson, Jacqueline Pflug, Scarlett Rogenkamp, and Patrick Scott Barker. Amazingly, three of them (Artzi, Pflug and Barker) survived.

COMMANDO RAID

Prime Minister Mifsud had played for high stakes in his negotiations, and it now looked as though he was losing. The US, France and Britain, all of whom had highly trained, experienced antiterrorist experts at their disposal, offered to send help, but Mifsud refused. Fearful of becoming entangled in a conflict between the US and the Arab world, the prime minister was trying to steer a neutral path, but dismally failed to resolve the crisis at hand. When Egypt offered to intervene, Mifsud jumped at the chance, allowing their troops to come in and take control of the situation. As it turned out, this proved to be the worst of his mistakes.

The Egyptians flew in a US-trained antiterrorist squad, the 777 Combat Unit, known as 'Al-Sa'iqa (Thunderbolt), under the leadership of Major-General Kamal Attia, who prepared to storm the plane in a commando-style raid on the morning of November 25. As their name suggested, the squad was not known for its delicacy or patience in situations of conflict. The negotiations continued, but the soldiers could not wait to spring into action and went on to storm the plane an hour and a half before the operation was supposed to take place. In an incredible display of stupidity, they tried to blast off the plane doors and the cargo hold with explosives, causing a fire on the plane that killed many of the passengers. They then stormed the aircraft, shooting at the hijackers and killing further passengers in the process. In a panic, the hijackers also let off hand grenades inside the aeroplane, which added to the carnage. By the end of the raid, 56 out of the 88 passengers who had managed to survive the ordeal so far, lay dead.

TRAGIC BLUNDERS

The blunders continued when the one surviving terrorist, Omar Resaq, who had led the operation, managed to escape. In the confusion of the raid, he was wounded, his lung pierced by a bullet, so he took off his mask, dumped his gun and hand grenades, and pretended to be a passenger. He was sent to the local hospital in an ambulance. It was only when he was in the hospital for treatment that other passengers recognized him as the perpetrator of the attack and reported him. Had they not done so, he might well have escaped detection and walked away a free man.

As the only surviving member of the hijacking team, Resaq was arrested and tried in Malta. He had been seriously injured in the attack, but he recovered enough to face trial there. He was charged on nine counts, including causing the deaths of Mendelson and Rogenkamp, and attempting to kill other passengers. He pleaded guilty to seven of the charges and was given a 25-year sentence. He was jailed in Malta, but actually only served seven years of his sentence before being released. He went to live in Ghana, before being tracked down by FBI agents in Nigeria, who extradited him and brought him to the US for trial. This time, he was given a life sentence without parole.

The hijacking of Egypt Air Flight 648 raised some extremely important issues in terms of the international handling of terror attacks. First, the issue of sky marshals. Should there have been an armed guard on the plane, and should he have opened fire? Many believe that the presence of armed guards on aeroplanes increases the risk of fatalities in terror attacks, either through direct killings as a result of crossfire, or through damaging the aeroplane itself. (Others point to the safety record of El Al, Israel's national carrier, which has a heavy presence of armed guards on its aircraft, but which has only sustained one terror attack, in 1968.) Next, the issue of negotiations: should countries handle their own talks with terrorists in situations of crisis, as happened in Malta, or should a politically neutral, international negotiating team be called in? And finally, the issue of commando-style armed raids: should they ever be used in situations like these? Or is the human cost of such operations simply too high – as happened in the case of Egypt Air Flight 648?

ENNISKILLEN MASSACRE

Remembrance Day had just begun,
To honour Ulsters fallen,
And ended in the massacre,
of Enniskillen town.

FROM 'THE POPPY DAY MASSACRE'

The Enniskillen Massacre, or Remembrance Day Bombing, as it is also called, took place on November 8, 1987, at the town of Enniskillen, Northern Ireland, during a Remembrance Day church service to commemorate the dead of World War I and II. In a vicious and completely un-expected bomb attack by the Irish Republican Army (IRA), 11 people were killed, and 63 injured. Afterwards, the attack was widely condemned by politicians of all persuasions in Northern Ireland and Britain, and it came to be seen as a turning point in the Northern Irish conflict, ushering in a new era of hope for peace.

Today, the Enniskillen massacre is generally held to be a major tactical error on the part of the IRA, because it thoroughly alienated the general public from the Republican cause. Although there may have been a political motivation for the bombing – one of those present was a reserve member of the Royal Ulster Constabulary (RUC) – the fact that the townspeople of Enniskillen were attacked when they were gathered together quietly with their families to commemorate the dead in a religious service pointed to the inhumanity of the IRA's campaign. Moreover, when the father of one of the victims publicly forgave his daughter's killers, the senseless brutality of the political conflict in Northern Ireland was brought into sharp focus, and the need for both sides to move towards a peaceful solution was shown to be more pressing than ever.

BURIED ALIVE

On the morning of Remembrance Sunday, a day dedicated to the memory of all those killed in World War I and II, a small crowd gathered in the centre of Enniskillen, Northern Ireland, to lay wreaths of poppies on the local war memorial. The red poppies were a reminder of the fields of northern France, where so much of the bloodshed took place. All over Britain, similar groups were gathering in towns and villages, in an atmosphere of solemn remembrance, to honour their dead.

The calm at Enniskillen was suddenly shattered

when, at 10.45 a.m., a bomb suddenly detonated. The blast caused the wall of a nearby building, St Michael's Reading Rooms, to collapse, showering huge chunks of rubble down onto the small group below. All at once, the atmosphere became one of chaos, panic and sheer horror as the scale of the atrocity became clear. Some of the victims were killed instantly; some staggered about bleeding until they died; and others were buried below the rubble, slowly suffocating as others tried to rescue them.

Unusually, the entire event was captured on video, by an amateur video enthusiast who had brought his equipment along to film the service. The scene of carnage from this video, later shown on television, shocked all who saw it. A more graphic example of the horrific results of sectarian violence could not have been devised, and it brought home just how pointlessly destructive the conflict in Northern Ireland had become.

THE SURVIVOR

All of the victims of the attack were Protestants, many of them elderly people and their families. Three members of the Armstrong family, Bertha, Wesley and Edward, were killed. Edward, aged 52, was a member of the 'Chosen Few' Orange Lodge and the Royal Ulster Constabulary Reserve. Jessie and Kitchener Johnson, both aged 70, died; as did William and Angus Mullen, also in their 70s. Among the other victims was Marie Wilson, the 20-year-old daughter of Gordon Wilson, who was also buried under the rubble with her but survived the ordeal.

Later, Gordon Wilson told how the force of the bomb blast had thrown him and his daughter forwards into the air, while stones and rubble rained down on them. A piece of falling masonry struck him on the shoulder, causing intense pain, and he then found himself lying under a pile of rubble 20 m (6 ft) high. He shouted to his daughter, who was still alive, and the pair held hands, although he could not see her. He asked her if she was all right and she replied yes, but then, after telling her father that she loved him, she fell silent. After a few minutes, Wilson and his daughter were pulled out of the wreckage and taken to hospital. Marie later died there.

A HUMAN TRAGEDY

After he was released from hospital, Gordon Wilson made a public statement that he did not bear a grudge towards his daughter's killers. 'Dirty sort of talk is not going to bring her back to life,' he said. He also mentioned that he would pray every night for the terrorists. His statement so impressed loyalist paramilitaries, who were intent on carrying out some form of retaliation, that they abandoned their plans for revenge. Wilson went on to become a spokesperson for peace, his courageous stance encouraging a general spirit of reconciliation in Northern Ireland.

Where the IRA had seriously miscalculated was to suppose that the Remembrance Day mourners in Enniskillen would be seen as a politically motivated group of Protestants with strong sectarian links, rather than as a group of ordinary citizens coming together to remember the many Irish men and women who had lost their lives in the World War I and II. In the public mind, the connection was made between the victims of the wars and the victims of the continuing troubles in Ireland; between the soldiers of the past who had no control over the political situation yet lost their lives, and modern-day civilians in Ireland who now found themselves in a similar situation, caught up as innocent victims in the horror of war.

SECTARIAN VIOLENCE

In fact, only one of the crowd who were present at the war memorial in Enniskillen that day was a politically motivated individual. Edward Armstrong, who lost his life, was a 52-year-old reserve member of the Royal Ulster Constabulary, which had come under heavy criticism from the IRA and others as a biased, anti-Catholic and often brutal state security force. In addition, he was a member of the 'Chosen Few' Orange Lodge. The Orange Order, as it sometimes called, is a Protestant organization that has been accused of anti-Catholic sectarianism, particularly with regard to its practise of marching through strongly Catholic areas in parades that celebrate Protestant culture and identity.

Thus, to some degree, there was a political aspect to the Remembrance Day bombing at Enniskillen, but it was hardly strong enough to warrant such a violently destructive act. Apart from Edward Armstrong, most of the victims that day were elderly or middle-aged people who had little or no connection with political activism. For this reason, the attack was seen as an example of the IRA's increasing tendency towards mindless violence. The fact that the attack took place on a day when the destructiveness of war was being quietly remembered all over the country made the crime seem doubly outrageous.

A BUNCH OF HOODLUMS

Not surprisingly, the Enniskillen attack was extremely damaging to the IRA's campaign. It was roundly condemned by all the leading political figures of the day, as well as by the media and members of the general public. This time, the rhetoric of the politicians had some real weight to it, and the public began to believe that, instead of agitating for a cause – the creation of an independent Republic of Ireland – the IRA were simply a bunch of hoodlums mired in violence and bitterness, dedicated to continuing age-old feuds and creating permanent civil war in the country. In response, the IRA claimed that the real target of the bomb had been a group of British soldiers, and that their leadership had not authorized the bombing. However, this was widely disbelieved.

It then emerged that a bomb had also been planted 32 km (20 miles) away, near a village called Pettigo, and that members of the Boys' Brigade, a religious organization for boys and young men, had gathered there to take part in a service for Remembrance Day. Thankfully, the bomb had failed to detonate, and no one had been injured. However, news of this attempted attack caused more outrage and further damaged the republican cause.

LEGACY OF PEACE

In 1997, on Remembrance Day, Sinn Fein leader Gerry Adams publicly apologized for the bombing on behalf of Sinn Fein, the political wing of the IRA. Three years later, Ronnie Hill, a victim of the bombing, finally died. He had been in a coma for 13 years as a result of his injuries at Enniskillen.

Gordon Wilson, whose daughter Marie was a victim of the Enniskillen bombing, and who later became a spokesman for peace in Northern Ireland, said after her death: 'I don't have an answer, but I know there has to be a plan. If I didn't think that, I would commit suicide. It's part of a greater plan.' His words were prophetic, at least to the degree that the Remembrance Day bombing at Enniskillen finally marked the moment when the general public lost sympathy with the IRA, and the conflict in Northern Ireland reached a turning point, making it possible for a peace process to begin.

PAN AM
FLIGHT 103

*To the little girl in the red dress who lies here
who made my flight from Frankfurt such fun.
You didn't deserve this. God Bless, Chas.*

A NOTE LEFT OUTSIDE LOCKERBIE TOWN HALL

The bombing of Pan Am Flight 103 – or the
Lockerbie Air Disaster as it is known in Britain –
was the largest and most destructive terror attack
on an American airline in the 20th century. It also
remains Britain's largest mass murder. It took place
on December 21, 1988, as many passengers were
flying home to celebrate Christmas with their
families, and not only killed the entire crew and
passengers of the plane, but also 11 people on the
ground, as it crashed into houses in the small
Scottish town of Lockerbie. In the wake of the
disaster, there were many theories as to who was
behind the attack, including claims that the Libyan
leader Muammar al-Gaddafi was responsible.

Eventually a security officer for Libyan Airlines, Abdelbaset Ali Mohmed Al-Megrahi, was brought to trial, convicted and given a life sentence for his part in the crime. Today, many believe that Al-Megrahi was just a pawn in an international game of conspiracy, and that the biggest players – believed to be heads of state and high-ranking politicians in the Arab world – have been allowed to escape justice.

THE BOMB EXPLODES

The flight from London to New York took off on a busy evening at Heathrow Airport, 25 minutes later than its scheduled departure time of 6.00 p.m. Earlier in the day, it had arrived from Frankfurt. There were a total of 243 passengers on board, and a crew of 16, led by Captain James MacQuarrie. Among the passengers were US intelligence officers Mathew Gannon, Daniel O'Connor, Chuck McKee and Ronald Lariviere. McKee had just returned from Beirut, Lebanon, where he had been involved in investigating the whereabouts of hostages held by the terrorist wing of the militant group Hezbollah. This later prompted suspicions that the bomb may have been aimed at the US officers, in response to antiterrorist defence initiatives.

Initially, the plane flew northwards, to Scotland, before heading out over the Atlantic Ocean. Just over half an hour into the journey, while in Scottish airspace, the pilot requested clearance to cross the

Atlantic from traffic controller Alan Topp. That was the last communication from the aircraft. As the plane moved off, Topp noticed that the small green square on his radar screen, with a cross in the middle indicating the aircraft's transponder code, had completely vanished, and in its place were several smaller squares. At first he thought that the radar was not picking up the signal correctly, but then the awful truth began to emerge: the blips on the screen were in fact exploded remnants of the aeroplane, flying through the sky.

SCENE OF CARNAGE

The traffic controller's worst fears were confirmed when, just one minute later, a wing section of the plane loaded with fuel dropped onto the ground in a quiet suburban area of the town of Lockerbie. The crash was immense, measuring 1.6 on the Richter scale for a seismic event, as the street became a fireball. The blast caused a crater in the ground, destroying several houses and killing 11 people. As the plane came down, the bodies of those aboard fell to the ground, scattering body parts around the area in a horrifying scene of carnage. The explosion scattered parts of the aeroplane for 2.190 sq km (845 sq miles) of land around Lockerbie. Not one of the 259 people aboard survived, although – amazingly – some landed intact, and two were even alive, but they died shortly afterwards.

The victims on the ground included a family, Jack

and Rosalind Somerville and their children Paul and Lynsey, whose house was hit in the explosion. Others died as more houses in the street exploded and the resulting fireball moved along the roads, scorching cars in its wake. For the drivers, the disaster had literally come out of the blue, and it was some time before people realized what had happened: many thought at first that a nearby nuclear reactor had melted down.

TRAIL OF EVIDENCE

The next grim task was to clear the wreckage, which proved another nightmare. So that exact details of what had happened could be established, many of the victims' bodies were left lying in streets and gardens for days, exactly as they had fallen. Residents complained of having to pass the same bodies, some of them small children, every day until forensic investigators finished their task. Meanwhile, relatives of the victims travelled to the town to identify their loved ones. In a touching gesture of friendship and solidarity in the face of their loss, volunteers from the town set up canteens for the relatives, offering food and company to those waiting to find out the worst. Once the forensic investigators had done their work, local people washed the clothing of the victims and returned it to their relatives. Many years later, friendships that were formed at that tragic time continued to be a source of comfort to both the people of Lockerbie who had lost loved ones and to the victims' families.

After the blast, local police from the Dumfries and Galloway Constabulary, the smallest police force in Britain, began the daunting task of trying to find out who was behind the largest terror attack in British aviation history. For almost two years, there was a high-level investigation into the crash, involving extensive forensic examination of the wreckage, as well as police inquiries in many countries. Little by little, a picture of what had happened began to emerge – however it was incomplete, and it remains so to this day.

A tiny fragment of the electrical device that detonated the bomb was found, and it was identified as part of a timer that was manufactured by a Swiss firm. When further investigations were made, the timer was found to have been exported to Libya as part of a consignment. This immediately suggested that the bombing was a politically motivated one, possibly sanctioned by the Libyan state under the leadership of Colonel Gaddafi.

REVENGE KILLING?

Gaddafi was already the subject of much suspicion, since there was a great deal of animosity between him and the US president, Ronald Reagan. In 1986, in response to a Libyan terror attack, the USA had bombed Tripoli, and in so doing, had managed to kill Gaddafi's adopted baby daughter, which had outraged leaders of the Arab states. Not only this, but only a few months before the Lockerbie incident, the USA had shot down a large Iranian passenger plane, Iran Air Flight 655, apparently by accident, thinking it to be an enemy aircraft. The plane had been filled with Islamic pilgrims travelling to Mecca, and the shooting, which killed 290 passengers, was perceived as a deliberate attack on the Arab world.

Thus, Libya and Iran, as well as other closely linked states such as Syria, had a good deal of reason for revenge. Many believed that the Ayatollah Khomeini had ordered the Pan Am Flight 103 bombing and had been helped by Syria. It was also thought that the bombing had been carried out by the Popular Front for the Liberation of Palestine, a Syrian-sponsored terrorist group.

THE FALL GUYS?

However, when the case came to trial, it was two unknown Libyans, Abdelbaset Ali Mohmed Al-Megrahi, and Al Amin Khalifa Fhimah, rather than heads of state or leaders of terrorist groups, who found themselves in the dock.

Al-Megrahi was a high-ranking Libyan intelligence officer who, it was alleged, had sent the bomb in a suitcase from Malta to Frankfurt, where it had been transferred to Heathrow and put on Pan Am Flight 103. Charred clothes wrapped round the bomb were traced to a Maltese shop, and the shopkeeper then identified Al-Megrahi as having bought clothes there shortly before the bombing. Al-Megrahi was also found to have arrived in Malta on a false passport, and he had travelled to Tripoli the following day.

On the basis of this evidence, on January 31, 2001, Al-Megrahi was convicted of murder and sentenced to life imprisonment. However, it proved more difficult to find any evidence against Al Fhimah, a close friend of Al-Megrahi's, and he was acquitted. Al-Megrahi immediately appealed against the judgement, but his appeal was turned down.

CONTROVERSY

Since then, the case has continued to be a controversial one, because many believe that Al-Megrahi and Al Fhimah were fall guys, and that the bomb was actually the work of the Iranian Khomeni regime. The theory is that the Iranians struck a deal with Libya whereby Al-Megrahi and Al Fhimah would take the rap for the bombing, and that Gaddafi concurred so that Libya could then resume normal relations with the international community.

Among the families of the victims themselves, there is some disagreement as to what really happened. The Americans are more inclined to accept the verdict that Al-Megrahi was responsible for the crime, while many of the British are not persuaded, viewing the bombing as a revenge attack masterminded by Iran, Syria and Libya, and carried out by Abu Nidal, a Palestinian political leader and the founder of Fatah – the Revolutionary Council or FRC. In addition, the British relatives want a full enquiry into the security arrangements at Heathrow Airport, to ensure that such a terrible tragedy could never happen again.

ATTACK ON THE ROYAL MARINE SCHOOL OF MUSIC

Even the people who say they support what the IRA calls its cause must be sickened by the way in which such death and injury is mercilessly inflicted.

NEIL KINNOCK

The Royal Marine School of Music in Deal, Kent, was the target of an explosion on September 22, 1989. Twenty-two men were injured and 11 people were killed, the majority of the victims being nothing more than teenagers.

INVOLVEMENT IN IRELAND

British security forces have been involved in the struggle in Northern Ireland since 1969, and the Royal Marines involvement goes back several centuries. As far back as 1916, a Royal Marines Battalion was called to Ireland in response to the 'Easter Uprising'. The rising was an attempt by militant Irish republicans to win independence from the UK. The Royal Marines' involvement lasted until the spring of 1922, following the establishment of the 'Free State'. The Irish Free State was formed on December 6, with six northern counties staying as part of the UK. As a result a civil war broke out between those supporting the Anglo-Irish Treaty and those who renounced it because they felt it would lead to the partitioning of the island. The Irish Republican Army (IRA), which at the time was led by Eamon de Valera, fought against the partition but did not succeed.

It was another 47 years before the Royal Marines would return to Northern Ireland, when they were asked to serve on the streets of Belfast in September 1969. Royal Marines Commando units were among the first troops drafted into Northern Ireland in 1969 and have served in the Province almost every year since, predominantly in the nationalist heartlands of West Belfast and South Armagh.

HITTING WHERE IT HURTS

The original Royal Naval School of Music was founded in 1903 to provide bands for the Royal Navy. The school itself was formed by the Royal Marines and later became an integral part of the Corps. Its original home was at the Eastney

Barracks in Portsmouth, but in 1930 it was transferred to the Royal Marines Depot in Deal. Deal is a town in Kent, which lies on the English Channel 13 km (8 miles) north-east of Dover. The barracks at Walmer consisted of the North, East and South (or Cavalry) barracks, and all were constructed shortly after the outbreak of the French revolution.

The 6.8 kg (15 lb) explosive device was planted in the recreation centre changing room at the Royal Marine School of Music on September 22, 1989. The blast, which happened just before 8.30 a.m., was so powerful that that it destroyed all three floors of the building and blew the roof completely off. Many houses in the neighbourhood were also damaged, and people who lived within a few kilometres of the barracks said they heard the blast quite clearly and it was very frightening.

As soon as the dust started to settle, rescue workers and marines alike worked furiously to try to clear the rubble. In desperation they grabbed at the debris with their bare hands, not wanting to wait until the heavy lifting equipment arrived in case their comrades were trapped underneath. The explosion had been so powerful that it wasn't until four hours later that rescuers found the body of a young man on top of a roof nearby.

Kent ambulance workers, who were on strike at the time, voluntarily agreed to stop their industrial action and started to take casualties to the nearby hospitals at Deal and Canterbury.

Musicians and buglers could join the Royal Marines School of Music from the age of 16 and onwards, so the majority of the victims in Deal were young men, most still in their teens. Prior to the explosion many of the recruits had been in the recreation area having breakfast, but by 8.30 a.m. they were undergoing marching practice and actually saw the roof lift off the building and the walls collapse. For days afterwards the young men were in a state of shock, unable to believe that so men of their friends had been needlessly killed.

In total 22 men were injured and 10 were killed. One of the young marines who had managed to survive the explosion, died one month later, bringing the total of deaths to 11.

Despite the advancement in forensic science, the police were not able to uncover enough evidence to bring about a conviction, and to this day no one has been arrested for the atrocity that occurred on September 22.

PART OF A CAMPAIGN

The Provisional Irish Republican Army claimed responsibility for the bombing, claiming that it was part of a campaign against the British armed forces who had been deployed in Northern Ireland for the past 20 years.

The nation was shocked at the attack because these were not ordinary soldiers but Royal Marines, and on top of that they were bandsmen. The Royal

Marines Bands provide military bands, orchestras and dance bands for state occasions, major national and service events, and for ship and shore ceremonial and social functions. They are dedicated musicians, not fighters, which meant the IRA had struck innocent victims in their fight to free their country of British involvement.

However, the Corps were not strangers to terror attacks, the Admiral of the Fleet, Earl Mountbatten of Burma, was murdered on August 27, 1979. A bomb exploded while his family were on a fishing trip in Mullaghmore in County Sligo. Other victims of the explosion were Dowager Lady Brabourne, his elder daughter's mother-in-law, the Earl's grandson, Nicholas, and a local boatman. Nicholas's twin brother, Timothy, and his mother and father were critically injured. The Irish National Liberation Army claimed responsibility for this attack.

In October 1981, the then Commandant General of the Royal Marines, Lt. Gen. Sir Steuart Pringle, was badly injured when he started his car, triggering off an explosive device hidden on the underside. When people rushed to his aid he was concerned that there might be a second device and told them not to come too close. The general's dog survived unscathed, but he lost a leg in the explosion, which the IRA claimed was their responsibility.

MARCHING AGAIN

Just one week after the explosion at the Royal Marines School of Music, the Band marched through the streets of Deal. To show support for their courage thousands of people lined the streets and applauded in appreciation. The members of the band left gaps in their ranks for each member that was no longer able to take part either due to death or injury.

In 1992 a memorial bandstand was erected in memory of those who died on that fateful day. The memorial itself stands on top of an ancient capstan on Walmer Green, and it bears the names of the 11 musicians 'who only ever wanted to play music'.

A memorial service is held every year at the site of the explosion, with one minute's silence held at 8.22 a.m., exactly the time the bomb went off.

The concert hall at the Deal barracks, which was originally a church, was badly damaged by fire in May 2003. The majority of the building had to be demolished as it was unsafe, but one single wall remains today, which is being retained as part of a memorial garden of remembrance.

The Royal Marines School of Music moved out of their barracks in the 1990s and now trains back in its original home in Portsmouth.

PART FIVE

1990–2006

THE MURDER OF
IAN GOW

*There are thousands of decent people who
want nothing more than to live in peace in
what I will always think of as God's own
province.*

TOM UTLEY

The murder of a British member of Parliament, Ian
Gow, by the Irish Republican Army (IRA),
illustrated the organization's contempt for democratic, or indeed, human values. Gow's mentor was
another British MP, Airey Neave, who was killed in
the House of Commons car park on March 30,
1979. Neave had had a remarkable life before he
became an MP. He was educated at Eton and
Oxford, and managed to escape from Colditz in
1942, and on returning to England was recruited as
an intelligence officer for M19. When he died he
was a Conservative MP for Abingdon and had
proved to be a prominent politician. His killers were
never caught and intrigue still hangs over his death.

Ian Gow was under no illusion that he had become a prime target by the IRA, by choosing to identify himself with Northern Ireland and for his support of the Unionist cause.

IAN GOW THE MP

Ian Gow was born on February 10, 1937. He married Jane Elizabeth Price in 1966 and they had one son. Gow was both a politician and a solicitor, and he joined the Conservative Party in February 1974 as member for Eastbourne, East Sussex. He soon made an impression on all his political colleages and his debating abilities on the floor of the Chamber became legendary.

Gow will go down in parliamentary history as the first person to speak in the House of Commons in front of television cameras. He was an articulate, intelligent and witty man and his speech was received well by both audiences – those in the chamber and the television viewers.

His early years in parliament were filled with difficult problems such as the Rhodesian negotiations and the Falklands War. However, Gow handled pressure well and proved to be a great asset.

Gow made his mark in the House of Commons when he assisted his associate, Airey Neaves, with Northern Ireland issues. In 1979, when Margaret Thatcher came into power, Gow was offered the position of Parliamentary Private Secretary.

In 1983, he left the doors of Number 10 to take

on a ministerial office, and he threw himself into the role as Minister for Housing with great verve. He showed his usual energy and enthusiasm and soon made his own impact on the problems of housing issues up and down the country.

In 1985, Gow moved on to the Treasury, but it was here that problems started to arise. His downfall was the fact that he was a staunch Unionist with a deep interest in the affairs of Ulster. He feelings ran so deep he was asked to resign in 1985 over the signing of the Anglo-Irish Agreement. It was an historic agreement signed by Margaret Thatcher and Garrett Fitzgerald, who was head of the government of the Republic of Ireland, on November 15, 1985, at Hillsborough Castle in County Down.

It was an agreement that was aimed at bringing an end to the troubles in Northern Ireland, but instead it plunged the area into turmoil. Unionists who had not been consulted, reacted with shock, anger and humiliation to the pact that offered Dublin a say in the affairs of Northern Ireland.

There were violent reactions all over Ireland to the agreement, which was vehemently rejected by the Republicans because it confirmed that Northern Ireland would remain part of the UK.

The Provisional IRA, who also refused to sign the agreement, continued their reign of terror. The national Fianna Fáil party in the Republic of Ireland rejected the agreement and the future President of Ireland, Mary Robinson, resigned from the Irish

Labour Party over the exclusion of the Unionists.

On the other side of the coin, the Unionists rejected the agreement because they felt it gave the Republic of Ireland an increased influence over Northern Ireland. The agreement not only failed to bring an end to the political violence in Northern Ireland, it did nothing to bring the two communities any closer to a reconciliation.

MURDER VICTIM

Ian Gow was preparing to leave his farmhouse near Eastbourne, East Sussex, on July 30, 1990. He climbed into the driver's seat of his Austin Montego, completely unaware that the IRA had planted a bomb underneath one of the seats. At exactly 8.39 a.m. the bomb exploded, leaving Gow with appalling injuries to the lower part of his body. His wife, who was inside the house at the time of the explosion, rushed out to see what had happened, but her husband died ten minutes later.

The IRA claimed responsibility for the attack, possibly hoping that the assassination would be a major setback to the Northern Ireland peace discussions. However, politicians on both sides remained resolute in trying to find a peaceful way to end the on-going dispute between the two countries.

Ian Gow's seat in the House of Commons was filled by David Bellotti, a Liberal Democrat. Ann Widdecombe, a Conservative MP who is known for her outspoken conservatism, stirred up a hornet's nest after Bellotti's election by saying, 'the IRA would be toasting their success'.

The police did question two IRA members over the murder of Ian Gow, but they have never been brought to trial.

IAN GOW MEMORIAL FUND

The former chancellor and foreign secretary, Geoffrey Howe, the former archbishop of Canterbury, Robert Runcie and the former chief of the general staff, Field Marshal Lord Bramall, set up a fund for Ian Gow. With Gow's deep love of Ulster in mind, the fund was an effort to promote understanding between the feuding communities in Ireland. It also invests in young people between the ages of 16 and 30 who are from a disadvantaged background, encouraging them to help themselves.

The fund has been in existence for 16 years now and has raised and distributed in excess of £850,000. More than 2,500 individuals have benefitted, including victims of the Omagh bomb in 1998, in which 28 people died.

The injustice of the death of Ian Gow seems overwhelming, in a country that is supposed to encourage freedom of speech it seems he had to pay for his criticism of the Irish peace process.

WORLD TRADE CENTER BOMBING

> *On February 26, 1993, a bomb set by*
> *terrorists exploded below this site. This*
> *horrible act of violence killed innocent people,*
> *injured thousands, and made victims of us all.*
>
> INSCRIPTION ON A GRANITE MEMORIAL FOUNTAIN

The bomb attack on the World Trade Center that took place on February 26, 1993, was a frightening warning of what was to come eight years later, when al-Qaeda launched its massive 9/11 offensive on the United States of America. In the 1993 New York attack, six people died and over 1,000 were wounded as a bomb exploded in an underground section of the North Tower, shutting down the lights inside the building and causing chaos. Later, a total of ten Islamic extremists were convicted of the attack and sentenced to life imprisonment, including the ringleader, Ramzi Yousef, who was described by the judge as 'an apostle of evil'.

CHAOS AND FEAR

The attack began at just after midday, when a Ryder self-hire removal truck packed with explosives detonated in the underground garage of the North Tower at the World Trade Center. The bomb made a tremendous hole in four levels of concrete, and cyanide gas was released into the air – however it burned up in the explosion. A good deal of damage was done to the building, and six people in the vicinity died, most of them workers at the Port Authority. There were serious injuries to hundreds more. Fortunately, the damage was much more limited than the bombers planned it to be: the North Tower did not collapse onto the neighbouring tower, as they had hoped, which would have caused the deaths of thousands of innocent victims.

Instead, the electricity grid to the center was cut off, and smoke rose high up into the buildings. The stairwells were plunged into darkness and a pall of acrid smoke rose up through them. Radio, television and telephone services were also disrupted, some of them for weeks afterwards. All in all, it was an extremely frightening experience, and one that deeply shocked New Yorkers, especially when it became known how damaging the attack might have been if all had gone according to the terrorists' plan.

After the incident, the New York authorities became aware that security was not tight enough in the World Trade Center and realized that emergency measures would have to be improved in future. Accordingly, among other measures, extra lighting was installed in the stairwells. This improvement is thought to have saved hundreds of lives eight years later, when the 9/11 attack on the twin towers occurred.

DEADLY BOMBS

After the 1993 attack, several suspects were arrested, some of whom were later freed and added to the US list of most wanted terrorirsts. Their testimony led to the arrest of Ramzi Yousef, a Kuwait-born Palestinian, who had travelled to the USA on a false passport, claiming political asylum. It was found that, once in the USA, he had made contact with several other terrorists, including Sheikh Omar Abdel-Rahman, later convicted as one of the perpetrators of 9/11.

Yousef and his associates began to make bombs at his home in New Jersey, putting together an unusually complex and deadly bomb for their attack on the World Trade Center. Their bomb included urea pellets and sodium cyanide, which Yousef hoped would travel through the ventilation shafts of the building and poison those above ground. Fortunately, the cyanide seems to have burnt up in the explosion, and his vicious plan was foiled.

VIOLENT THUG

Prior to the attack on the World Trade Center,

Yousef contacted several New York newspapers, identifying himself as the Fifth Battalion of the Liberation Army, and demanding an end to diplomatic relations between Israel and the USA. He accused Israel of state terrorism and announced that its actions would be met with terrorism. Yousef also threatened that the attack on the World Trade Center would be the first of many Islamic actions around the world if his demands were not met.

Yousef was not bluffing. After escaping from New York in the aftermath of the bombing, using a Pakistani passport, he travelled to Pakistan. In the summer of that year, he attempted the assassination of the Pakistani Prime Minister, Benazir Bhutto, at the behest of a terrorist organization called Sipah Sahaba. This was a group of Sunni Muslims known for their violent acts, such as beheadings, against other Muslims sects. When Yousef and an accomplice, Abdul Hakim Murad, were discovered planting the bomb outside the Prime Minister's residence, the bomb blew up, injuring Yousef, who was taken to hospital by Murad, and recovered.

The following year, Yousef travelled to Bangkok, where he took part in the attempted bombing of the Israeli embassy. While driving towards the embassy, his truck crashed into a motorcyclist, and the plan was aborted. After the debacle, Yousef went back to Pakistan, where he helped to mastermind the notorious Bonjinka plot.

OPERATION BOJINKA

Bojinka, meaning 'bang' or 'explosion', was a plan to mount a number of terror attacks against the West in an all-out bombing offensive. The plot was bankrolled by the terrorist organization al-Qaeda, and the money laundered through Filipino girlfriends of the terrorists. The outrageous plan, which presaged the attacks of 9/11, was to blow up 11 aeroplanes, to assassinate Pope John Paul II, and to crash a plane into the headquarters of the CIA in Virginia. Thankfully, the plot was discovered before any of these attacks actually took place; however, al-Qaeda learned a great deal from the experience of mounting this major offensive, which they later used in the attacks of 2001.

Operating under the name of Adam Sali and living in Manila, Philippines, Yousef began to make and test bombs in his apartment in an ordinary residential area of the city. One of the bombs was placed in a Manila theatre, injuring several people, and another was hidden aboard a Boeing 747, which killed one passenger. Amazingly, the plane made an emergency landing and the other passengers survived.

Having checked that these small-scale bombs worked, Yousef and his co-conspirators began to test their plans for attacking the airlines, smuggling explosives onto a United States airlines to see if they could get through security. This was terrorism on a scale never seen before, and had the plan worked, it is estimated that several thousand people would have been killed.

However, Operation Bojinka was abandoned when a fire broke out at Yousef's apartment in Manila. When firefighters arrived, Yousef and his accomplice Murad fled, and police searched the apartment, finding huge quantities of chemicals and electrical timers there. The evidence could not have been more compelling. Bubbling away in the kitchen sink was a cocktail of explosive chemicals, and beside it was a handbook on how to build a liquid bomb, written in Arabic. Moreover, when Yousef's computer was switched on, it was full of files about Operation Bojinka: everything from plane timetables to names of associates to terrorist political statements. The police had stumbled on a bomb factory. The search was now on for the two terrorists who had abandoned it.

THE CULPRITS

It did not take long to find the culprits. When Murad returned to retrieve the computer, he was arrested. After being subjected to torture by the police, he was extradited to the United States, where he gave evidence that helped to convict Yousef. Yousef himself was picked up as he hid in a hotel room in Islamabad, Pakistan; and another accomplice, Wali Khan Amin Shah, who had bankrolled the operation, was arrested in Malaysia. All were tried in the USA and received life sentences.

Despite his pose as a political radical, during his trial Yousef emerged as a thoroughly destructive, and in some ways incompetent thug, dedicated to bloodshed, violence and revenge, rather than to the establishment of a new order. He was alleged to have been personally violent towards his several wives, often beating them when he was angry. After being sentenced, he refused to show any remorse for his actions and commented in court that he was proud of being a terrorist.

AFTERMATH

After the bombing of the World Trade Center in 1993, a memorial fountain was built on Austin J. Tobin Plaza, just above where the explosion took place, to commemorate the victims of the attack. On it was engraved the names of the six people who lost their lives and an inscription that claimed the bomb made us all victims. The words proved to be prophetic. In 2001, both of the World Trade Center towers were completely destroyed in the attacks of 9/11, also blowing up the memorial fountain. A small piece of it was later recovered, and found to bear the word 'John'. Strangely, almost everything around the fragment had been reduced to dust by the enormous blast of the bomb and the falling masonry that day. Currently, the fragment is set to be used as the central motif in a new memorial to the victims of 9/11, so that the victims of the first bombing will be forever remembered along with them.

WARRINGTON
BOMB ATTACKS

*The first explosion drove panicking shoppers
into the path of the next blast just seconds
later.*

EYEWITNESS

Warrington is the main town situated between
Manchester and Liverpool, and the largest town in
Cheshire. On March 20, 1993, two bombs exploded
in the town centre killing two young boys, which
provoked widespread condemnation of the Irish
Republican Army (IRA), the Irish terrorist
organization responsible.

The onset of the troubles in Warrington started
on Thursday, February 25, 1993, when three IRA
terrrorists broke into a Warrington gas storage
depot. After planting several Semtex bombs, the
three men attempted to get away, but they were
spotted by a patrolling police officer, Mark Toker,
who was shot in the chase. Luckily the majority of
the bombs failed to detonate, and apart from a huge

fireball there were no casualties. However, if the citizens of Warrington thought they had had a lucky escape they were wrong. The three IRA men were arrested and taken into custody, but little did the police realize that the IRA would want revenge.

REVENGE

The shopping mall at Warrington was packed with shoppers who had been brought out by a spell of warm spring weather. It was March 20, the day before Mother's Day, and people were out looking for cards and gifts.

At just around midday the charity help-line of the Samaritans received a coded message that a bomb was going to explode outside the Boots shop in Liverpool, which was approximately 24 km (15 miles) from Warrington. The Merseyside police leapt into action, also warning the Cheshire police in Warrington of the threat. By the time the message got through, however, it was too late to act, as a bomb exploded in Bridge street outside the Boots store. Just minutes later a second bomb exploded outside the Argos catalogue shop. People ran in panic after the first bomb exploded, only to run into the path of the second.

The bombs had been left in two separate cast-iron litter bins, which turned them into the equivalent of two large hand grenades. As they exploded they sent small amounts of shrapnel flying through the air. There were casualties everywhere, some even lost limbs in the explosion. Those people that were not too shocked, rushed to their aid.

Buses were arranged to take people away from the area and paramedics started to arrive to administer on-the-spot treatment. In the end, crews from 17 ambulances had to deal with the casualties, and plastic surgeons were bought to Warrington General Hospital from the regional burns unit at Whiston hospital, 10 km (6 miles) away. In total there were 56 casualties.

The news that sickened the nation the most was the unnecessary death of two small boys. Jonathan Ball was only three when he died, and an only child. He was out with his babysitter in Warrington, helping her choose a Mother's Day card. He died at the scene of the explosion and Jonathan's father, Wilf Ball, still grieves a decade later. He said, 'It's hard not to be bitter. They took something away that you were living for.'

The second child was 12-year-old Tim Parry, who had been sitting on the bin at the time and took the full force of the blast. Tim was still alive when he arrived at hospital and was put on a life support machine for five days, but his little body eventually gave up fighting.

Despite the biggest murder hunt that Cheshire had ever seen, the police were unable to turn up any positive evidence and no one has ever been caught.

THE AFTERMATH

Colin and Wendy Parry, Tim's parents, campaigned to build a peace centre within months of their son's death. On the seventh anniversary of the explosions, the Tim Parry–Jonathan Ball Young People's Centre was opened. It is dedicated to working with adults, children and peace organizations that aim to resolve conflicts at a local, national and international level. The centre is run by the NSPCC and includes accommodation for visiting groups from around the world.

The River of Life project was also developed in the aftermath of the Warrington bombs. The project was an effort to bring new hope to the community and to act as a reminder of what happened on Bridge Street that day. The central design of the River of Life is a tear-shaped water feature in which water emerges from a broken glacial boulder. It then cascades onto a bronze dome, which bears the imprints of the hands of local school children. Around the dome is a disc of etched copper showing the faces of children, including those of Tim and Jonathan.

JOHN KINSELLA

One of the three men arrested for the Warrington gas works bombing was a petty thief by the name of John Kinsella. At his trial in 1994, Kinsella was sentenced to 20 years for possession of an explosive substance. He claimed that he stashed a bag of Semtex, which was to be used for future IRA operations, on an allotment, because he believed it contained some stolen silver. He denied any involvement with the IRA. He told the court that he was eager to make some extra cash and was told that if he would hide the bag he would be well rewarded.

Inmates had warned Kinsella that the IRA did not forgive informants. While he was on remand he tried to commit suicide by slashing his neck on the lid of a salmon tin.

The supposed leader of the IRA unit that carried out the gas works bombings was Páiric MacFhloinn, who was given 35 years for his part. MacFhloinn gave important evidence claiming that Kinsella had been fooled by the IRA, and Kinsella's case was referred to the Court of Appeal. Unfortunately when the case was due to be heard, MacFhloinn backed down and told the police that the IRA leadership had told him that they did not wish him to give evidence at the appeal.

During the appeal, the Crown Court felt it was unlikely that Kinsella was a member of the IRA, as he would never have led the police to the stash of explosives. The only link with the IRA that had been found during investigations were three photographs in a family album, which included a display commemorating the death of an IRA volunteer in Belfast in 1972. After the appeal John Kinsella's sentence was reduced from 25 to 16 years.

Following the Good Friday Agreement John Kinsella was released in 1999 as part of the early release programme agreement between Ireland and the UK.

The Good Friday Agreement was a historic breakthrough, which addressed relationships between both parts of Ireland and England, Scotland and Wales. However, the process of arriving at the agreement was gruelling and very hard to put into practise, and at this stage it is still too early to say whether this document will mark a final break from the past.

ALAS CHIRICANAS
FLIGHT 00901

Fight against a nation, revenge a nation; and this jihad of our nation will liberate Muslims captivity and humiliation

ANSAR ALLAH

The bombing of a small aeroplane, Alas Chiricanas Flight 00901, thought to have been carried out by a suicide bomber, was one of several horrifying anti-Israeli terror attacks to take place in 1994. All the 21 people on board, many of them Jewish business-men, were killed when the bomb exploded. The previous day, a large bomb had been placed in the Asociacion Mutua Israelita Argentina (AMIA), a Jewish centre in Buenos Aires, killing 86 people. In the same year, the Israeli embassy in London was attacked, injuring 20 people, and a car bomb outside a Jewish charity shop exploded. In addition, two years earlier, there had been a major attack on the Israeli Embassy in Buenos Aires, killing 29 people.

The perpetrators of these atrocities were widely held to be the work of Palestinians linked to Hezbollah, the militant Lebanese group. In some cases, the culprits were arrested, tried and convicted. However, in the case of the Alas Chiricanas Flight, no one was ever brought to justice.

On July 19, 1994, a twin-propeller Panamanian plane set off on its usual route between Francis Field, Colon, and Panama City, at 4.30 p.m. There was nothing to suppose that the voyage was anything out of the ordinary, or that terrorists could have any reason to attack such a small domestic service. However, as the plane flew over the Santa Rita Mountains there was a massive explosion on board, and the plane was blown into numerous pieces. The wreckage was scattered over the mountains below. Later, despite the difficulties of working in such terrain, the emergency services managed to recover the remains of the victims, numbering 21 people in all. All of these were claimed by their families, except one: that of a passenger named Jamal Lya.

Had it not been for the fact that, the day before, a bomb had exploded in Buenos Aires, killing 86 people, many of them Jewish, the tragedy that befell the Alas Chiricanas flight might have been deemed a mysterious accident, rather than a terror attack. But as it was, suspicions were immediately aroused, particularly when it became clear that a large number of passengers on the plane were Jewish. (The Buenos Aires bomb had been targeted to kill

Jews at the Argentine–Jewish Mutual Association in the city.)

Jamal Lya, the passenger whose remains were not claimed by his family, was described by ground staff as aged about 25 to 28, and having a Middle Eastern appearance. He was light-skinned with black hair, brown eyes and thick eyebrows. He apparently did not speak English or Spanish, and he communicated by using hand signals and by writing notes on occasion.

Lya boarded the plane under a false passport, carrying a briefcase containing a Motorola radio packed with semtex plastic explosives, which later blew up as he held it on his lap. However, since no one came forward to identify him, little more is known about him.

After the bombing, a mysterious organization called Ansar Allah (The Helpers of God, in Arabic) issued a statement to the press, supporting the action. They did not, however, claim direct responsibility for it. They also announced their approval of the Buenos Aires bombing the day before.

Because of this anti-Jewish link, it was widely supposed that the bombing was the work of Hezbollah, the Lebanese militant Arab group, or possibly some other pro-Palestinian organization. However, no proper investigation was launched, and despite pressure from the international community, the Panamanian authorities have, to this day, done little to find out the details of what happened, or to bring any co-conspirators to justice. By contrast, the AMIA bombing in Argentina has been the subject of a high-profile, controversial trial. It was hoped that, during the course of that trial, some light would be shed on the Alas Chiricanas tragedy, but as yet, the crime is still unsolved.

GENOCIDE IN
RWANDA

*In their greatest hour of need, the world failed
the people of Rwanda.*

KOFI ANNAN

Rwanda is one of the smallest countries located in
Central Africa, with a population of around
7,000,000 people. In 1994, the Hutu government
and its extremist allies almost succeeded in wiping
out the entire Tutsi minority.

Rwanda is divided into two main ethnic groups,
the Hutu and the Tutsi, and for years there has been
tension, which gradually reached a peak while the
country was under Belgian colonial rule. The Hutus
account for around 90 per cent of the population,
but in the past the Tutsi minority were considered
the aristocracy who dominated the Hutu peasants
for decades. Originally, there was little difference
between the two groups – they spoke the same
language, inhabited the same areas and followed the
same traditions. However, when the Belgian

colonists arrived in 1916, they saw the two groups as entirely different entities, even resorting to producing identity cards according to their ethnic origin. The Belgians treated the Tutsis as the superior group and because of this they enjoyed superior education and employment than their neighbours, the Hutus.

Bit by bit resentment grew among the Hutu people, which culminated in a series of riots in 1959. They killed more than 20,000 Tutsis, and many more fled to the surrounding countries of Burundi, Tanzania and Uganda.

When Rwanda became independent from Belgium in 1962, the Hutus seized power and started to take control, oppressing the minority Tutsis with outbreaks of extreme violence.

PREPARING TO ATTACK

Hutu President Juvénal Habyarimana, who was coming to the end of two decades in power, was starting to lose popularity among the Rwandans as the economic situation deteriorated. Tutsi refugees who had fled to Uganda, with the aid of some moderate Hutus, formed the Rwandan Patriotic Front (RPF), with the aim of overthrowing the president and regaining their homeland.

At first Habyarimana did not see the newly formed rebel group as a threat, but saw it as a way of bringing dissident Hutus back to his side. He started to accuse Tutsis who were still living in

Rwanda as RPF collaborators and in a campaign to create hatred between the two ethnic groups, Habyarimana played on the memories of early Tutsi domination. Tutsis were easily recognized by their appearance, and most Rwandan residents knew who they were even without looking at their identification cards.

By 1992, Habyarimana had started to provide military training to members of his party, and they formed into a militia that became known as the *Interahamwe* (Those Who Stand Together or Those Who Attack Together). Attacks against Tutsis became commonplace and any violence committed by the Interahamwe became accepted as it was considered to be for political gain.

Gradually, through the use of violence, harmful propaganda and persistent political tactics, Habyarimana and his band of militia widened the gap between the Hutus and the Tutsis. Aware that it would be too expensive to arm all of the president's supporters with firearms, it was decided to import a large numbers of machetes. This provided approximately every third adult Hutu male with some sort of weapon.

Aware of the political activity, the RPF prepared themselves for further conflict. They started to recruit more supporters and, despite the peace agreement signed between Habyarimana and the RPF in 1993, they increased their soldiers and firepower. The horrific turn of events that took place in 1994 was sparked off by the death of Habyarimana on April 6, when his plane was shot down just above Kigali airport. Travelling with Habyarimana was the president of Burundi and various other chief members of staff, and the perpetrator of this crime has never been established. Whoever was behind the crime, the effect was both catastrophic and immediate.

GENOCIDE BEGINS

The Presidential Guard in the capital of Kigali, backed by the militia, and led by Colonel Bagosora, instantaneously started to take their revenge. They murdered leaders of the political opposition and Hutu government officials, leaving space for Bagosora and his men to take control.

Within 24 hours of Habyarimana's jet being shot down, roadblocks sprang up all around Kigali. Recruits were despatched all over the little country to carry out a horrendous wave of killings, separating Tutsis from Hutus and hacking them to death with machetes at the roadside. Those who could afford to pay, chose to die from a bullet. The Interahamwe encouraged locals to join in, often forcing them to kill their Tutsi neighbours. Participants were offered bribes to encourage them to take part, using money and food as incentives, even telling them that they could keep the land of any Tutsis they killed.

UN troops were powerless to stop the killings and after the slaughter of ten of their own soldiers, they decided to withdraw their troops. Rwanda's first female prime minister, Agathe Uwilingiyimana, was murdered despite her guard of Belgian soldiers. These soldiers were arrested, disarmed, tortured and murdered in the hope that it would force the Belgians to withdraw their troops. Just as the rebels intended, the Belgians decided to remove the remainder of its UN troops from Rwanda.

The genocide spread with incredible speed, expanding from Kigali out into the more remote parts of the countryside. Government radio broadcasts encouraged the Tutsis to take refuge in churches, schools and sports stadiums, but this only made it easier for the rebels as their targets were congregated in larger groups. The Tutsis tried their hardest to fight off the Hutu rebels, but only armed with sticks and stones, they made little, if any, impact against the grenades and machine guns of the Rwandan army and presidential guard.

Within 13 weeks of April 6, 1994, the slaughter of at least 500,000 Tutsis and moderate Hutus had taken place. The stench of decomposing bodies hung heavily in the air, and everywhere there was the gruesome evidence of what had taken place. Twisted bodies lay by the roadside, some were heaped on top of one another and others, which had been brutally mutilated, were thrown down a steep hillside. A decapitated torso of a child lying on the steps of a church surrounded fragments of clothing – all these things a grim reminder of the devastation wrought by the tribal violence.

Karubamba, 48 km (30 miles) northeast of Kigali, was described as a vision from hell. It was a nauseating scene of human wreckage, with signs of agony on the faces of the dead. Every window, every door, told its own incomprehensible story – a schoolboy lying dead across his desk, a couple covered in blood underneath a picture of Jesus. Every few hundred kilometres along the red-clay road, bodies lay in heaped, decaying piles. The church, which the locals thought would be a safe refuge, was a scene of complete carnage. What was once a fertile valley of terraced hills, was now a carpet of bloodshed in every direction.

THE AFTERMATH

By July the RPF had managed to take control of Kigali, crushing the Rwandan government and eventually bringing a halt to the genocide by July 18. When it became obvious that the RPF was victorious, it is estimated that as many as 2,000,000 Hutus fled to Zaire (the present Democratic Republic of Congo). There were large-scale reprisal killings against Hutus who were alleged to have taken part in the massacre, and the UN returned to Rwanda to help restore order and basic services.

A new multi-ethnic government was formed on July 19, which promised a safe return to all refugees. Pasteur Bizimungu, who was a Hutu, was appointed president with many prominent cabinet posts being taken by members of the RPF.

Although the massacres were over, there was still a concentrated search to find all of those people who were involved. By 2001, 100,000 people were being held in prison and another 500 were sentenced to death for their part in the genocide.

Rwanda, which was already one of the poorest nations in the world, is still suffering today, with little hope of a quick recovery. They are still in desperate need of decent roads, bridges and telephone lines, and education is suffering due to a shortage of schools, teachers and educational material. To make matters worse, food production has been ravaged not only by war, but also by drought, leaving many Rwandans desperate for nourishment and relying on aid from the UN.

It would be nice to think that the atrocities of 1994 are just a distant memory for Rwanda, but today the scars remain and the Tutsis are still convinced that the only way to ensure their survival is to repress the Hutus. The Hutus, themselves, feel they are being treated unfairly under the Tutsi-led government and extremists on both sides still believe that the only solution is the annihilation of the other. As the warring ethnic groups remain prepared for future struggles, we can only hope that this does not lead to another wave of mass killings.

The genocide was a direct result of a small section of the Rwandan government, who believed that an extermination campaign would restore the solidarity of the Hutu under their leadership. Using their power they incited the impoverished population of Rwanda to take up arms and fight for their benefit. One aspect of the genocide, which perhaps has been overlooked, is the fact that it was not only men who were recruited to fight. A substantial number of women, and even young girls, were involved in a number of ways. Not only did they assist in the slaughter, but they also inflicted extraordinary cruelty on fellow women and children. This was another move by the perpetrators to involve the whole of the population – people who were already swayed by past fear and hatred.

A human rights report, which was released in March 1999, stated that the USA, Belgium, France and the United Nations were all given previous warnings of the 1994 genocide, and that it could have been prevented. Over a decade later world leaders have denounced what happened in Rwanda and are shamed by their failure to intervene to halt the slaughter. If another Rwanda happened, has the world learned by its mistakes and would it respond any differently? One thing is for certain: the alarm signals were ignored, and people are still angry at the world's callous characterization of the Rwanda genocide.

HOTEL RWANDA

The atrocities of 1994 are documented in a 2004 film entitled *Hotel Rwanda,* directed by Irish filmmaker Terry George. It is based on the true events that took place during the genocidal violence, and the central character is Paul Rusesabagina (played by Don Cheadle), a Hutu, who managed the four-star Sabena-owned *Hôtel des Mille Collines* in Kigali. Through his bravery and management skills he was able to save the lives of 1,200 people, making his hotel a place of refuge against all odds.

KIZLYAR HOSPITAL SIEGE

Chechnya declared independence 11 years ago. Hostage taking, hijacking and bloodshed have been the rule – not the exception – ever since.

TIME MAGAZINE, OCTOBER 2002

The siege of the hospital at Kizlyar, a town in Dagestan, Russia, took place in 1996 as part of a series of attacks by Chechen rebels to draw attention to their claims for a separate state, independent from Russian rule. In one of the biggest attacks of its kind, rebel warlord Salman Raduyev held 3,000 hostages captive in the local hospital. After releasing the majority of the hostages, the rebels fled to the Chechen border, where the Russian army opened fire, killing some of the remaining hostages in the process. The situation worsened when, in support of the rebels, gunmen hijacked a passenger ferry on the Black Sea, demanding that the Russians cease their offensive. Thankfully, after four days, the hijackers surrendered and the 255 hostages on the ship were safely returned.

MASS DEPORTATION

The siege was just one episode in a history of conflict between Chechnya and its foreign rulers, which had continued since the reign of the Ottoman Turks in the 15th century. From the 18th century on, Chechen warlords resisted the Russians, who took over the province, and took every opportunity they could to oust their new rulers. Naturally enough, the Chechens were especially rebellious whenever there was internal unrest in Russia itself – for example during the Russian revolution and during the period of enforced Collectivization.

With the advent of the World War II, the Chechens threatened to help the Germans against the Soviet Union, so Stalin ordered the deportation of virtually the whole population to Kazakhstan and Siberia, in the process causing thousands of deaths. It is now thought that roughly one-quarter of the Chechen population died in this way. After the war, there was a continuing programme of 'Russification' among the Chechens, forcing them to use Russian as the main language, which proved another source of resentment.

ROUGH JUSTICE

It was not surprising, then, that when the Soviet Union began to collapse in 1990, the Chechens were among the first to take advantage of the situation. By now, Chechnya was an economically deprived, backward region presided over by a group of renegade warlords with different motives and ideals: some of them genuinely fought for independence, progress, and modernization, while others sought merely to line their own pockets. Whatever their motivation, most of these men were no strangers to violence and had grown up with a rough and ready idea of justice. When they began to mount a series of terrorist attacks in the republic, to draw attention to the plight of their people, they proved to be formidable enemies.

As the former Soviet Union began to break up, Russia sent forces into the rebel republic to maintain its authority there. The warlords, led by Shamil Basayev, responded by seizing the town of Budyonnovsk, in Southern Russia, on June 14, 1995, and taking control for six days. They captured the local town hall and police station before commandeering a hospital, where they held more than 1,000 people hostage. Basayev issued a statement demanding the withdrawal of troops from Chechnya and an end to the war between the Chechens and the Russians. He also tried to force authorities to hold a press conference in the hospital, and when his demand was refused, he killed five policemen that had been held hostage.

Eventually, the Russians sent in commando troops, and a battle between them and the rebels raged for two days, before a ceasefire was agreed. Some hostages were released as a result, but many lost their lives in the battle. A second Russian raid failed to resolve the situation, and in the end Russia was forced to agree to ending hostilities with the Chechens in return for the hostages. The president of Russia at the time, Boris Yeltsin, met with a great deal of criticism, both at home and abroad, for allowing the Chechen terrorists to go largely unpunished. The Chechen leader Dzhokhar Dudayev disclaimed responsibility for the action and sought to distance himself from the rebels.

THREE THOUSAND HOSTAGES

However, this was by no means the end of the story. Six months later, in January 1996, Chechen terrorists again mounted a terror attack, this time in the town of Kizlyar, on the Terek River delta in Dagestan, Russia. The leader of the attack was Salman Raduyev, who assembled a force of around 250 militants, apparently with the support of Dudayev. The rebel fighters attacked a military base at Kizlyar, and then took hostages, commandering the local hospital. The attack was similar to the one in Budyonnovsk, only more hostages were taken: 3,000 people were herded into the hospital and held captive there while the rebels issued their demands.

Once again, the terrorists demanded the withdrawal of Russian troops from Chechnya.

After releasing most of the hostages, the Chechen rebels made their way back to Chechnya, taking with them hundreds of remaining hostages. They managed to get to the border, at the village of Pervomaiskoye, where they were blocked by Russian troops. They entrenched themselves at the village, and were surrounded by Russian special forces, who tried to overcome them. When they failed, Interior Minister Anatoly Kulikov announced that the hostages had all been executed by the rebels and ordered the Russian troops to open fire. Despite appeals from the hostages, who were still very much alive, the soldiers began to fire off rockets into the village. After an eight-day battle in which more hostages died, Raduyev and the rebels managed to escape from the village, taking hostages with them.

To make matters worse, a separate action was taken when another group of Chechen terrorists hijacked a passenger ferry on the Black Sea and held the crew at gunpoint. Demanding that the Russians should cease their attack at Kizlyar, they threatened to detonate a bomb on board the ferry, which would have killed more than 200 people on board. However, after a siege that lasted four days, the gunmen were forced to surrender, and the hostages were free to return home, much to the relief of their families.

<u>WILD WEST</u>

The mayhem continued when, at the end of the first war between Russian and Chechen forces, the region became a kind of Wild West. The Chechen president, Aslan Maskhadov, ceased to have any control over the warlords, who began to kidnap individuals at random, often extorting money as well as demanding political changes. The rebels' cruelty became legendary, and there were instances of hostages being beheaded. For example, four engineers were taken hostage and later found with their heads cut off. Aid workers and missionaries also became targets for the rebels, though luckily they survived: Herbert Gregg, an American missionary, went through the ordeal of being held hostage for seven months. After his release, it emerged that the rebels had taken a video of one of them cutting Gregg's finger off. Gregg himself claimed that he had been reasonably well treated, though this was hard to square with the evidence. In another incident Camilla Carr and John James, two British aid workers, were held captive for a year, but they were fortunately released unharmed.

Sadly, in the new millennium, the continuing conflict between Russia and Chechnya has led to further terrorist incidents. In March 2001, Chechen rebels hijacked an Istanbul plane bound for Moscow. When security forces raided the plane, three people were killed. Not long afterwards, a series of relatively small scale, but nonetheless frightening, attacks were mounted by rebel individuals operating independently. In one of them, tourists in a hotel in Istanbul were held captive in protest at the war; in another, 30 people on a bus were imprisoned in the heat as a Chechen rebel demanded the release of Chechen prisoners held for their part in a previous attack. However, the most daring and horrifying of these attacks took place at a Moscow theatre in 2002, when Chechen terrorists stormed a theatre and held the audience captive before being subjected to a commando-style raid by Russian troops, which killed a large percentage of the hostages.

DEATH OF A WARLORD

In 2002, the leader of the Kizlyar raid, Salman Raduyev, died in jail in Russia. The year before, he had been sentenced to life imprisonment for terrorist acts. The circumstances of his death were somewhat mysterious, the cause of death being given as 'internal bleeding'. Many suspect that what actually happened is that he was beaten to death, although the Russian authorities vehemently denied this at the time. Amnesty International, aware of the many instances of torture and ill-treatment within the Russian penal system, has called for a full, impartial investigation into his death.

Today, Raduyev remains a controversial figure in Chechen history. For many, he was simply a thug, refusing to abide by the wishes of the Chechen rulers and continuing to carry out terrorist attacks independently. For some, he was a hero: after almost losing his life in a car bomb assassination attempt in 1998, he earned the nickname 'Titanic', because of the steel plates planted in his head to reconstruct his skull. Others, such as the incoming Chechen president in 1997, believed that he was mentally ill. He was probably a combination of all three: violent, brave and perhaps somewhat deranged; and, perhaps, it was only the injustices inflicted on him and the Chechen people by the Russian state that gave him any credibility as a freedom fighter.

DOCKLANDS
DEVASTATION

I looked out of my window towards Canary Wharf to see a huge pall of smoke.
OFFICE WORKER, PAUL BARGERY

On February 9, 1996, a large area of London's Docklands was ripped apart by a massive explosion. The blast was centred on an area known as the South Quay and it was caused by a lorry that was loaded with explosives.

The London Docklands was formerly part of the Port of London, which at one time was the largest port in the world. The demise of the docks came about between 1960 and 1970, when the port was unable to cope with the much larger vessels needed for the newly adopted container system of cargo. The shipping industry gradually moved to deep-water ports such as Tilbury and Felixstowe, and one by one the docks closed. The redevelopment of the area, which was principally for commercial and residential use, took almost 17 years to complete.

The 22 sq km (8H sq mile) area, which stretches across the East End boroughs of Southward, Tower Hamlets and Newham, has been transformed and has attracted much worldwide attention.

BOMB ENDS CEASEFIRE

The South Quay in the London Docklands is a railway station for the Docklands Light Railway on the Isle of Dogs, which opened in 1987. On February 9, at about 7.01 p.m., a 500 kg (1,000 lb) bomb, left in a small lorry about 73 m (80 yds) from the station exploded, causing approximately £85 million worth of damage. The lorry was parked underneath Marsh Wall, a bridge at a point where the tracks crossed. The station itself was extensively damaged, along with three nearby buildings – the Midland Bank and South Quay Plaza I and II.

Dublin and Belfast media had received a coded telephone warning regarding the bomb, and consequently the buildings and road nearby were evacuated. Unfortunately, two men working in a newsagent shop directly opposite Marsh Wall, Inam Bashir and John Jeffries, were not warned, and they both died in the explosion. A further 39 people required hospital treatment due to blast injuries and falling glass.

Local residents said they heard an almighty bang and then their windows seemed to bow under the pressure. Another resident reported that even though she lived several kilometres from the explosion, glasses in her china cabinet shook when the bomb actually went off.

Windows in the nearby housing estate imploded and gas mains were ruptured, triggering off a second, smaller blast. Customers who were having a quiet drink in the nearby Trade Winds wine bar, dove to the floor as radiators literally popped off the walls and ceiling tiles started to fall down.

Firemen worked through the night to clear up the devastation, searching carefully through the rubble in case there were more bodies. The secondary gas explosion hampered their rescue efforts, and it wasn't until the following morning that the police found the bodies of the two men.

The bomb at London Docklands marked the end of a 17-month ceasefire by the Irish Republican Army (IRA), and the return of violence took most people by surprise. During the ceasefire British, Irish and American leaders worked at trying to come up with a political solution to end the troubles in Northern Ireland. The problem was the Unionists never wanted a negotiated settlement at all. The deposed Unionist leader, Jim Molyneaux, complained at the time of the IRA cessation that 'the cease-fire had destabilised the situation'. Conversely, Gerry Adams, the leader of the political wing of the IRA known as the Sinn Fein, spoke out about the need to continue the peace process.

Although the IRA claimed responsibility for the bomb at the Docklands, they made a statement that the 'regrettable injuries' could have been avoided if the police had responded promptly to their warnings, which, according to the IRA, were both clear and specific.

The IRA have been waging a war against British authorities and the Protestant majority for more than 25 years, with the ultimate goal of getting the British rulers out of Northern Ireland and reuniting it with the Republic of Ireland to the south. However, the Protestant paramilitary organizations, who were determined to keep Northern Ireland British, joined in the battle with their own terror attacks. In the subsequent violence, more than 3,000 people have been killed.

Police investigations into the Docklands bombing led to the arrest of James McArdle, a 29-year-old bricklayer from County Armagh. He was tried and found guilty of conspiracy to cause explosions in June 1998 and was jailed for 25 years. Murder charges for the deaths of the two men killed in the explosion, had to be dropped when the judge dismissed the jury over concerns of unfair press coverage.

The IRA agreed to another ceasefire 18 months after the bombing. Peace was finally established with the signing of the Good Friday Agreement on April 10, 1998. The agreement set out a plan for devolved government in Northern Ireland on a stable and inclusive basis and provided for the creation of Human Rights and Equality commissions. However, it also provided for the early release of terrorist prisoners and, under the terms of this agreement, James McArdle was released in July 2000.

FURTHER ATTACKS ON LONDON

During police investigations of the London Dock-lands bombing, they uncovered plans that the IRA were preparing to set bombs in London to coincide with Bill Clinton's, the then president of the USA, visit to London and Northern Ireland in November 1995. They uncovered a considerable amount of bomb-making equipment, which included Semtex, detonators and incendiary equipment, from Edward O'Brien's London apartment. Edward O'Brien was a former member of the IRA who died later on when a double-decker bus exploded in the heart of London's West End on February 18, 1996. It emerged that he was blown up and killed by his own device when it accidentally detonated while, the police think, he was carrying it to another destination.

The police managed to trace the lorry that was involved in the Docklands bombing to rural Northern Ireland, where they discovered it was being refitted for its new mission to take place some time the following year.

Earlier in 1995, on May 30, a faulty detonator had failed to trigger a bomb that had been planted under the Hammersmith Bridge in London. The bomb, 14.5 kg (32 lbs) of Semtex, was the largest high-explosive devise ever planted on the British mainland and was large enough to have wrecked the bridge and would have possibly taken several hundred lives. The explosion was planned to

coincide with the 80th anniversary of the start of
the Easter Rising, which was the 1916 rebellion
against British rule in Dublin.

ACTEAL MASSACRE

Intimidation, harassment and violent attacks against indigenous communities are frequent occurrences in countries including Honduras, Brazil, Colombia, Guatemala, Mexico and Venezuela

FROM A NEWS RELEASE ISSUED BY THE
INTERNATIONAL SECRETARIAT OF AMNESTY
INTERNATIONAL – AUGUST 9, 2001

The Acteal Massacre, which took place on December 22, 1997, in a small village in the state of Chiapas, Mexico, is one of the most shameful episodes of the ongoing civil war in the region. On that day, pro-government paramilitary troops forced their way into a Catholic chapel, where a service was taking place among the local Mayan people, and shot to death all those inside. They then rounded up those who had managed to escape and shot them as well. The death toll numbered nine men, 21 women and 15 children. Of the women, four were pregnant. Afterwards, the Mexican government was accused of ordering the massacre, or at least of involvement with it, and an investigation was mounted. However, to date it has been a slow, laborious process and many have accused the authorities of stalling.

The village of Acteal stands high in the mountainous area of Chiapas state, a region in the southeast of Mexico, bordered by the states of Veracruz, Oaxaca and Tabasco. In ancient times, Chiapas was part of the Mayan civilization, and many extraordinary ruins in the area bear witness to its glorious past. Today, however, Chiapas is one of the poorest states in Mexico, with a malnutrition rate of over 40 per cent. A large proportion of the population are of Mayan descent, working as peasant farmers and speaking their own language.

CIVIL WAR

Not only is the region extremely backward, but civil war has been waged there since 1994, causing yet more suffering to its poverty-stricken people. The combatants are, on the one hand, the Mexican government, and on the other, the Zapatista Army of National Liberation (EZLN), often known as the 'Zapatistas'. Although armed, the Zapatistas profess to adhere to a doctrine of nonviolence, and since their initial uprising, they have not been in the habit of using armed force to pursue their political aims, a strategy that has made them popular among the local people. The Zapatistas have set up their own autonomous communities in the state, which have a precarious relationship with the Mexican authorities.

It was against this background of tension that the Acteal Massacre took place. On that day, a pacifist group of Mayan Roman Catholics, calling themselves *Las Abejas* (The Bees), had gathered together in the local chapel to attend a prayer meeting. The Mayans were Tzotzils, direct descendants of the classic Maya civilization, who for centuries had been exploited as peasant labourers on European sugar and coffee plantations. However, with the collapse of the coffee trade in the 1980s, they were now an unemployed, uneducated community, eking out a subsistence in the mountainous regions of the state. Resented by other inhabitants of the area, the Tzotzils looked to the Zapatistas to advance their cause, especially as many of the Zapatistas themselves were indigenous Tzotzil. On this fateful day, however, the Zapatistas could not protect them.

CHILDREN AND BABIES SHOT

Ironically, the Las Abejas group praying in the chapel at Acteal that day were pacifists, among them refugees from nearby communities who had recently undergone the traumatic experience of fleeing from paramilitary violence and becoming refugees at the village. As they offered up their prayers for peace, the chapel was surrounded by 70 armed men wearing dark blue uniforms – they belonged to an unknown paramilitary force that had been stalking the area, waiting for a chance to attack.

As the soldiers opened fire and stormed the church, the congregation scattered, running to hiding places in the mountains, cornfields and along the side of the river. However, those who managed to get away were hunted down by the paramilitaries and shot in cold blood, many of them at point-blank range. The soldiers even shot children and babies, following their frightened cries as they hid with their mothers in caves along the riverside.

Meanwhile, special police forces callously observed the events from a distance, failing to intervene and stop the bloodshed. Instead, they tried to hide what had happened, pushing the bodies into the caves and into a nearby ravine so that the massacre would not be discovered.

SHEER BRUTALITY

All in all, the massacre took five hours, as the terrorists roamed the mountainsides, unearthing the villagers from their hiding places. According to some reports, after being shot, the pregnant women were disembowelled and their unborn children displayed for all to see. The sheer level of brutality at the Acteal raid shocked even the most hardened inhabitants of Chiapas, who had become accustomed to the violence of paramilitary groups in the region.

After the incident, there was outrage in the

international community at what had happened. The massacre brought to attention what many aid workers, human rights organizations and others already knew – that the Tzotzil, along with the Chole, Mame, Tojalobal and Tzeltal indigenous peoples – had long been the subject of mass persecution in the region, and that the Mexican authorities condoned, if not encouraged, the violence of the paramilitary groups terrorizing the people there. Any attempt on the part of the indigenous groups to politicize and organize themselves had been met with brute force, and they had remained desperately poor, with no hope of a better future for themselves and their families.

REIGN OF TERROR

With the focus now on the massacre, it also came to light that, over several years, more than 1,000 people in the northern region of Chiapas had been murdered for political reasons. About one-third of the Mexican army were stationed in Chiapas, and trained paramilitary groups there had created a reign of terror. Over 10,000 people had become refugees, especially in the region of Chenalho, where families had fled from the communities set up by the Zapatistas, hounded out by the paramilitaries. Not only this, but despite its rich natural wealth, in terms of fertile agricultural land, the whole state was utterly impoverished, through a combination of civil war, unemployment and under-investment. Many people in the state continued to live without running water, sewage or electricity; and only half the population were literate. Moreover, there was virtually no state health care, and many children died of common diseases – especially refugees, who in some areas were homeless and dying of starvation. However, for the most part, the plight of the Chiapas indigenous people had received very little interest from the international press.

The Mexican government initially refused to take any responsibility for the massacre and have attempted since then to downplay the political and social issues raised by such an atrocity. Their attitude was that this was a feud between local families, caused by a dispute over a sand pit, an explanation that few believe and which caused ridicule in the Mexican press at the time. They also tried to pin the blame on the Zapatistas. But many believe that government-backed forces are still targeting indigenous communities in Chiapas, despite the fact that the government has signed peace agreements with the Zapatistas, giving them the right to self-government. They point to the fact that the army presence in the region has increased massively, and there are constant reports of their brutality towards, and harassment of, indigenous people there.

KILLING MACHINE

There are also reports that other countries are involved in the fighting. In the preliminary report into the Acteal Massacre, it was pointed out that disembowelling pregnant women is a trademark ritual of the notorious 'Kaibiles', soldiers of the Guatemalan military who are known for their brutality. The Kaibiles wear distinctive maroon berets with an insignia showing a blazing sword and bearing the words, 'If I go forwards, follow me. If I stop, urge me on. If I turn back, kill me.' There is also well-documented evidence that, as part of their training, recruits are forced to kill an animal, eat its flesh raw and drink its blood. The brutality of the Kaibiles' training and general ethos has prompted the conclusion that the special force is 'a killing machine', and they have been held responsible for several other massacres, including one at Dos Erres, Guatemala, in 1982, in which over 200 civilians were murdered.

There are also accusations that the USA has also been involved in the subjugation of the Mayans and other indigenous peoples in Chiapas, through supplying the Mexican army with weapons, and through training its soldiers in counter-insurgency techniques. Although the Acteal Massacre has focussed attention on the plight of the Tzotzils, and the Zapatistas have taken over several towns in the area, the native peoples have suffered growing repression since that time. Many of the survivors of

Acteal are now refugees with nowhere to live. They have no access to clean water, sanitation, medical care or employment and rely on aid and other international assistance for their daily needs. However, despite their troubles, the native peoples have continued to support the Zapatistas. The group's international reputation has grown since they set up their autonomous zones, working peacefully to provide basic amenities for the peasants there, and using modern innovations as the Internet and satellite phones, rather than armed force, to publicize their anti-globalization, pro-environmental message.

SEPTEMBER 11

Thousands of lives were suddenly ended by evil, despicable acts of terror. The pictures of airplanes flying into buildings, fires burning, huge structures collapsing, have filled us with disbelief, terrible sadness and a quiet, unyielding anger.

GEORGE W. BUSH

The terror attacks that took place on September 11, 2001, undoubtedly changed the course of history. These horrifying attacks, which killed around 3,000 people in total, were reported live as they occurred, so that viewers all over the world watched in amazement as the unthinkable occurred: two planes crashed into the Twin Towers, in the heart of Manhattan, creating an inferno of fire and smoke; a third plane crashed into the Pentagon, headquarters of the US Department of Defense; while a fourth crashed into a field in Pennsylvania, after an apparent fight for control on board. Never, since the attack on Pearl Harbor during World War II, had such a massive, co-ordinated attack been made on

American soil, causing so much damage and loss of life.

Yet, as it emerged later, the September 11 attacks were not perpetrated by a large, powerful army with state backing: they were the work of a small, renegade band of Islamic fundamentalists, armed only with such weapons as box-cutter knives and pepper spray. That a ramshackle band of religious fanatics could create devastation on such an enormous scale defied belief, and in the aftermath of the events, many questions were asked as to how security services could have failed to stop the attacks.

But as it transpired, the terrorists had a trump card that even the most sophisticated security systems were unable to beat: the hijackers were prepared to commit suicide in the pursuit of their ends and go down with the planes themselves. In the aftermath of 9/11, with other attacks against Western interests now taking place around the world on a regular basis, it is this aspect of terrorism that has remained the most perplexing and terrifying: how to understand the pathology of fanatics who are prepared to die for their cause – and more importantly, how to defend ourselves against them.

ENGULFED IN FIRE

On the morning of September 11 in Manhattan, the weather was warm and the sky a clear blue: a perfect day marking the end of summer. Nearby the

Twin Towers, a couple of planes flew low overhead, noticed by New Yorkers as they scurried along the streets of the financial district around the World Trade Center. Seconds later, disaster struck: at 8.46 a.m., one of the planes crashed into the North Tower of the Center, followed by another, at 9.03 a.m., which crashed into the South Tower. The buildings were engulfed in fire and smoke, and emergency services rushed to the rescue. There was pandemonium in the streets below as people ran for their lives. Office workers trapped in the buildings began to throw themselves out of the windows to their deaths, rather than be burnt alive in the flames or suffocated by smoke.

The authorities responded to the attack as quickly as they could, closing all roads into the city and grounding all domestic flights. There were fears that the attacks were not yet over, because along with the two flights that had crashed into the towers (American Airlines Flight 11 and United Airlines Flight 175), two other flights had also been hijacked that morning (American Airlines Flight 77 and United Airlines Flight 93).

At 9.45 a.m., news came in of a hijacked aeroplane that had crashed into the Pentagon headquarters at Arlington County, Virginia. Meanwhile, at 10.05 a.m., the South Tower came crashing down, dredging the streets of New York with dust and ash, killing hundreds, and creating chaos in the heart of the city. In the face of this massive assault on the USA's most prestigious landmarks, the security services ordered the immediate evacuation of the White House. Minutes later, at 10.10 a.m., a large section of the Pentagon building collapsed. At exactly the same time, the fourth hijacked plane crashed into a field in Pennsylvania, killing the entire crew and passengers, as well as the hijackers themselves.

STATE OF SHOCK

The United States of America, and the rest of the world, was left reeling from shock. The idea of using planes as bombs, simply flying them into buildings to create maximum damage, including the deaths of all those aboard the plane, was unprecedented. It was clear that the Western world was dealing with a new kind of enemy.

As the emergency services set about clearing up the wreckage in New York, Virginia and Pennsylvania, a picture of what had happened began to emerge. Passengers and crew members aboard the hijacked planes had been able, in some cases, to use their mobile phones to report what was going on. A commission was set up to further investigate the events, and it reported that in the case of the fourth plane, the passengers and crew had attempted to wrest control of the plane from the hijackers, resulting in the crash. It was also revealed that other attacks had been planned by members of the terrorist group al-Qaeda, but they had been aborted.

Besides grieving for the victims killed in the attacks, New Yorkers, and Americans generally, were in a profound state of shock. For some, the attacks provoked questioning and self-doubt: what could their country have done to warrant such violence? Was the USA, as the world's leading capitalist nation, guilty of oppressing other nations through economic and cultural imperialism? Or was this an unprovoked attack by fanatic religious elements in the Arab world, bent on destroying the democracy, equality, freedom and prosperity of the West?

'AXIS OF EVIL'

President George W. Bush responded, rather late in the day, by pointing to Osama Bin Laden, the leader of an Islamic fundamentalist group known as al-Qaeda, as the architect of the destruction. (Bin Laden's now familiar name was, for most people at the time, quite unknown.) Bush resolved to dedicate all the resources at his disposal to finding Bin Laden, wherever he might be, and bringing him to justice.

Instead of limiting his rhetoric to describing a small, vicious band of nihilists who had to be tracked down and incarcerated for the safety of the public. Bush took the opportunity to declare a 'war on terror' against an 'axis of evil', implying that other powerful elements in the Arab world were also to blame. Eventually, the 9/11 attacks were used to justify US invasions of other countries such as Afghanistan and Iraq, resulting in an escalation of conflict between the Arab and Western worlds and further terrorist acts, which some feel might have been avoided had al-Qaeda been seen for what it was at the time: a tiny, extremist organization of fanatical terrorists, bankrolled by the megalomaniac son of an oil millionaire, which had little support among the majority of the Arab nations.

THE TERRORISTS

After the events of 9/11, a special commission was set up to enquire into what had happened. Eventually, after three years of investigation, the report identified 19 hijackers, all of whom belonged to al-Qaeda, as well as eight terrorists who tried and failed to take part in the attack. There are currently various disputes as to the findings of the report, but it is thought that the pilots of the planes were Mohammed Atta, who crashed Flight 11 into the North Tower; Marwan al-Shehhi, who crashed Flight 175 into the South Tower; Hani Hanjour, who crashed Flight 77 into the Pentagon; and Ziad Jarrah, who crashed Flight 93 into a field in Pennsylvania. Two other men, Khalid al-Mihdhar and Nawaf al-Hazmi, were also leading organizers. The terrorists mostly came from Saudi Arabia, but also from the United Arab Emirates, Lebanon and Egypt, and they had entered the USA earlier that year. Others involved included Abu Zubaydah, Mohammed Zammar, Ramzi Binalshibh, and Zacarias Moussaoui, the so-called 'twentieth hijacker' who received a life sentence for his terrorist activities in 2006.

All of the terrorists had been trained by the terrorist group al-Qaeda, some of them forming a cell in Hamburg, Germany, and fleeing from there before the attacks. The attacks had been planned in detail by Khalid Sheik Mohammed, a leading figure in al-Qaeda until his eventual capture in Pakistan in 2003. He was also responsible for other atrocities. The plan had the full approval and backing of Osama Bin Laden, the leader of al-Qaeda.

OSAMA BIN LADEN

The shadowy figure of Osama Bin Laden has continued to haunt the West since he was identified as the mastermind behind the 9/11 attacks. He is also believed to have been involved in several other major terrorist attacks, including many US embassy bombings, Bali nightclub bombings and the Madrid bombings. However, to date the FBI does not have enough hard evidence to link him to the events of September 11, and he has not been captured. His whereabouts are unknown, although he is thought to be living in rural Afghanistan. There have also been reports of his death, though these are unsubstantiated.

Bin Laden was born in Riyadh, Saudi Arabia, on March 10, 1957. His father, Muhammed Awad bin Laden, worked for the Saudi royal family in construction, amassing a huge fortune in the 1950s.

Muhammed had many wives, and Osama was one of 55 children. His mother was a Syrian-born woman who divorced his father shortly after his birth, marrying a man who worked for Muhammed. Osama became part of a new step-family, and was raised as a devout Sunni Muslim. At school and university, he came under the influence of religious dissidents, some of whom preached a philosophy of anti-Western 'jihad'. As a young man, he married several times, divorcing once, and fathered more than 20 children. Described as soft-spoken, gentle and polite, he nevertheless aligned himself with the most militant elements in the Muslim world.

TERRORIST TRAINING CAMP

Bin Laden was a strong supporter of the Muslim fundamentalist regime of Ayatollah Khomeini, who had ousted the Shah from the throne in Iran, and he also supported the Muslim guerrillas, or 'muhajideen' fighting against the Soviets in Afghanistan. He set up an organization known as Maktab al-Khadamat (MAK) to channel funds, arms and trained soldiers into Afghanistan. He then broke away from MAK and set up a new group, al-Qaeda, publicly denouncing the Saudi government for allowing US military bases in the country. Eventually, in 1991, the Saudi government expelled Bin Laden to Sudan, where he established a base for his future terrorist activities, training Islamic militants in all aspects of terrorist warfare.

In May 1996, Bin Laden was expelled from Sudan, and went to Afghanistan, befriending leaders of the Taliban government there. He then masterminded a series of terrorist attacks around the world, including the failed 'Bojinka' plot, a 9/11-style multi-target attack involving hijacked aeroplanes. He also issued a 'fatwa' declaring a holy war against all Americans for crimes committed against Arab peoples, in particular criticizing American support for Israel.

CAVE HIDEOUT

In response, the US government ordered the arrest or assassination of Bin Laden and froze all assets linked to him. They also sent over cruise missiles to kill him, but he escaped – however, many other people were killed. Sanctions against Afghanistan were imposed, but the Taliban refused to give up Bin Laden, even when he became the prime suspect in the 9/11 attacks. Since then, despite strenuous attempts to link Bin Laden directly to the events of September 11, no conclusive evidence has been found against him.

Today, Bin Laden is still in hiding. His large extended family have disowned him, and he is thought to be living in caves on the border between Pakistan and Afghanistan. It is also believed that Bin Laden has serious health problems and suffers from a kidney disease that needs to be treated with advanced medical equipment. Over the years, several sightings of him have been reported, but none of them have yet led to his capture. Some accounts even suggest that Osama Bin Laden is in reality dead, and that it is a continuing myth that he is hiding in the rugged landscape of Afghanistan. But whatever the truth, the fact remains that, five years after the 9/11 attacks, the mastermind behind the atrocities has still not been caught, and it looks unlikely that he will be brought to justice in the near future.

MOSCOW THEATRE HOSTAGE CRISIS

Every nation has the right to their fate.
Russia has taken away this right from the
Chechens and today we want to reclaim these
rights, which Allah has given us, in the same
way he has given it to other nations. Allah
has given us the right of freedom and the
right to choose our destiny.

The Moscow Theatre Hostage crisis, in which Chechen rebels stormed a Moscow theatre and held over 900 audience members hostage, is in many ways a tragic story. The hostages endured a three-day ordeal, and were then 'rescued' by Russian troops using a mystery gas, which unfortunately caused the deaths of a 130 of them. Afterwards, the Russian authorities refused to say what the gas was and were slow to administer an antidote, which meant that many died, and those who survived were, in many cases, left with memory loss and other damage. For these reasons, the Moscow Theatre Hostage crisis remains a controversial issue, and many questions surrounding the event remain unanswered.

HUMAN TIME BOMBS

The attack on the theatre, named the House of Culture and situated in the Dubrovka area of the city, began on October 23, 2002, during a performance of the popular Russian musical Nord-Ost. During the second act, 42 terrorists, 18 of them women, stormed the theatre and held up the audience at gunpoint. They were led by Movsar Barayev, the nephew of a Chechen military leader who had died in combat. Barayev announced that the terrorists had placed mines around the theatre and would blow it up unless Russia withdrew troops from the rebel republic of Chechnya. Some of the terrorists were reported to have explosives strapped to their own bodies. It was also claimed that the women among them were widows of Chechen men killed by Russian forces.

Backstage, some of the performers who had been waiting to take part in the musical managed to escape through a window. They immediately called the police and informed them that the theatre had been taken over by force, mentioning that some of the terrorists were women. Inside the building, some hostages managed to phone family and friends on their mobile phones, but in many cases this simply added to the tension. One hostage, for example, described how he was sitting beside a bomb that one of the terrorists was threatening to detonate. Further anxiety was caused when the terrorists issued media announcements with a video, in which some of the gunmen swore that they were willing to die to avenge their country's honour.

SUMMARY EXECUTIONS

During the first day, the terrorists released a man suffering from a heart condition and let several children go. They also freed all Muslim members of the audience. In addition, several hostages managed to slip out of the building, through open windows. However, the terrorists refused to release foreign (non-Russian) members of the audience, despite the authorities' pleas to do so as soon as possible.

On the second day of the siege, a member of the public barged her way through the Russian soldiers surrounding the building, and berated the hostages, telling them to stand up to the terrorists. The gunmen pushed her into a side room and three shots were heard, which suggested that she had been executed. The following day, another member of the public fought his way into the building, claiming that he had come to fetch his son. He met with the same chilling fate.

For almost three days, the Chechen terrorists held the people inside the theatre to ransom. The producer of the musical, Georgy Vasilyev, later described what happened as a bardak, a slang

Russian word meaning 'utter chaos'. Naturally, the hostages feared for their lives, either at the hands of the gunmen, or through an explosion of one of the mines planted in the building. It seemed that the gunmen were not at all well organized or clear about their plans, and an atmosphere of panic prevailed.

KILLER GAS

Early on the Saturday morning, the Russian government decided to act. They sent in the 'Spetsnaz', a team of special forces, in a commando-style raid on the building. Unusually, the soldiers sprayed an anaesthetic gas into the building before entering. Although many of the hostages and their captors fell asleep, some of them remained alert, and a terrifying gun battle between the security forces and the terrorists ensued, with the hostages in the auditorium caught in the crossfire.

In the immediate aftermath of the crisis, the situation did not seem to improve a great deal. Many of the hostages suffering from the effects of the gas were taken to hospitals around the city, but there were delays in finding antidotes for them, and some died of gas poisoning. Relatives were given little or no information as to what was going on, causing a great deal of ill feeling towards the soldiers and the authorities. Outside some of the hospitals, members of the public shouted, 'Hostages again!' as they waited for news of their loved ones. Their anger intensified when Moscow's senior medical official announced that the 120 hostages who had died had all been victims of the gas, rather than dying of gunshot wounds.

Defending his government's decisions, President Vladimir Putin claimed that the raid had been extremely successful and had saved many lives. He declared a day of mourning for the victims and expressed his sorrow that the security forces had not been able to rescue all of them.

Later, it emerged that the Russian authorities had refused to let doctors at the hospitals know what kind of gas the victims had been poisoned with. Despite pressure from foreign embassies, they had been unwilling to divulge the exact nature of the gas that the security forces had used. This meant that there had been delays in resuscitating the patients, which led to many deaths.

Eventually, the Health minister, Yuri Shevchenko, was pressured into identifying the gas. He claimed that it was a type of Fentanyl, an extremely powerful morphine-based drug. In Germany, using evidence from a urine sample provided by one of the survivors of the attack, the gas was identified as halothane, a type of anaesthetic. However, there continues to be some dispute as to whether this was the case. Whatever the truth, the gas was administered at levels much too high for the average person to survive.

SERIES OF ATTACKS

Not surprisingly, the Russian government were extremely defensive about what appears to have been a major error on the security forces' part. Putin insisted that the raid had been a success, and he tightened restrictions on media coverage of terrorist events. He also vetoed the setting up of an inquiry into what had happened during the raid. Moreover, military action against Chechnya was stepped up and security measures tightened. Although the Chechen rebel leader who had seized the theatre, Shamil Basayev, claimed he had no connection with the Chechen president, Aslan Maskhadov, there were many in the Russian government who doubted this was the case, and relations between Russia and Chechnya went on to deteriorate considerably.

The Moscow Theatre Hostage Crisis was just one episode, albeit perhaps the most dramatic, in a series of Chechen terrorist actions designed to draw attention to the republic's fight for self-government and independence from Russia. Two years later, in September 2004, another crisis broke out when Chechen rebels, once again led by Shamil Besayev, stormed a school at Beslan, killing hundreds of civilians, many of them children (see page 399).

The attack drew condemnation from the West, but there have also been criticisms of Russia and the way it has handled the Chechnyan issue. Some commentators point to a certain degree of hypocrisy in the way that Russia has been criticized by the Western media for its response to Chechen terrorism, while the USA has been praised for a similar, indeed some would say much more far-reaching, response to attacks by al-Qaeda. While we are often encouraged to look at the underlying causes of Chechen rebellion, no such sympathy is extended towards examining the motivation of Islamic fundamentalist groups.

What remains clear is that the Chechen rebels often operate in an extremely brutal way, frequently towards innocent victims who have no connection whatsoever to the political situation they are fighting to improve. This brutality carries with it a lack of respect for basic human rights, as their treatment of hostages in the Moscow Theatre Crisis shows. The rebels' willingness to die for their cause can be seen as gloriously brave, or – perhaps more persuasively – as evidence of a certain degree of nihilism, or even mental instability.

How such an ethos comes about, and how such a pathology develops, is a subject that has not been analyzed extensively in this context, but it seems likely that the Chechen warlords' history and culture of living outside the law has contributed to their rough and ready approach to justice. To this degree, they are not very different, on the face of it, to the operatives of al-Qaeda, or indeed to any other contemporary terrorist groups who seek to gain their ends by brute force. Thus, as some commentators have suggested, calling the Chechen hostage-takers 'rebels' and 'warlords' lends a certain degree of respect to people who are, in the end, simply terrorists, just like those of al-Qaeda and other groups who threaten the stability of the West.

THE BALI BOMBING

*We fight terrorism because we love freedom;
because we share the values of other countries
that are in the war against terrorism; and
because it's evil and you do not seek to reach
an accommodation with those who would
destroy your sons and daughters and take
away the security and the stability of
this country.*

QUOTE FROM *THE AUSTRALIAN*, OCTOBER 2002

The bomb explosions on the Indonesian island of
Bali in October 2002 killed a total of 202 people,
most of them tourists enjoying a night out on the
Kuta tourist strip there. This was the deadliest terror
attack ever to take place in Indonesia, and it is
thought to be the work of Jemaah Islamiah, a
militant terrorist group with links to al-Qaeda,
which seeks to impose a fundamentalist theocracy
in South East Asia. Among others, Abu Bakar
Bashir, a Muslim cleric with extreme fundamentalist
views, was eventually convicted, but he only served

a short prison sentence, causing a great deal of controversy, especially in Australia, where many of the victims had hailed from.

SCENE OF CARNAGE

The evening of October 12, 2002, in the tourist town of Kuta, Bali, was much like any other. Crowds of foreign tourists gathered, as they did every night, to dance and drink in the many clubs and bars lining the main street. Among them were many young Australians, for whom the island of Bali was a favourite holiday spot. Unbeknown to them, a terrible drama was about to unfold.

At just after 11.00 p.m., a bomb detonated in a bar known as Paddy's Bar. The bomb was stowed away in a backpack worn by an individual, who was killed outright. Many of the people in the bar were injured by the bomb and rushed out into the street. Seconds later, another bomb exploded, just outside the Sari Club, which served a mainly Western clientele. This time, the bomb was detonated via remote control and was a far bigger device. It had been hidden in a white van just outside the club, and its force blew a crater in the ground and caused windows of the buildings nearby to blow out.

The scene was one of carnage, as body parts were blown around the street. Many of those who were injured could not get immediate medical attention, as the local hospital was too small to deal with such a disaster. Some of the victims were flown to

Australia for specialist treatment, in an emergency rescue launched by the Australian air force. Meanwhile, another bomb went off just outside the American Consulate, but thankfully no one was killed in this attack.

ISLAMIC TERRORISTS

The reaction to the attacks was one of horror, sadness and anger. Most of the tourists were young men and women, enjoying the summer nightlife of Bali. It seemed incredible that someone could launch an attack on such innocent victims. And not only did foreign tourists lose their lives: a large number of Balinese and Indonesian workers and residents were also killed in the attack.

As the investigation began, it became clear that the attacks were made by a terrorist organization. The bomb was found to be manufactured of ammonium nitrate, which is used as a type of fertiliser in Indonesia, suggesting that the perpetrators were local rather than from a foreign country. Suspicion immediately fell on an outspoken cleric named Abu Bakar Bashir, leader of the Indonesian Mujaheeden Council, who had repeatedly made anti-Western statements and was known to be a strong critic of the Indonesian government. He was also alleged to be the spiritual leader of the Islamic terrorist organization Jemaah Islamiah and to have links with al-Qaeda. However, he denied these connections and stated that the bombs were planted by the United States intelligence agencies, a theory that few believed. Other suspects included Aris Munandar, an associate of Bashir's, and Mohammad Abdullah Sughayer, who was thought to be bankrolling Abu Sayyaf, a guerrilla organization from the Philippines.

NO REMORSE

In April 2003, Abu Bakar Bashir was charged with treason for attempting to overthrow the government and set up an Islamic theocracy in its place. The complex case against him involved charges relating to a series of bomb attacks in South-East Asia, including a series of attacks on Christian churches in Indonesia, which claimed 18 victims. However, there was not enough evidence presented at court to convict him of the crimes, although he was jailed for immigration offences.

In October 2004, Bashir was once again arrested and charged, this time for his part in an attack at the Marriott Hotel in Jarkarta the year before, which resulted in the deaths of 14 people. As well as the charges relating to the Marriott Hotel attack, there were secondary charges regarding conspiracy in the Bali bomb attack of 2002. Once again, there was not enough evidence to convict him for the main charges, but he was convicted of conspiracy in the 2002 attack. Bashire was given a sentence of two and a half years' imprisonment.

There was dismay in Australia and the USA that

Bashir was not given a longer sentence, and there was also outrage when he was released four months earlier than the sentence imposed. Showing no remorse, Bashir came out of prison to cheering crowds. He was escorted by numerous bodyguards, waving a book that he had published to coincide with his release. Afterwards, he told the press that the Australian prime minister, John Howard, should convert to Islam, and that if he did not, he would go to hell.

DEATH BY FIRING SQUAD

The authorities did, however, manage to gain some convictions in the Bali bombing, much to the relief of those who had lost their loved ones in the attack. The individuals named were Amrozi bin Haji Nurhasyim, who was accused of procuring the explosives and the van used to store them outside the Sari Club, his brothers Ali Imron and Ali Ghufron, and Imam Samudra.

Amrozi, as he came to be known, was the fifth of 13 children, who became well known for his confident air during the trial. In fact, he appeared so calm and untroubled by his situation that he came to be known as 'the smiling assassin'. Amrozi denied being a member of Jemaah Islamiya, but he said that he had done his duty to God, in support of all Muslims around the world. He was sentenced to death by firing squad. However, this method of execution has since been ruled illegal in Indonesia, so he has remained in prison.

Imam Samudra, apparently the intellectual of the group, was sentenced to death for organizing the bombings. Remembered as a quiet, studious child in his native village of Serang, West Java, he later became a religious teacher and then travelled to Afghanistan to fight for the Islamic fundamentalist Taliban regime there. Chillingly, after the bombs went off, he stayed in the Kuta area for several days to witness the devastation caused.

Ali Gufron, also known as Mukhlas, was also sentenced to death. The older brother of Amrozi, he was a preacher, and he is thought to have persuaded his brothers to become terrorists. As the trial progressed, it became clear that he was the mastermind behind the whole plot, and also that he was firmly convinced that he was fighting a 'jihad', or holy war, against the West. He stated that the attacks were made in order to avenge Muslims for the United States' tyranny against them in the Middle East, and he claimed that he was the head of Jemaah Islamiyah. He also said that he knew Osama bin Laden personally, and had fought with the Mujahideen in Afghanistan.

REMORSEFUL TEARS

Unlike his two brothers, the other man accused, Ali Imron, had a change of heart after the bombings, and during his trial he showed a great deal of remorse for his crimes. He apologized to the relatives of the victims, even dissolving into tears at some points, and co-operated as much as he could with the prosecution throughout. However, despite his expressions of regret, he was given a life sentence. His part in the crime had been a central one, mixing and packing the explosives for the bomb, and training the two suicide bombers who had mounted the attack.

Also suspected of playing a part in the 2002 attack was Riduan Isamuddin, known as Hambali. Hambali is thought to have been the leader of Jemaah Islamiyah and the main contact for al-Qaeda in South-East Asia. He was arrested in Ayutthaya, near Bangkok, by American and Thai intelligence, and he has been kept in American custody ever since. Reports suggest that the USA does not want to hand Hambali over to the authorities in Indonesia, for fear his sentence will not be harsh enough. Today, his whereabouts are kept secret, but it is thought that he may be held in Jordan.

MUSLIM SUPERPOWER

From what is known of Hambali, it appears that he wanted to create a Muslim theocracy across the whole of South-East Asia, with himself at the head of it. This superpower, with a population of around 420 million and a massive army, would have been able to have military power of the region, and control all trade, shipping and other interests there.

As a major operator in terrorist circles, Hambali

was friendly with Khalid Shaikh Mohammed, who was behind the September 11 attacks. After the 2002 Bali bombing, Hambali became a top terrorist suspect, and he was eventually tracked down and arrested. However, he has not yet been brought to trial.

To date, none of those convicted of the 2002 Bali bombing have been put to death. In Australia, there is no death penalty, but a recent poll showed that a majority of citizens there feel that the Indonesian courts should impose the death sentence for the crimes the terrorists have committed. The Australian government have also agreed not to ask Indonesia to withhold the death penalty in this instance.

GULF WAR NUMBER THREE

We declared jihad against the US government,
because the US government is unjust, criminal
and tyrannical. It has committed acts that are
extremely unjust, hideous and criminal
whether directly or through its support of
the Israeli occupation.

OSAMA BIN LADEN

The US invasion of Iraq in 2003 has been the subject of much controversy since it took place. Using the terror attacks of 9/11 as the justification for a 'war on terror' against what he called an 'axis of evil', President Bush launched a generalized offensive against elements of the Arab world, invading Afghanistan and Iraq. Some argued that, in the case of Afghanistan, this was a legitimate course of action, since the Islamic Taliban regime there was thought to be harbouring Osama bin Laden, who had been identified as the mastermind behind the 9/11 attacks. However, in the case of Iraq, no such obvious link between the government and the terrorists appeared to exist; indeed, Saddam Hussein and the Islamic fundamentalists who were behind the 9/11 attacks appeared to be polar opposites in terms of Arab culture. (Hussein's regime was firmly secular, with strong links to the West, while bin Laden's followers were entirely separatist and fundamentalist in outlook.)

SUPPORT FOR TERROR ATTACKS

Even so, President Bush managed to persuade the American public that Hussein and his regime were linked to the attacks, and that Hussein had funded terrorist organizations to commit such atrocities as 9/11. The USA, aided by the UK, thus launched an invasion of Iraq, citing Hussein's flouting of international laws regarding weapons of mass destruction, human rights abuses and alleged support of terrorist organizations, as reasons for doing so. Many critics felt that the US behaved opportunistically in this instance, arguing that the real reason for the invasion was to do with seizing control of the oil fields of Iraq.

Whatever the truth of the matter, there is little doubt that the invasion of Iraq provoked many of the Arab nations to regard the USA and the West with tremendous hostility, and that it has had the effect of ratcheting up the tension between the cultures to an alarming degree. This has shown itself in increased support for terrorist attacks among Islamic peoples who had not, before, espoused terrorist violence as a means to protecting Muslim culture and its way of life.

It is also clear that the US invasion of Iraq has done a great deal of damage to relations between the Islamic world and the West. Some commentators go further and claim that the invasion itself was a terrorist attack: that it had no legitimacy and was a form of state terrorism itself. This argument holds that the invasion of Iraq was an unprovoked attack on an independent country, and that as such it was a breach of international law.

WEAPONS OF MASS DESTRUCTION

The invasion of Iraq began on March 20, with a coalition force of American, British and Kurdish troops, as well as involvement from other nations in the form of equipment, security forces and troops. The given reason for the invasion was that the government of Iraq had not complied with international law, which required them to reveal their weapons arsenal to UN inspectors. The theory was that Iraq had a powerful arsenal of nuclear, biological and other weapons that could be used at any time to launch an attack on the USA or the UK, and that Hussein was planning to do so. As such, Hussein's regime posed an intolerable threat to the West, which needed to be dealt with by invading the country as soon as possible.

As it transpired, these weapons of mass destruction were never found, and it is doubtful whether they ever existed. Prior to the invasion, UN inspection teams were asking for more time to find these supposed weapons, but their requests were ignored by the US and UK governments.

There was a massive worldwide demonstration on February 15, 2003, protesting against the imminent invasion, in which around 10,000,000 people took to the streets in more than 60 countries, demanding peace. However, the voices of the people went unheard, and the invasion went ahead, despite the enormous opposition that it generated around the world.

CREATION OF A TYRANT

One of the most disturbing aspects of the invasion was that it was not ratified by the United Nations (UN) Security Council. It had become clear that France, Russia and China would block any attempt by the USA to gain permission to launch the invasion. France in particular had strong links with the Iraqi government, having helped to arm Saddam Hussein in the first place. The irony of the situation was that Saddam Hussein had established a strong regime in Iraq with the help of the Western powers, who had seen his secular, modernizing government as a bulwark against anti-Western, anti-capitalist, fundamentalist elements in the Arab world. Moreover, during that time, the Western powers had turned a blind eye to Hussein's many appalling human rights abuses, especially regarding his treatment of the Kurds in the north of the country. Now, having supported Saddam's regime from its inception, the Western powers found that they had created a tyrant who would no longer do their bidding.

In October 2002, the United States Congress authorized the invasion of Iraq, citing Hussein's refusal to abide by UN resolutions on weapons of mass destruction, human rights, terrorism and treatment of prisoners of war. The following month, the UN offered Iraq a final chance, under resolution 1441, to comply with its disarmament obligations and reveal its weapons of mass destruction. The resolution warned that there would be grave consequences if this were not done.

In response, Iraq claimed that it had abided by the resolution and had disarmed as required. Hans Blix, the head of the UN weapons inspectors team, asked the UN for more time to check whether this was actually the case. Meanwhile, the USA and UK were demanding a further resolution authorizing the use of force in Iraq if, as they believed, there were still weapons of mass destruction there. They never received this final resolution, and the invasion began without it.

'OPERATION IRAQI FREEDOM'

The USA and UK defended themselves by claiming that the use of force was implicit in resolution 1441.

However, the UN Security Council pointed out that it was not up to individual members of the council to determine how resolutions were enforced. Several years after the event, the legality of the Coalition invasion under the terms of resolution 1441 is still being disputed, especially as after the invasion, no weapons of mass destruction were ever found.

The invasion of Iraq was conducted under the code name of 'Operation Iraqi Freedom', and ir deployed 100,000 soldiers and marines from the USA. The UK sent more than 26,000 troops, and there were also forces from other nations, such as Australia. A large force from Iraqi Kurdish militia was also present, numbering more than 50,000. The Coalition forces had hoped to set up a base in Turkey, but in the event, the Turkish government refused to allow this.

On the other side of the conflict, the combined Iraqi armed forces numbered over 300,000, but they were poorly equipped and managed. For many years before the invasion, there had been sanctions against Iraq, and the entire infrastructure and organization of the country was extremely poor. The Iraqi troops had also been fighting low-level battles against US and UK air patrols for several years, in the aftermath of the 1991 Gulf War. These hostilities were stepped up in the months prior to the invasion, to allow Coalition forces to enter Iraq without detection.

<u>HUSSEIN CAPTURED</u>

The formal attack on March 20, 2003, was marked by a series of explosions in Baghdad in the early hours of the morning. Meanwhile, Coalition troops were swarming into Iraq from Kuwait and elsewhere. Their aim was to destroy the Iraqi military and to secure the Iraqi oilfields rather than to decimate cities and harm civilians. Within about three weeks, they achieved their aim; the Iraqi military, and with it the Iraqi government, had completely collapsed. US forces then moved into Baghdad, launching an attack on the Palaces of Saddam Hussein and taking control of the city. On April 9, 2003, the city was formally declared occupied by the USA.

When Saddam Hussein was eventually captured on December 13, 2003, it became clear that his brutal regime was over for good. In a matter of weeks, with relatively little loss of civilian life, the Coalition forces had managed to overrun the country, take over the government and win the war. At the time, this seemed like a triumph, and the USA and UK were jubilant at their victory.

However, once the war was over, the picture began to cloud. As it transpired, it was not so easy to quell the many conflicts that ensued once the regime had fallen. With the collapse of the government, Iraqi tribes began to fight among themselves to establish their dominance in the new order. Thus, the Coalition troops now found themselves involved in constant fighting between different factions in various cities, all taking place in a run-down country ravaged by sanctions and war. The Coalition invasion may have been a success, in military terms, however, the aftermath of the war proved to be a long and tortuous ordeal.

GUERRILLA WARFARE

Iraq was a country in disarray, with rogue elements from the military still fighting and looting; in addition, the hospitals, water supply and basic amenities had broken down, or were at breaking point. Not only this, the country's great museums, housing ancient treasures of immense cultural significance, in a region once held to be the cradle of civilization, had been ransacked, while other important historical buildings had been permanently damaged.

There was a threat to the Coalition soldiers as well as to the local population. Dangerous weapons and ammunition were stashed all over the countryside, hidden by insurgents. In a guerrilla war that included improvised explosions, suicide bombing, sabotage of oil wells, water and electricity, and grenade attacks, the opposing enthnic and political factions of Iraqi society continued to do battle with each other.

To date, the problems in Iraq continue to beset its inhabitants, both local people and foreign troops. Many critics point out that, although the invasion itself was carefully planned, the USA did not give a great deal of thought as to how post-war unrest in Iraq could be controlled, and they have not deployed enough troops or resources to rebuild the country in a viable way. Thus, with Iraq still in crisis, and its people still suffering the ravages of war, not to mention the increasing threat of terrorism around the world that many feel has been the result of the invasion, it seems that the winning of Gulf War Three has, in many ways, been a hollow victory for the West.

CHECHNYA 'BLACK WIDOWS'

We didn't come here to go home again, we
came here to die. We are all suicide fighters.
CHECHEN REBELS REPORT TO THE BBC

The Black Widows come from Russia and are a group of female suicide bombers, usually of Chechen origin. They got the title 'Black Widows' due to the fact that the majority of the women lost male members of their families in the Chechen wars against Russia. They are dressed from head-to-toe in black and wear the so-called 'martyr's belt' that is filled with explosives. The first Black Widow was Khava Barayeva, who blew herself up at a military base in Chechyna in June 2000.

The woman who is thought to be the main recruiter for the Black Widows is a mysterious, dark-eyed, middle-aged woman with a hooked nose and dark hair, popularly known as 'Black Fatima'. She has reportedly been spotted lurking in areas where terrorist bombings have taken place during the ongoing tensions between Russia and the break-away republic of Chechyna.

A resident in Grozny, Russia, Medna Bayrakova, told reporters that she remembers clearly the day that a middle-aged woman showed up at her front door. She asked if she could speak to her 26-year-old daughter, Zareta and, not aware that anything was wrong, Bayrakova let the visitor into her house. Her daughter and the stranger spent half an hour in the bedroom, and then her daughter left, saying she was walking the woman to the bus stop. One hour later Bayrakova's daughter had still not returned, and several men in camouflage uniform knocked at the door of the family's apartment. They told the woman that they had taken her daughter away as she had agreed to marry one of their members. Bayrakova protested violently, saying that her daughter was a sick girl, suffering from tuberculosis. They told her that they would give her medication and make sure she was well looked after, then they turned and left.

The next time Bayrakova and her husand saw their daughter was 24 days later, when Chechen rebels seized the Dubrovka Theatre in Moscow. Zareta's unmistakable dark eyes were visible above a black veil, as a television company showed a number of the rebels during one of their broadcasts. Her hands were clasped firmly below a belt of powerful explosives. Zareta Bayrakova was just another one of a string of women who had agreed to join the band of Black Widows.

Chechen terrorists have become a major threat to the security of the Russian people, as they have targeted rock concerts, subways and commuter trains full of students. In total the Black Widow suicide attacks have killed as many as 100 people and wounded several hundred more. It is believed that the women turn themselves into live bombs because they want to avenge loved ones killed in Chechnya's ten-year war with Russia.

DUBROVKA THEATRE SIEGE

The Black Widows made their first entrance into the world of terrorists on October 23, 2002, when Chechen rebels stormed a Moscow theatre during a performance of the musical *Nord-Ost*. The siege at the Dubrovka Theatre started at around 9.00 a.m., when a blast was heard near the building and witnesses said they heard some gunfire. The rebel group consisted of 40–50 gunmen, but they were also accompanied by several Chechen women, who were strapped with explosives.

It is estimated that as many as 900 people were taken hostage during the siege, including 90 members of the theatre staff. The talks between the rebels and the Russian authorities lasted for three days, in which time a total of 200 hostages were released. After the release of the first few hostages, the rebels demanded that Russian military forces be pulled out of Chechnya within one week. They said if the federal forces attempted a counterattack on the theatre, they would simply blow up the building. The rebels used the hostages they had freed to communicate with the negotiators, and said that they would release the children if they were allowed to speak to the media. At about midnight, the crews of the NTV television network were allowed to broadcast some comments from the rebels. Later that night, two Chechen representatives in Russia's parliament succeeded in getting inside the theatre, and attempted to negotiate with the captors. However, these negotiations were unsuccessful, and antiwar protests started to break out all over Moscow, as relatives of the hostages appealed for the rebels' demands to be met.

On the third day of the negotiations, at about 5.00 a.m., the Russian Special Forces stormed the theatre, believing that the rebels had already started to kill several of the hostages. After getting inside the building, the Special Forces released a narcotic gas to try to subdue the terrorists, and they managed to kill all of the terrorists in the ensuing shoot-out. However, it was not only the rebels that were killed: 129 of the hostages died, all but two of them due to the gas used by the the federal forces. By 7.00 a.m. the hostages were taken from the building and loaded onto buses to be taken to various hospitals in the locality.

The 18 women who were involved in the siege were regarded as real heroines, and they even received sympathy from the Russian survivors. Whatever the truth about these women, whether they were there of their own free will, or whether they were forced, they were certainly willing to lose their lives in revenge for the killing of their families.

The year after the theatre siege, former hostages started to file lawsuits and over 60 plaintiffs claimed millions of dollars in compensation from the Moscow government. On the first anniversary, a monument was unveiled in memory of the victims who lost their lives.

ASSASSINATION ATTEMPT

In May 2003, a Black Widow suicide bomber killed 14 people and wounded 150 as the pro-Moscow Chechen administrator, Akhmad Kadyrov, was addressing thousands of Muslim pilgrims at a crowded festival in Ilaskhan-Yurt. The attack was timed to coincide with the birthday of the Prophet Muhammad, and the intended target was Kadyrov himself and all the religious figures who support Putin's peace plan.

Witnesses said that the woman who carried out the attack had first asked to speak to Kadyrov, saying that three of her sons had disappeared. But the security guards simply turned her away, and she blew herself up only a few metres away from Kadyrov. The woman was later identified as Shakhida Baimuratova – whose first name translates as 'martyrdom' – a 46-year-old rebel fighter, whose husband had been killed in 1999. Dressed in black, with her hair tucked into a hijab, or Muslim headscarf, Baimuratova arrived at the festival with roughly 400 g (14 oz) of explosives strapped to her waist. A second woman, who had failed to detonate her explosives, also died in the blast.

Although Kadyrov was not injured in the attack, five of his bodyguards were killed, and he stated that he was concerned that there would be further attacks by the new breed of suicide bombers. He described the attack as a frightening new form of rebel action in a decade-old conflict. Just two days earlier another woman was part of an attack in the region's usually peaceful north, when she drove a truck packed with explosives into a government complex. Russia was now taking the threat of the Black Widows seriously as attacks were happening on an almost daily basis.

BUS BLAST

A woman, believed to be a 25-year-old Chechen, threw herself under a bus carrying members of Russia's military on Thursday, June 5, 2003. The attacker was wearing a white coat, the normal uniform for medical personnel. The blast killed 17 people and injured at least 15 critically.

The attack took place at 7.36 a.m. on the outskirts of Mozdok air base, a major military installation in Russia's North Ossetia province. The woman waited until the bus slowed down for a railway pass, and then approached the vehicle and blew herself up. So far the suicide bomber has not been identified.

ROCK CONCERT BOMBERS

On July 6, 2003, two women strapped with explosives blew themselves up at a crowded outdoor rock festival, killing at least 16 people. The first blast went off at one of the entrances to the festival at the Tushino airfield in Moscow. Another went off ten minutes later, as spectators were filing there way out of one of the exit gates.

The annual festival called *Krylya* 'Wings' is popular with young people, and there were about 20,000 people in attendance. Although a number of people were evacuated following the explosions, the concert continued in the hope of preventing mass panic.

Guards at the festival entrances were suspicious of the two women and stopped them from entering the grounds. Had they been able to gain access, it is feared that the casualty figures would have been far higher. As the two women approached the gate, the guards said their agitation was clearly visible. As soon as they were told they were not allowed to go into the concert, the first woman triggered her explosive-packed belt. Police immediately tried to direct the panicking crowed through another exit, which is where the second bomb was detonated, and this is where most of the casualties occurred.

Helicopters flew over the area looking for anything suspicious, while ambulances and police streamed into the airfield. Another bomb was discovered near one of the festival entrances, but the police managed to defuse it before any harm was done.

Although no one claimed responsibility for the attack, it was suggested that it was connected with the announcement made by the Russian president, Vladimir Putin, the day before, stating that presidential elections would be held in Chechnya in October.

ATTACK ON A COMMUTER TRAIN

In December 2003, a suicide bomber was responsible for killing at least 46 people and injured over 100 others when he blew himself up on a commuter train in southern Russia during the morning rush hour, when the train was packed with people. The male bomber was assisted by three women, two of whom managed to jump from the moving train and fled the scene. The third woman, who didn't manage to escape, was seriously wounded.

The explosion occurred just as the train had left Yessentuki station and, as a result of the blast, the train was derailed. The majority of those injured were students on their way to school in Mineralniye Vodi. Investigators believed that it was explosives attached to the belt of the woman terrorist that caused the main explosion. The male suicide bomber also detonated grenades that he had strapped to his legs, and a bag containing further explosives was found on board the train.

The timing of the attack was significant, as it came only two days before major parliamentary elections in Russia. Officials believed that the attack was an effort to try and destabilize the situation and possibly even disrupt the elections. President Putin was determined that the terrorists would not achieve their aims, and the elections took place unhindered.

Although initially no group claimed responsibility, on December 23, members of the Chechen Black Widow Brigade said they had carried out the terror attack on the commuter train. They defended their actions and said they would not stop until hostilities against their region were stopped.

GOVERNMENT TARGET

On December 9, 2003, just a few hundred metres from the Kremlin, a bomb exploded outside the National Hotel in the heart of Moscow. The terror attack was thought to be the work of a female suicide bomber and one other accomplice. It is thought that the bomb exploded too early, as their main target was the State Duma building and not the hotel. Just before the bomb exploded one of the bombers had reportedly asked directions to the Duma building. At the scene, police found a briefcase, which they believed had contained explosives that had been detonated by a robotic device. They also found additional explosives on a headless female body, which they believed to be one of the primary suicide bombers, which had also been detonated by a robot.

Russian police started a search to find a third

woman, who they believed to be an accomplice, and possibly the one who had activated the explosives. The attack came just two days after Putin's supporters won the legislative elections, in what many felt were unfair and biased elections. At the time of the explosion several Council of Europe members were near the hotel, but they escaped injury. However, six people died and at least 13 others were injured in the blast.

On December 23, the Chechen Black Widows claimed responsibility for the attack. Later that year one of the suicide bombers was identified as Khadishat Mangeriyeva, the second wife of Ruslan Mangeriyev, who had been killed the previous summer. Both Mangeriyev's sister and his third wife had already avenged his death in a similar manner.

BOMB EXPERT KILLED

A Russian bomb specialist was killed while trying to defuse an explosive device outside a café in central Moscow on Friday, February 6, 2004. He was well-known for his work with explosives, and was one of the men who had been called to the rock concert in 2003. A woman, who was believed to be in her 20s, had tried to enter the café, but because of her suspicious behaviour was not allowed in. When she was approached by a security officer, the woman became agitated and started to threaten the officers, saying, 'I'm going to blow this place up.'

The security officers removed her bag, covered it

with flak jackets and waited for members of Russia's Federal Security Services to arrive. However, efforts to defuse the device using robots and water cannons failed. The bomb expert was killed as he approached the bag and, although he was wearing a special protective suit, the explosive force of 400 g (14 oz) proved to be too powerful.

No one claimed responsibility for the attack, but Russian police and security officials are certain that the attack was linked to Chechen rebels, in particular the Black Widows.

SABOTAGE ON PASSENGER PLANES

Two Russian passenger planes that crashed in 2004 are believed to have been the targets of the Black Widow Brigade. Officials have discovered the remains of two Chechen women, thought to be suicide bombers, and traces of explosives in the wreckage. The loss of the two planes, which blew up just three minutes apart, was the first successful attack on passenger aircraft by Islamic extremists since September 11.

The smaller of the two planes, a Tu-134, carrying 44 people, crashed near Tula in the south of Moscow. The Chechen woman on board this plane was identified as Amanta Nagayeva, who only bought her ticket one hour before the flight took off. Although her body was completely destroyed by the blast, experts managed to find two tiny fragments 2.4 km (1½ miles) apart. She was the only person on board that flight who did not have her remains claimed. Nagayeva was born in 1977 near Vedeno, which was the home of the militant Chechen warlord, Shamil Basayev, and lived in Grozny, the Chechen capital.

The larger jet exploded near the Russian city of Rostov, killing 46 people, and among the wreckage, experts found traces of the military explosive hexogen. Another Chechen woman, named as S. Djerbikhanova, who was initially booked on another flight, changed her ticket at the last minute to the smaller evening flight. She sat in seat number 19F, which was just nine rows from the tail, which is considered to be the most vulnerable part of a plane. Once again hers were the only remains that remained unclaimed.

These last two attacks were an embarassment for President Putin, who had gained power on a promise to try and eradicate Chechen violence and to bring renewed security to Russia. It is still uncertain how Djerbikhanova managed to get through passport control, as she had given no personal details when she bought her ticket, and Putin made a statement that all airport security would now have to be tightened in the wake of the recent events.

WEB OF VIOLENCE

The face of the female terrorist in Chechnya is a relatively new phenomenon, even though the use of women for deadly terrorist attacks has existed in Lebanon, Israel, Syria, Sri Lanka and Turkey possibly since the 1980s. The Black Widow women are known as *shakhidki*, or martyrs, who are driven by intimately personal motives of fear and terror of what has happened to their husbands, brothers, fathers or sons at the hands of the Russian federal troops.

The ranks of the Black Widow are filled mainly by young women, many only 15–16 years old. Not all the women were widows, for some of the younger ones had not even married, and they came from totally different social backgrounds. Some had professional careers, while others were unemployed and came from families severely affected by poverty. One thing they did all have in common though, was the hatred and disgust of what was happening to Chechyna with its ongoing war with Russia. They were all trained in special camps by psychologists and experts in explosives. Some were voluntarily recruited, while others joined after having been 'sold' to rebel groups. They were subjected to drugs, rape, blackmail and brainwashing, until eventually they were ready to commit suicide for their cause.

Although the Black Widows generally work on their own or in small groups, it must be remembered that they are part of a much larger web of violence and always act on behalf of their rebel group. The groups often pinpoint women who have suffered extreme personal distress, because not only are they more willing to act as a suicide bomber, but the sheer fact that they are women 'martyrs' attracts a wider media coverage. They hope that by presenting black widows in a sympathetic light, it will give them more support from the community.

What is still puzzling the authorities is who exactly is ordering the terror attacks, and do they have any links to al-Qaeda and other jihad organizations outside of Russia? There has been a history of such links going back more than a decade, and there is also little doubt that Osama bin Laden used the Chechen cause to his own aim. Although there is no proof that al-Qaeda is the driving force behind the recent spell of Black Widow terror attacks, in the world of international terror, no one is prepared to rule it out.

BESLAN SCHOOL HOSTAGE CRISIS

This generation will lead us to freedom.
SHAMIL BASAYEV

The Beslan School Hostage Crisis was internationally condemned as one of the worst terrorist
atrocities ever to take place. The fact that a large
number of children were taken hostage and killed,
and that a total of 344 civilians died, provoked
outrage across the political spectrum. Any
sympathy that onlookers around the world might
have had for the Chechen rebels evaporated when
the true extent of the terrorists' brutality during the
siege became known: children had been raped,
tortured and murdered by the armed gunmen;
mothers had been forcibly separated from their
children, often forced to choose which ones to stay
with and which ones to leave behind; infants,
children, parents and teachers had been crammed
into a hot, overcrowded gymnasium wired with
explosives for days on end; and the terrorists had

refused to allow the removal of dead bodies that lay rotting on the ground during the ordeal. The surviving hostages' ordeal proved so appalling that some committed suicide after they were set free, while others suffered permanent psychological damage.

As many commentators pointed out, there could be no political cause that could possibly warrant such brutal behaviour, especially towards innocent children and infants. As UN Secretary Kofi Annan announced after the crisis was over:

> *The brutal and senseless slaughter of children only served to emphasize the need for the world community to come together in confronting terrorism.*

EXPLOSIVES WIRED UP

The siege began on September 1, 2004, at School Number One in Beslan, a Russian town in North Ossetia. The school was no stranger to political unrest, having served as a detention centre for the Muslim Ingush people during a period of civil war in 1992. At that time, the Ossetians had killed several of the Ingush. The Ingush were closely allied to the Chechnyans, by religion, culture and a history of oppression. Thus, the stage was already set for further conflict.

In Russia, September 1 is traditionally celebrated as a 'Day of Knowledge' by children and their extended families. Parents and relatives often accompany their children to school to take part in a ceremony in which the younger children give flowers to the older children, and the older children take the younger ones into their classes. It was on this day in 2004, when the children and their families were enjoying this innocent ritual at School Number One, that a group of armed terrorists decided to strike.

At 9.30 a.m., 32 terrorists invaded the school, disguising themselves with black masks and wearing belts loaded with explosives. The police were called, and a gun battle immediately broke out, causing terror and panic among the staff, children and relatives at the school. During the battle, five policemen were shot dead, while only one terrorist was killed. The nightmare continued as the terrorists herded 1,300 hostages into the school gym, many of them children. Then, in front of the terrified staff, children and families, the gunmen mined the gym with explosives, circling it with tripwire so that nobody could escape.

BODIES IN THE PLAYGROUND

About 50 hostages had managed to escape during the police shoot-out, but the others were now stuck in the gym, which was becoming hotter and hotter. Government security forces surrounded the school, but there was little they could do, since the gunmen were threatening to kill large numbers of the hostages should the soldiers attack. And their threats proved to have substance when, later that day, the terrorists killed 20 hostages (all of them men) and threw their bodies out onto the playground outside.

Terrified of further reprisals, the Russian government agreed to veto any show of force and attempted to negotiate a peaceful end to the crisis. Leonid Roshal, a paediatrican who had helped to negotiate the release of children in the Moscow Theatre Hostage Crisis (see page 376), was called in to help. The United Nations Security Council was convened at Russia's request, to see if any conclusion could be negotiated in this way. But these efforts proved fruitless: the terrorists would not allow medicines, food, or even water to be taken into the school for the hostages. In addition, they refused to let medical workers in to the school grounds to dispose of the bodies.

RAPE AND MURDER

Not only this, but the terrorists then began to abuse the children further. Many of them were by now sweltering in the heat and, becoming dehydrated through lack of drinking water, they took off their clothes. The terrorists then raped some of them, including adolescent girls, while their families were forced to listen to their screams ringing down the corridors of the school.

After negotiations with Ingush leader Ruslan

Aushev, the terrorists agreed to release 26 breast-feeding mothers and their babies. In one case, a baby was released on its own, because its mother did not want to leave her other children at the school to suffer at the hands of the terrorists. In other cases, mothers with babies were given no choice in the matter and forced to leave their older children behind at the school. Tragically, some of these older children were later killed.

It was now becoming obvious that the government was dealing with terrorists who were cruel, barbaric and possibly insane. The terrorists now agreed to the removal of bodies by medical workers, but proceeded to shoot two medical workers dead when they entered the school. They also began to fire at the security personnel surrounding the school. A bomb then went off in the gymnasium, and a wall collapsed. In the chaos that ensued, dozens of hostages escaped, but others were killed in the shoot-out between the terrorists and the security forces.

TANKS AND FLAME-THROWERS

As mayhem broke out, local citizens joined in the fray, appearing at the school with guns and other weapons. The explosives that had been set up in the gymnasium began to detonate, and the building caught on fire. Meanwhile, the Russian army began to deploy tanks and flame-throwers against the terrorists, and a major battle took place. Many hostages were trapped inside the school, unable to escape; others were killed and wounded as the hostilities escalated. Fighting continued into the evening, until the majority of the terrorists were dead; one of them was reported to have been ambushed and beaten to death by angry parents as he was being taken to hospital.

In the aftermath of the battle, the true extent of the damage was assessed, and it became clear that hundreds of hostages, both children and adults, had died during the siege. The Russian government came under criticism for attacking the school with heavy artillery while the hostages were still inside; they argued, however, that the main attack had not commenced until most of the hostages were safe. Be that as it may, an enormous number of innocent civilians, many of them children, had been killed; and also, there was a disturbingly high casualty rate among the security forces.

ARAB OPERATIVES?

After the siege was over, two days of national mourning took place. Thousands of people joined a rally organized by the government in Moscow, to protest at the scourge of terrorism. Yet there was still some confusion as to who, exactly, was behind the attack. A couple of weeks after the crisis, Chechen warlord Shamil Basayev claimed responsibility for it; Magomet Yevloyev, an Ingush terrorist, was also suspected of involvement.

On the face of it, the Beslan school siege was very similar to the Moscow Theatre Hostage Crisis and the Kizlyar Hospital Siege, both of which Basayev had been involved in. Yet some suggested that the terrorists in the Beslan incident were not Chechens, because they did not understand the Chechen language and asked to communicate in Russian. The Russian government believes that Arab al-Qaeda operatives were among the terrorists, but this claim is yet to be substantiated.

LYNCH MOB

The only person to be tried in a court of law for the crime was Nur-Pashi Kulayev. He was thought to be the only terrorist who had survived the siege (although Chechen warlord Basayev claimed that several more had escaped). Kulayev was a 24-year-old unemployed Chechen carpenter, whose brother Han-Pashi had once worked as a bodyguard for Basayev. Nur-Pashi had attempted to escape after the siege by posing as a hostage, but he was recognized by members of the crowd, who tried to beat him to death. Security forces eventually came to his rescue.

Kulayev's defence rested on the claim that he had been recruited by Chechen rebels to attack a military target and had no idea before the siege that he would be asked to take children in a school as hostages. He also claimed that he had not shot anyone during the siege and had saved the life of one young girl. However, there were reports that he had intimidated the hostages, running around with his gun and shouting curses at them. Eventually, he was convicted of committing an act of terrorism and murder, and given a sentence of life imprisonment.

BRUTAL KILLER

Whatever Kulayev's true role, it is clear that he was not one of the major players in the drama. It is thought that, although he did not take part in the actual attack, the Chechen terrorist Shamil Basayev organized and financed it. Basayev had claimed responsibility for this and numerous other horrific terror attacks in Russia and elsewhere, and was one of the world's most wanted terrorists. On July 10, 2006, he finally met a fitting end, at the village of Ekazhevo, Ingushetia. As he rode along in a truck packed full of explosives, about to commit another terrorist attack, a bomb detonated, killing him instantly. His remains were identified by DNA analysis. The Russians claimed that their agents had planted the bomb, while Chechen rebels declared that the explosion was an accident. Whatever the truth of the matter, there were few who mourned the passing of such a brutal killer.

MADRID BOMBINGS

*The government's position is one of caution, of
prudence . . . After so many years of horror
and terror [it] will be a long and difficult
process.*
JOSÉ LUIS RODRIGUEZ ZAPATERO,
SPANISH PRIME MINISTER

The Madrid bombings of March 11, 2004, were the
most destructive terrorist attacks ever to take place
in Spain. The city's complex commuter train system
became the target of several co-ordinated bomb
attacks, which killed a total of 192 people, and
injured more than 2,000. The bombings took place
three days before the Spanish general elections,
prompting suspicions that it was the work of ETA,
the terrorist Basque separatist organisation. The
Spanish government under President Aznar immediately blamed the attacks on ETA, but it later
became clear that Islamic militants from Morocco
were behind the bombings. The Spanish people
were so angry at the way the government had

manipulated the situation that they voted Aznar out and a Socialist government took over, who condemned the war in Iraq and threatened to pull Spanish troops out of the conflict. Thus, the attack had immediate political effects in Spain and around the world, particularly because of its timing just before the national elections.

A SCENE FROM HELL

The morning of March 11, 2004, was a busy one as usual in the Spanish capital, as thousands of people made their way to work in the morning rush hour. However, as a series of explosions ripped through the commuter railway system, everything came to a standstill. At the centre of the attack was Atocha, one of Madrid's main train stations. Eyewitnesses told how pieces of train flew into the air, and how bodies could be seen trapped in the wreckage of twisted iron. There were huge holes in the train carriages where the bombs had blasted through them. Dead bodies lay on the railway line while the walking wounded, covered in blood, stepped over them to safety. There were clouds of smoke and an acrid smell of burning plastic everywhere. People were screaming and crying in shock as they witnessed horrific injuries and saw people die in front of them. As one commentator remarked: 'It was a scene from from hell.'

When the dust settled, what had happened began to become clear. At just after 6.30 a.m., four bombs had exploded on a train entering Atocha station, killing and injuring dozens of people. Three explosions on a train standing inside the station had killed further commuters. Only 15 minutes later, at El Pozo station, two explosions caused further death and destructions, and a minute after that, an explosion at Santa Eugenia Station killed more people. Not only that, but well over 1,000 people in total were injured by the blasts. Later, three more unexploded bombs were found, hidden in backpacks, and were safely detonated by police from bomb disposal units.

BRUTAL TERRORISTS

After the bombings, the government immediately issued a statement naming the Basque separatist group ETA (Euskadi Ta Askatasuna) as the culprits. Since the 1960s, ETA had mounted numerous bomb attacks in Spain in the past, killing and injuring dozens of people. Their campaign had reached a peak from the 1980s as car bomb attacks, attempted assassinations, brutal shootings and kidnappings increased. Most Spaniards condemned ETA for their violent tactics, and there was not a great deal of sympathy for their cause, even among the Basque people themselves. In recent years, ETA had begun to alienate themselves still further from their own people by murdering, kidnapping and blackmailing Basque politicians, newspaper editors and others who spoke out against their terrorist attacks.

THE TRAINS OF DEATH

However, it soon became clear that, in this instance, ETA was not to blame for the bombings. A stolen van was found near the scene of one of the station bombings, containing a supply of detonators and a tape in the Arabic language. Not only this, but soon after the event, a letter was sent to an Arabic newspaper in London, claiming that the attacks were mounted by Abu Hafs al-Masri Brigades, a group thought to be associated with al-Qaeda. The group, named after a former terrorist, had in the past claimed responsibility for a number of attacks around the world. They referred to the attacks as 'The Trains of Death Operation'. Later, another organization, The Lions of Al-Mufridun, also claimed responsibility for the attack.

The claims of these groups were regarded with some scepticism at first, but then more evidence came to light. A bag of explosives that failed to detonate was found, and in it was a mobile phone. The phone was traced to Jamal Zougam, a Moroccan thought to have links with Abu Dahdah, the suspected leader of an al-Qaeda cell in Madrid. Several more arrests were made, including Moroccan and Indian nationals, all of whom were thought to be connected to the bombings in some way. Zougam, who ran a mobile phone shop, was suspected of being involved in the making of the bombs. He was already under surveillance as a suspect in the suicide bombings of Casablanca in

May, when 33 people were killed in an anti-Jewish attack. The Casablanca atrocity was attributed to Salafia Jihadia, a Moroccan-based Islamic fundamentalist group with links to al-Qaeda. Zougam had also been mentioned in connection with the attacks of 9/11 in the USA.

PROTESTS AGAINST TERRORISM

Meanwhile, forensic evidence was beginning to emerge that the bombs were unlike any other bombs that had been detonated by ETA in the past. The attack was also on a much larger scale than any that ETA had hitherto mounted. Nevertheless, the Spanish government had immediately blamed the Basque separatists, in a move that was now seen as opportunistic and mainly motivated by its desire to win the upcoming election.

As a result of these complications, the Madrid bombings became the subject of much political controversy, and there were angry demonstrations protesting against the manipulative behaviour of the government in dealing with this tragic situation. To this day, there continues to be many differing accounts of who exactly was to blame and why the attack took place.

On the day following the blasts, millions of Spanish people took to the streets to protest against ETA, who were presumed to be behind these latest atrocities. Later on, it became clear that it was Islamic fundamentalists, not Basque separatists, who were behind the attacks, and a major investigation was launched to try to bring the culprits to justice.

SUICIDE BLAST

The first suspects were rounded up on March 13, 2004. The seven men, three of them Moroccan, two Indian and two Spanish, were alleged to have provided support for the perpetrators of the attack. On March 18, five more suspects were picked up, all of them, except one, Moroccans. There were more arrests on March 22, and the trail led to a Moroccan national, Abdelkrim Mejjati, who was alleged to be the mastermind behind both the Casablanca attack and the Madrid bombings.

The following month, police began to close in on a group of Moroccans in an apartment block in Leganés, a town near Madrid. As they did so, they evacuated the residents of the block and the surrounding areas, fearing a shoot-out. Then there was a massive explosion, which killed a special forces agent and injured several other policemen. It appeared that the Moroccan terrorists had blown themselves up. They were later identified as Jamal Ahmidan, Abdennabi Kounjaa, Asri Rifat Anouar and Sarhane Ben Abdelmajid Fakhet. Fahket was a Tunisian, and he was thought to be the main perpetrator of the Madrid bombings.

MASS MURDER

More arrests followed as police in Milan caught up with Rabei Osman el Sayed Ahmed, suspected of planning the Madrid bombings with co-conspirator Fahket. In Serbia, Abdelmajid Bouchar was picked up and identified as one of the other terrorists involved, and a request was made to extradite him from the country. Meanwhile, the Spanish judiciary charged the three Moroccans who had first been arrested with murder – not of one or two people, but a 190 in total – and of the attempted murder of 1,400 people. In addition, the men were accused of belonging to a terrorist organization. The two Indian suspects, Suresh Kumar and Vinay Kohly, were charged with collaborating with terrorists and falsifying documents.

Under Spanish law, the five suspects could be held in jail for up to two years while the prosecution gathered evidence for the case against them. Accordingly, they were taken to prison to await trial. That same year, more suspects, José Emilio Suarez, Abderrahim Zbakh, Abdelouahid Berrak and Mohamed El Hadi Chedadi, were charged with a variety of crimes, from murder and robbery to collaboration with terrorists.

The terrorist bombings in Madrid exposed many of the deep political rifts within the country, and they continue to do so. While on one level the government, the authorities, the media and the public were united in grief at the tragic loss of so many ordinary citizens of Madrid, it was also clear that there was a great deal of political capital to be made out of the attack, coming as it did just before a national election, and in the context of ETA terrorism, which had in recent years been a major issue in the country. Because of this, the attack had major repercussions on the political scene in Spain, and it continues to be a major source of controversy both there and internationally.

THE JULY 2005 LONDON BOMBINGS

I think we all know what they are trying to do – they are trying to use the slaughter of innocent people to cower us, to frighten us out of doing the things that we want to do, of trying to stop us going about our business as normal, as we are entitled to do, and they should not, and they must not, succeed.

TONY BLAIR

The London Bombings of July 2005 confirmed what everyone had feared since the attacks of 9/11 in New York: that the UK, as well as the USA, was now a major target for Islamic fundamentalist terror attacks. On Thursday, July 7, 2005, a co-ordinated attack of four bombs, three on the underground and one on a bus, killed 52 people and injured 700 more. This was the scenario that the public, the security services and the government had been dreading for months, years even – a direct attack on London's massive, overcrowded public transport system during a peak rush-hour period.

BLOOD, DUST AND DEBRIS

As the emergency services moved in, the full horror of the scenes below ground, and in the street where the bus exploded, began to become clear. Underground, emergency workers braved the darkness, smoke and carnage to rescue those who were still alive and to retrieve the bodies of those who had died. Above ground, the remains of the bus bore witness to the blast that had taken place on board, as victims staggered about the streets covered in blood, dust and debris. Such scenes horrified the nation when pictures of the atrocity began to be released on television and in the newspapers.

Yet, characteristically, the British public reacted calmly on the whole, and it was not long before Londoners resumed their normal lives. Later, when the details of those who had died were published, it became clear just how indiscriminate the attacks had been, and an unexpectedly moving picture emerged of London as a tolerant community in which people of all races, backgrounds and faiths lived and worked side by side. Far from attracting sympathy to their cause, the bombers had merely succeeded in showing how well integrated the community of the city was on a day-to-day level, offering a snapshot of people from all over the world who had come to London to pursue their careers and build successful lives. In contrast, the bombers could only be seen as a retrogressive force dedicated to a nihilistic death cult set on destroying modern civilization.

SUICIDE BOMBERS

Exactly two weeks after the bombings, four attempted bombings took place in London. Like the earlier attacks, there were three bombs placed on underground trains and one on a bus. Thankfully, the attacks were foiled by the security services and none of the bombs were detonated, but they served as a frightening reminder that terror attacks were still a threat to the lives of everyone in the nation's capital city.

When the suicide bombers of July 7 were eventually identified – all of the terrorists died in the attacks – new questions were raised as to the pathology of the culprits. For the most part, the bombers were young men from relatively stable backgrounds; they were not people whose lives had been fragmented by war, loss and poverty. So why had these individuals turned against their families and their society in this way, condemning themselves to their own deaths in the process? The pathology of the suicide bombers was perplexing, and it is still an issue that is under-researched in the discussion of the phenomenon of terrorism in the 21st century.

HOME-MADE BOMBS

Thursday July 7, 2005, in central London was busy as usual, with the underground and bus services working at full stretch. Just before the rush hour began to draw to a close at 8.50 a.m., three bombs hidden on underground trains detonated: the first on an underground train near Liverpool Street, the second near Edgware Road, and the third on a train as it travelled through a tunnel between King's Cross and Russell Square. An hour later, at 9.47 a.m., there was another explosion, this time on a double-decker bus at Tavistock Square, near King's Cross. In all, there were 26 victims at Russell Square; 13 died at Tavistock Place; seven at Aldgate; and six at Edgware Road.

The first bomb, on a Circle Line train, also damaged the Hammersmith and City Line from Liverpool Street to Aldgate East; while the second bomb, again on the Circle Line, damaged other trains as it passed by. The third bomb exploded at the rear of the first carriage in a train on the Piccadilly Line, damaging two carriages and the tunnel around it. The bomb on the bus, which was a number 30 travelling between Marble Arch and Hackney Wick, exploded as the bus took a diverted route. Ironically, people who had been evacuated from the tube had boarded the bus as an alternative method of transport.

The blast ripped off the roof of the bus and destroyed the rear section. Those at the front mostly survived, including the driver, but most of the unlucky victims at the rear were killed. In many cases, their bodies were so badly damaged that it took a long time to identify them. Since the bomb exploded near the offices of the British Medical Association, a number of doctors were on hand to provide immediate medical attention to the victims of the bus explosion.

TERRORIST ATTACK

Immediately after the underground bombs exploded, there was confusion as to what had happened. Initially, the authorities reported that there had been a power surge on the underground. Some now believe that this was an explanation designed to prevent an outbreak of mass panic on the trains, which would have resulted in chaos. Others argue that the way in which the bombs detonated caused power failures at certain points on the lines, prompting the theory that circuit breakers had come into operation as a result of a power surge. Whatever the truth, within two hours, the police admitted that the explosions were in fact the result of a major terrorist attack on central London.

Forensic examinations of the scenes of the crime yielded the information that the bombs were home-made devices using easily obtainable materials. Each of the bombs contained 4.5kg (10lb) of high explosive, using acetone peroxide. According to some reports, the bombs were placed in such a way that the explosions would form a 'cross of fire', centred on King's Cross, thus symbolically representing the destruction of the Christian Western world.

THE CULPRITS

Using a combination of evidence from CCTV footage and forensic evidence, police tracked the bombers down and conducted raids on houses in the Leeds area, as well as in Aylesbury, Buckinghamshire. The bombers were identified as: Hasib Hussain, Shehzad Tanweer, Mohammad Sidique Khan and Germaine Lindsay. Initially, it was confirmed that they had all died in the attacks, but it was not until later that they were said to be suicide bombers. None of them had previously been identified as violent extremists, and in most cases their families, friends and acquaintances expressed extreme shock and dismay that they had been involved in the bombings.

FAMILY MEN

Three of the men were from the north of England: Mohammed Sidique Khan was from Dewsbury, where he lived with his pregnant wife and young child; Shehzad Tanweer was from Leeds, where he worked in a fish and chip shop, living with his mother and father; and Hasib Hussain was also from Leeds, and lived with his brother and sister.

The fourth, Germaine Lindsay lived in Aylesbury, Buckingham, with his pregnant wife, who had converted to Islam.

The bombings took place at a significant time in Britain, while Prime Minister Tony Blair was hosting the G8 summit, and just after London had won the contract for the 2012 Olympics. In addition, there had recently been a huge *Live 8* concert in London for the victims of famine in Africa. The bombings also coincided with the anniversary of race riots in the north of England, in Bradford, four years earlier, and with the beginning of the trial of a noted Islamic fundamentalist, Abu Hamza al-Masri.

MISTAKEN IDENTITY

One of the most troubling aspects of police response to the bombings was the shooting of an innocent man on July 22, 2005, in a case of mistaken identity. The incident occurred the day after a series of attempted bombings in the capital, and police had mounted a huge antiterror operation, hoping to catch the perpetrators before they escaped. That day, they were searching for suspects, using information obtained from unexploded packages.

The trail of clues led them to a block of apartments in Tulse Hill, where they watched the block until a young man emerged. He was a Brazilian electrician, Jean Charles de Menezes, who turned out to be entirely unconnected to terrorism of any kind. The Brazilian had come to London to earn money, hoping to return home and start a ranch with his savings. However, he bore an unfortunate passing resemblance to one of the suspects, which was never properly verified.

SHOT IN THE HEAD

That day, Menezes was setting off to mend a broken fire alarm in Kilburn. As he began his journey, he was followed by several plain-clothes policemen, and after riding on a bus, he entered a tube station. Menezes sat down in a train, waiting for it to move off, but before it could do so, officers rushed onto the train, grabbed him and shot him dead. They fired a total of 11 shots into his head and shoulder, in full view of witnesses on the train.

Afterwards, the police claimed that Menezes was trying to resist arrest, but eventually they admitted this was not the case and that a tragic error had been made. The Metropolitan Police subsequently issued a full apology for the incident and the British public had mixed reactions to what had happened. Many sympathized with the need for the police to make a split-second decision, while others condemned the killing as police brutality.

Demonstrations later took place in Brazil, but as some commentators pointed out, the record for police brutality in that country was considerably worse than it was in Britain. Even so, both July 2005 bombings and the police reaction to them, in the shape of the killing of Charles de Menezes, have proved a serious threat to the capital's reputation as a safe city in which law and order can be relied on to prevail.

BOMBS ROCK EGYPT

The perpetrators of these heinous acts of terrorism will be tracked down and punished.
HOSNI MUBARAK, EGYPTIAN PRESIDENT

Since 1992, Egypt has suffered a series of terror attacks largely aimed at tourists in the country. Today, tourism in Egypt represents the most lucrative part of the country's economy, so such attacks are extremely damaging. The attacks have been mounted by various Moslem militant groups, some of whose members are thought to be directly connected to Osama bin Laden and al-Qaeda. However, in many cases, it is not entirely clear who was responsible for the attacks, and exactly why they were carried out. In general, it seems that the attacks are part of a generalized Islamic funda-mentalist offensive against the westernization of Egypt. In recent years, the country has rapidly been transformed into a modern capitalist economy, with tourist resorts featuring luxury hotels, swimming pools, golf courses and the like. While for many this has been a positive development, bringing jobs and prosperity to the region, there are also those who feel that large sections of the indigenous Egyptian population have been ignored, and they continue to live in poverty while surrounded by foreign wealth.

In addition, the regime of President Hosni Mubarak has been widely criticized as being autocratic. Following the assassination of his predecessor Anwar Sadat in 1981, Mubarak declared a state of emergency in the country, giving himself and his government wide constitutional powers. Today, 25 years later, this 'state of emergency' is still in effect, and Mubarak continues to rule the country with a rod of iron. The difficulty of mounting an effective opposition to Mubarak's government within a democratic framework may perhaps go some way to explaining why Egypt has experienced a series of terror attacks whose motive is somewhat obscure. However, it is also possible that these attacks would have occurred whatever the country's political system, since they appear to have been perpetrated by Islamic groups who are fundamentally opposed to any form of Western democracy.

BUS AMBUSH

It was in 1992 that the series of bomb attacks on Egyptian targets began, with a warning from the main Islamic militant group Gama'a al-Islamiya that tourists should not enter the province of Qena, renowned for its ancient archaeological treasures from the times of the Pharaohs. The warning came in September, and in October, gunmen opened fire on a ship cruising along the Nile filled with German tourists. No one was killed, but the Egyptian crew were injured. Next, in the same month, came the ambush of a tourist bus, in which a British woman was killed and two British men injured. This was the first time a foreign tourist had been killed as a result of terrorist attacks in Egypt.

Bomb attacks continued into the following year, targeting tourist buses and cruise boats. The terrorists also began to bomb restaurants and hotels in Cairo, the nation's capital. Many were injured in the attacks, some seriously, while nine people in all were killed: a Turk, a Swede, an Italian, a Frenchman, two Americans and three Egyptians. In some cases, Gama'a al-Islamiya claimed responsibility; in others, such as the attack on a luxury hotel in Cairo, the assailant was thought to be mentally disturbed. Whatever the case, Egypt was becoming a dangerous place for tourists to visit, a situation that threatened to do lasting damage to the country's well-established, successful tourist industry.

TOURIST WARNING

In 1994, the assaults on tourists continued: five people died, and many more were injured as gunmen ambushed buses, opened fire on cruise boats, attacked trains and made raids on holiday resorts. In most cases, Gama'a al-Islayamiya claimed responsibility. Yet little was known about the group, other than that they were dedicated to the overthrow of Mubarak's undemocratic government. It also became clear that they focused their attacks on their enemies within Egypt, rather than taking on American or international targets, who would have been very powerful adversaries.

In 1995, the random attacks continued, killing two European tourists on a train and wounding many more. At this stage, Gama'a issued a warning to all foreign tourists to leave the country immediately. The following year, 17 Greek tourists and an Egyptian were gunned down outside a hotel in Cairo in the worst atrocity the country had seen so far. But there was a great deal worse to come.

MASSACRE AT LUXOR

Up to this point, the random snipings at tourist targets had been seen as a problem for travellers in Egypt, but not an insuperable one. In 1997, all that changed. In September, there was another attack, killing several tourists; but on 17 November, came an all-out offensive at Luxor. Muslim terrorists launched an attack on tourists at Deir el-Bahri, who were visiting the famous memorial temple to the female pharaoh Hatshepsut there. During the morning, six gunmen armed with automatic guns and knives, posing as security officers, followed a group of visitors to the temple, and proceeded to launch a ferocious attack on them. According to reports, the assailants actually beheaded and disembowelled many of their victims. When Egyptian police arrived, a gun battle ensued, in which all six of the terrorists were killed.

This horrifying event was met with worldwide outrage. Most of the tourists killed were Swiss, but there were also Japanese, British, German, French, Colombian and Bulgarian victims. Several Egyptians also died. President Mubarak reacted angrily to international criticism, blaming Great Britain for granting political asylum to Egyptian terrorists, but he also made changes in his cabinet after the event. Security was also tightened round all tourist centres.

Not surprisingly, there was a large downturn in tourism after the Luxor massacre, and the industry did not begin to recover for several years afterwards. During this time, having achieved their aim, the militants remained silent – until 2004, when the trouble began once again.

SUICIDE MOTORCYCLE BOMBER

The killings began once more in 2004 in the Red Sea villages of Taba and Ras Shitan, where 34 people, mostly visitors from Israel, met their deaths and over 100 people were injured. The following year, on April 7, a spectacular attack horrified onlookers as a suicide bomber drove his motorcyle into the bazaar of Khan al-Khalili and a home-made nail bomb detonated, killing two tourists and injuring around 18 people. Body parts and debris were scattered over the bazaar in a scene of carnage. This time, a previously unknown extremist group calling itself the Islamic Brigades of Pride claimed responsibility.

Then, on April 30, a suspected bomber who was being chased by the police, jumped off a bridge in Cairo, detonating a bomb as he did and killing himself. Two hours later, two female militants opened fire on a bus in Cairo and wounded two passengers, before turning their guns on themselves. A group known as the Abdullah Azzam Brigades, named after a Palestinian militant, claimed responsibility, stating that the attacks were in revenge for arrests of Islamic militants that had been made in connection with the Red Sea attacks.

EXPLODING CARS

The situation in Egypt was clearly becoming more and more tense, and it was only a matter of time before another appalling atrocity was committed. It took place at the Red Sea resort of Sharma el-Sheikh, ironically known as the 'city of peace' because of its relaxing atmosphere, and also because several international peace conferences had been held there.

On July 22, Egypt's National Day, a suicide car bomber struck the Old Market district of the city at 1.00 a.m., killing 17 Egyptians gathered in a coffee house there. Meanwhile, not far away, another suicide bomber rammed his car, packed with explosives, into Ghazala Garden Hotel. Not long afterwards, a bomb planted a few streets away in a car park near the beach detonated. The bombs all went off in the night, when the streets, bars and markets were packed with people. The total death toll of the Sharma el-Sheikh atrocities was 88, with more than 200 people injured.

PEACE PROTEST

After the bombings, the local population took to the streets in protest, marching past the wreckage and demanding an end to terrorism. Yet less than a year later, another bombing occurred, this time at the Red Sea resort of Dahab, in which three bomb blasts killed 20 people and injured almost 100 people.

Currently, there is some debate, both within Egypt and internationally, about the aims of the terrorists. Some believe that the militant groups, which include Gama'a al-Islayama, the Egyptian Islamic Jihad, the Islamic Brigades of Pride and the Abdullah Azzam Brigades, seek first and foremost to overthrow the Mubarak regime, which they see as oppressive and corrupt. (Many other nonviolent, democratically inclined political opponents of Mubarak share this view of his regime, of course.) Other commentators argue that the terrorists are no longer just targeting foreign tourists in general, but that the attacks are specifically anti-American in nature – significantly, many of the attacks have occurred since the incarceration of Egyptian cleric Omar Abdel-Rahman, the spiritual leader of Gama'a al-Islayama, for his part in the 1993 bombing of the World Trade Centre. But whatever the truth, the fact remains that in the near future, terror attacks in Egypt look set to continue; and that innocent people, both Egyptian nationals and foreigners, will continue to pay the price for ideological conflict there.

MUMBAI MASSACRE

---

*The series of blasts . . . are shocking and
cowardly attempts to spread a feeling of fear
and terror among our citizens. My heart
reaches out and grieves for all those affected
by these blasts and who have lost their near
and dear ones . . .*

MANMOHAN SINGH, INDIAN PRIME MINISTER

On July 11, 2006, a series of bombs exploded on the
Western Railway, Mumbai, in the suburbs of the
city. It was the worst attack to take place in Mumbai
for over a decade: 207 people died, and hundreds
more were injured, some severely. Afterwards a
terrorist organization called Lashkar-e-Qahhar
claimed responsibility for the bombing, apparently
as retaliation for the political oppression of Muslim
minorities in the regions of Kashmir and Gujrat.
However, Lashkar later denied that any of their
members were involved, as did another radical
group, the Student Islamic Movement of India
(SIMI). Eventually, police arrested four men, one a
member of Lashkar and three members of SIMI.

A LIVING NIGHTMARE

Mumbai, formerly Bombay, is the financial capital of India and has one of the largest and busiest commuter railway systems in the world, carrying more than 6,000,0000 people to work and back every day. On the evening of July 11, the usual rush hour crush began as office workers made their way home to the suburbs on the city's Western railway. Suddenly, between 6.24 and 6.35 p.m. local time, seven bombs detonated, causing complete pandemonium. Eyewitnesses spoke of bodies being flung onto the railway tracks by the force of the blast, while many of those still alive tried to jump off the trains, only to be run over by trains coming in the other direction. (Most of the trains were moving when the bombs went off.) A shopkeeper living near one of the railway tracks said that the explosion he heard was so powerful he thought he had been struck by lightning. Thus, in just over 10 minutes, what had been an ordinary evening on the public railway had become a living nightmare.

As television crews moved in, viewers across the world saw images of trains whose doors and windows had been blown off by the blasts, and railway tracks with luggage, clothes and shoes scattered all over them. They watched as dazed commuters, covered in blood, walked from the wreckage, and emergency workers fought through the piles of twisted metal to rescue those who had been trapped below. Hospitals around the city were inundated with casualties, and many found it difficult to cope. Further chaos was caused by the collapse of the mobile phone network, so that emergency services could not communicate with each other, and stranded commuters were left unable to phone home.

To compound the problems, Mumbai was experiencing heavy rains in the monsoon season, and there was flooding in many parts of the city. This initially hampered the rescue operation considerably, but the situation improved when citizens who had been unharmed in the attacks began to help the victims, walking them to ambulances and giving them first aid where possible.

HIGH ALERT

The bombs had all been hidden in trains running from Churchgate, in the city centre, to residential areas in the suburbs of the city. They had been placed in the first-class 'general' carriages, rather than the 'ladies' carriages reserved for women only. When they went off, the trains were nearing their destinations, at Borivali, Bhayandar, Jogeshwari, Khar Road, Bandra, Mahim and Matunga Road. Later, a bomb disposal unit defused another bomb planted at Borivali.

Immediately after the bombs detonated, authorities closed down the entire Mumbai railway system, and the city was put on high alert. India's capital city, Delhi, was also put on high alert as the government and security services struggled to find out what was happening. Hundreds of thousands of commuters in Mumbai were left stranded, while an atmosphere of panic began to build up. The Prime Minister of India, Manmohan Singh appealed to the public to keep calm, and comdemned the attacks as 'shocking and cowardly attempts to spread a feeling of fear and terror among our citizens'. In Pakistan, political leaders also denounced the attack as 'a despicable act of terrorism'. But as yet, no one knew who was responsible.

BOMB TARGET

Initially, Home Minister Shivrah Patil told the media that no one had immediately claimed responsibility for the attack. He added that the government had received some information before-hand that an attack was going to take place; however, the place and the time of the attack had not been divulged, so the authorities had been at a loss as to how to react.

Mumbai had been a target for bomb attacks in the past: in 1993, a series of bomb blasts in the city had killed more than 250 people. Bombings in various parts of India had continued since that time; just hours before the Mumbai attack, a string of grenade bombs had been thrown in the city of Srinagar, killing seven people.

In the days that followed this latest atrocity, police detained around 350 people for questioning.

Suspects included members of the Students Islamic Movement of India (SIMI), which was outlawed by the Indian government in 2002 because of suspected involvement in terror attacks across the country; and Lashkar-e-Toiba ('the army of the pure'), one of the largest terrorist organisations in Jammu and Kashmir, which had also been outlawed by the government.

MORE ATTACKS THREATENED

On July 14, a hitherto little-known Islamic fundamentalist organization calling itself Lashkar-e-Qahhar sent an email to an Indian television channel claiming responsibility for the bombing. It also threatened attacks on important symbolic sites such as the Gateway of India in Mumbai, the Red Fort in New Delhi and the Taj Mahal in Agra. The authorities investigated the claim and tried to track down the sender of the e-mail, but no firm evidence emerged.

Next, a spokesperson for the international Islamic fundamentalist group al-Qaeda made a telephone call claiming that the attack had been made in response to 'Indian oppression and suppression of minorities, particularly Muslims'. However, this claim was not substantiated either.

When forensic experts examined the bombs planted, using up-to-date chromatography and scanning techniques, they concluded that all the bombs had been planted at the central Churchgate station, where all the trains had been departing from on the evening of July 11. However, the forensic investigation as yet has yielded no more clues as to who was behind the attack.

SUSPECTED TERRORISTS

On the basis of their investigations, police made three arrests on July 21. Two of the men were arrested in the state of Bihar, while the third was picked up in Mumbai. A fourth suspect, Abdel Karim Tunda, was arrested in Kenya. Tunda was high on the list of India's most wanted terrorists and was thought to be a major player in the Islamic fundamentalist group Lashkar-e-Toiba.

Lashkar-e-Toiba is the subject of a great deal of controversy between India and Pakistan. In January 2002, President Pervez Musharraf of Pakistan banned the group, under international pressure in the wake of the 9/11 attacks; however, up to that time, the group had been allowed to operate openly in Pakistan, raising funds, recruiting members and training soldiers.

Initially, Lashkar's main area of operation was in the Indian state of Kashmir, where revolutionaries were fighting against Indian troops to secure their independence. However, as conflict between Islamic fundamentalists and the USA mounted, Lashkar is also thought to have become involved in generalised anti-American operations, and eventually it was accused of attacks against the Pakistani government itself. In 2002, to counter these claims, the party renamed itself Jama'at ud Dawa (Party of the Calling) and vowed to keep its focus in Kashmir. However, the group remained officially banned, although in practise, according to many sources, their activities were allowed to resume.

ARMED RAID

Following a spate of bomb attacks in India, Lashkar was again accused of terrorism, and the group actually admitted to being responsible for bombing an army barracks at the Red Fort, Delhi, which killed three people. However, it denied involvement in another Delhi bomb attack, which killed more than 50 civilians. The group again came under suspicion when, in December 2001, there was an armed raid on the Indian parliament; and again in August 2003, when a series of explosions rocked Mumbai, killing more than 50 and injuring 180 others. With the latest attack on the Mumbai railway in 2006, which appears to have been extremely well planned and cleverly co-ordinated, Lashkar was once again accused of responsibility; but as ever, the group has denied involvement.

Whether or not Lashkar is behind all these acts of terrorism, the fact remains that it has become the centre of a bitter dispute between India and Pakistan. India has accused its neighbour of harbouring terrorists, and Pakistan has come under international scrutiny as a state that may have sponsored or condoned acts of terrorism. In particular, the armed raid on the Indian parliament brought relations between the two nations to a peak of tension and nearly sparked off a war between them.

SUICIDE ATTACKS

In recent years, Lashkar has become notorious for its audacious suicide attacks on army bases, and for its extreme brutality, not only of soldiers but of civilians; stories abound of massacres where defenceless babies and children, as well as adult men and women, have been killed.

Many suspect the Pakistani government, through its Inter-Services Intelligence agency (ISI), of supporting the terrorists, and the issue continues to be an extremely controversial one in India, and the rest of the world. Whether or not this latest act of terrorism in Mumbai will throw any further light on the situation, when the perpetrators of the crime are brought to justice, remains to be seen.

Meanwhile, the people of Mumbai have been left to pick up the pieces and carry on with their lives. On July 18, they remembered the victims of the bombings with a special memorial service and a two-minute silence, gathering around the railway stations on the city's Western line to light candles and place wreaths for the dead in the places where they fell.

ISRAEL–LEBANON TERROR

*Those who call us terrorists wish to prevent
world public opinion from discovering the
truth about us and from seeing the justice on
our faces. They seek to hide the terrorism and
tyranny of their acts, and our own posture of
self-defence.*

YASSER ARAFAT'S SPEECH TO UNITED NATIONS

The Israel–Lebanon conflict has been an ongoing
situation since 1978, but its roots go far deeper. As
far back as 1948, five Arab nations, including
Lebanon, decided to invade Israel in the hope of
stopping the formation of the Jewish nation on land
that they believed belonged to the Arabs. The
Arabs named the land they occupied as Palestine
and the inhabitants Palestinians. However, due to
continual outbreaks of war, thousands fled to
neighbouring Arab countries. A Palestian guerilla
army formed and, using terrorist tactics, it started
retaliating by attacking Israel. Their attacks

prompted further retaliation, this time on the Palestinian host nations, Jordan and Lebanon. It wasn't long before the Palestinians became a force to be reckoned with in Jordan, and a civil war broke out in 1970, forcing the expulsion of the Palestinians. Not to be beaten, the Palestinian forces moved to another location on Israel's border, Lebanon.

In their new location, the Palestine forces regrouped under the leadership of Yasser Arafat and his Palestine Liberation Organization (PLO). Their relocation caused major disruption for Lebanon, however, as it brought a violent response from Israel. Lebanon became the subject of violent attacks, leaving behind a trail of death and destruction. The second major effect was on the balance of the population, due to the fact that the Palestinians were Muslims, who now greatly outnumbered the Christians in the Lebanese population.

By 1975, the tension had mounted to fever pitch between the Lebanese Christians and the Lebanese Muslims, who were supported by the PLO. It resulted in a bloody war, which caused the dissolution of the Lebanese government and army as the two nations rivalled for what they felt was rightfully theirs. The conflict did not just stay within the borders of Lebanon; neighbouring nations intervened. Syria sent a 40,000-strong peacekeeping force into eastern Lebanon, while the Syrians took the side of the Muslims and the PLO. Israel started to assist the anti-Muslim forces by supplying them with weapons and offering them extra manpower.

War raged on and by 1978, with southern Lebanon now completely occupied by the Palestinians, Israel decided to attack.

TIMELINE OF THE CONFLICT

March 11, 1978
PLO terrorists made a sea landing in Haifa, Israel, took over a bus and then drove towards Tel Aviv, firing from the windows. By the end of the day the IDF had killed nine terrorists, who had murdered 37 Israeli civilians. Four days later the Israelis retaliated.

March 14, 1978
Operation Litani was the official name of the Israel Defence Forces (IDF) invasion of Lebanon up to the Litani river. The purpose of the operation was to force the PLO away from the positions they held on the border and to bolster the strength of the SLA. The IDF managed to take control of an area about 10 km (6 miles) and then continued north and captured all of Lebanon south of the Litani river.

It is estimated that 285,000 Lebanese and Palestinian civilians were taken refugees due to Operation Litani, and the death toll of civilians was between 1,000 and 2,000 people. Twenty Israeli soldiers were killed and the PLO suffered an unknown number of casualties. On the one hand the Israelis considered the operation to be a military success, as they succeeded in driving the PLO forces north of the river, but on the other hand they had not succeeded in stopping their retreat. As a result of the operation the Lebanese government created the UNIFIL peacekeeping force, and this brought about a partial withdrawal of Israeli troops from Lebanon.

June, 1978
The Israeli forces withdrew from southern Lebanon and turned over control of the area to the South Lebanon Army (SLA), which was led by Major Saad Haddad. Haddad was a renegade Lebanese officer who had formed his own militia, and during this time he was involved in frequent conflicts with the PLO.

June, 1981
In response to PLO rocket attacks, Israeli forces started a heavy bombing campaign of PLO targets in Lebanon. The president of Lebanon asked Islamic leaders if they could use their influence to stop the endless death, destruction and displacement of his people. After a four-day conference leaders of 37 Islamic countries and the PLO called for an immediate cease-fire.

July 1981–June 1982
The PLO decided to interpet the cease-fire in its own way and, after a short break, it carried out several attacks from Jordan and also attacked Jewish targets in Europe. During this period 26 Israelis were killed and 264 were injured.

On April 3, 1982, Ya'acov Bar-Simantov, second secretary of Israel's embassy in France and a Mossad officer, is shot dead in Paris. The Lebanese Armed Revolutionary Factions claimed responsibility, but Israel blamed the PLO and labelled the murder a violation of the terms of the July 1981 cease-fire.

On June 3, 1982, an attempt was made on the life of the Israeli ambassador in London, Shlomo Argov. He was shot as he was leaving a diplomatic affair at the Dorchester Hotel in the centre of London. The terrorists fired a burst from a sub-machine gun at Argov, wounding the 52-year-old father of three in the head and, although he survived the attack, he was left completely paralyzed. This last attack proved to be the final straw, and in June 1982 Israel launched a large-scale invasion of Lebanon, which became known as *Operation Peace for Galilee*. The PLO responded with a massive artillery attack on the Israeli population of Galilee. On June 6, the IDF moved into Lebanon to drive out the terrorists.

Israeli forces, who allowed the Palestinians to leave Lebanon, remained in control of south Lebanon until 2,000, when their troops were withdrawn to try to put a stop to the ongoing guerilla war with the Shi'ite Lebanese militia called Hezbollah.

July 25–31, 1983

As a direct result of attacks by the Hezbollah and the PLO in June, Israeli forces launched *Operation*

Accountability. This conflict is known as 'The Seven Day War' by the Lebanese. It lasted for seven days and they targeted Shi'ite towns and villages of south Lebanon in the fiercest attack since 1982. During the operation Israeli forces destroyed or damaged thousands of houses or buildings, causing as many as 300,000 Lebanese and Palestinian civilians to migrate to areas outside of the combat zone. The Israelis targeted Lebanese power stations, bridges and roadways, which is a tactic that would be repeated in future attacks on Hezbollah and Lebanon. Hezbollah responded with more rocket attacks causing the death of at least 118 Israeli civilians.

The USA negotiated a cease-fire, which ended the week-long campaign in Lebanon. An oral agreement was reached in which the Israelis agreed to refrain from attacking civilian targets in Lebanon, while the Hezbollah pledged to stop firing rockets into northern Israel. However, this agreement was only a temporary respite to the violence and in April 1996 the IDF was forced to launch another major offensive.

April 11–27, 1996

By the spring of 1996 the situation had become intolerable, and the Israeli government could not fail to react to the repeated attacks. They approved a massive bombing of south Lebanon, known as *Operation Grapes of Wrath*, which resulted in 1,100 air raids and the firing of over 25,000 shells at Hezbollah targets. In addition to the air raids, the

South Lebanese Army (which was a mixture of Christian and Shi'ite Muslim militia under the command of Haddad), was also engaged in ground fighting. A United Nations camp at Qana was hit by Israeli shelling, killing 118 Lebanese civilians who had taken refuge there. During the 16-day period, at least 350 civilians were wounded in Lebanon, and 62 Israeli civilians were wounded in Israel.

On April 26, the US Secretary of State, Warren Christopher, was able to bring about an understanding between Israel, Lebanon, the Hezbollah and Syria, which effectively ended the operation. The Israeli government would not admit that Hezbollah were part of the agreement, as officially it would have been admitting to negotiating with terrorists.

OPERATION TRUE PROMISE

The latest chapter in the ongoing saga between Israel and Lebanon took place on July 12, 2006, when the Hezbollah launched *Operation True Promise*. The attack started with a diversionary attack of rockets and mortar shells on Israeli settlements and military posts close to the Israel–Lebanon border. Hezbollah troops then crossed into Israel and attacked an IDF patrol, killing three Israeli soldiers and capturing two others. The guerillas returned to southern Lebanon with their prisoners, Ehud Goldwasser and Eldad Regev, where the Hezbollah leader, Hassan

Nasrallah, said they had taken the men in order to set up a prisoner exchange with Israel.

An Israeli Merkava Mark II tank, which was stationed close to where the attack happened, tried to follow the captors into Lebanon, but it was hit by an explosive device that killed all four occupants. Another Israeli soldier, who attempted to rescue the soldiers from the burning tank, also died.

Israel's prime minister, Ehud Olmert, promised retaliatory action as he considered their latest assault to be an 'act of war'. The Israeli forces immediately launched air, naval and ground attacks at Hezbollah targets across Lebanon. The Hezbollah responded by launching hundreds of rockets into northern Israel, reaching as far as Haifa. An Israeli warship was damaged 16 km (10 miles) off the Lebanese coast by an Iranian-made unmanned drone, which rammed the ship and exploded on impact.

Both sides continued to attack, but the most damage, as usual, was to innocent civilians. Israel attempted to cut off any supplies that Hezbollah might receive from Syrian or Iran and, as the war entered its second full week, Israel issued three terms of condition in a hope of ending the hostilities. The first was the release of any captured soldiers, the second an immediate end to the war and the third was the return of the Lebanese national army to southern Lebanon to disarm the Hezbollah.

For the first time since 1980, US marines landed in Beirut to help evacuate citizens from Lebanon and other western nations evacuated their nationals from the war zone, including the UK, France and Italy.

WILL IT EVER END?

As the repercussions from the Israel–Lebanon conflict spread further and further, the question on everyone's mind must be, 'will it ever end?' There is a long list of terror acts for which Hezbollah are suspected of being involved in, right back to the suicide truck bombings of the American embassy and marine barracks in Beirut in 1983. They are also suspected of hijacking a TWA flight in which a US navy diver was killed, and it is thought they are behind the attacks on the Israeli embassy and cultural centre in Argentina in the 1990s. The Hezbollah have also kidnapped Israeli soldiers before when, in 2000, disguised as UN soldiers, they took three IDF soldiers and a reservist. Nasrallah used them as a trade-off for militants held in Israel and, although it took three years, his strategy worked. Israel released 430 prisoners from Lebanon, Jordan and territories occupied by the Palestinians in return for three dead bodies!

DAYS LEADING UP TO THE CEASE-FIRE

At the beginning of August 2006, Israeli troops deployed near the Lebanese town of Baalbeck in the Bekaa Valley, while Hezbollah increased their rocket attacks from areas north of the Litani river.

On August 2, Hezbollah fires 215 rockets on northern Israel, which was the highest number recorded in one day, killing one civilian. Ten people die in an Israeli raid on a Baalbeck hospital that the IDF believed to be a Hezbollah headquarters.

The following day a further eight civilians die when Hezbollah fires over 200 rockets at northern Israel. Israel resumed its attack of Beirut's southern suburbs and the IDF is reported to have carried out 120 airstrikes on Lebanon during the night. Four Israeli soldiers, and four Hezbollah fighters are killed during a ground fight.

August 4, in Qaa, an Israeli air strike kills more than 20 people at a site selling fruit and vegetables. Israeli forces continue to bombard Beirut's southern suburbs and bomb routes out of the northern part of the city. Hezbollah fires more than 200 rockets into Israel, reaching deeper than previously recorded.

The UN Security Council put together a draught agreement to end the violence and bring about a permanent cease-fire, while Hezbollah continue to hit Israel with rockets.

Sunday, August 6, Hezbollah launches over 180 rockets into northern Israel. Twelve Israeli army reservists are killed near Kfar Giladi and three civilians are killed in Haifa. The IDF report that they have captured a Hezbollah fighter who was responsible for the July 12 kidnappings of the two Israeli soldiers.

The fighting continues in this way throughout the early part of August with a UN cease-fire resolution set to take effect on Monday, August 14. Since the renewed fighting began on July 12, 2006, Lebanese security forces say that 880 people have died and the IDF reports 136 deaths.

SILENCE

For the first time in five weeks there was no sound of gunfire across southern Lebanon as the UN-planned cease-fire took effect on August 14. Fighting continued right up until the beginning of the truce, then as if by magic, both sides stopped. Lebanese civilians defied the Israeli ban on travel and started to stream back into their homes in the war-ravaged areas. For the first time in a month no Hezbollah rockets could be seen lighting the sky, even though the Israeli army said that six Hezbollah fighters had been killed in three clashes after the cease-fire took effect. Although Israel started to withdraw its troops from the area, they warned that some would stay in place until a UN peacekeeping force arrived.

NO QUICK SOLUTION

There will be no quick and easy solution to ending the Israel-Lebanon conflict and, even if the UN-imposed cease-fire holds, the road ahead will be fraught with difficulties. The disagreements continue because Israel refuses to withdraw before the UN peacekeepers and Lebanese troops arrive in the south and Hezbollah move north of the Litani river. The Lebanese army also say they won't deploy the area while Hezbollah is still there, and the guerillas continue to refuse to give up their weapons in the south.

Hezbollah, who initially rejected all of Siniora's ideas, is now thought to be showing signs of flexibility. Lebanon has rejected the proposed plan as it does not call for an immediate Israeli withdrawal from southern Lebanon, nor in fact an immediate cease-fire. At present, Israel still has about 10,000 troops in the Lebanon and the Lebanese people still do not have high expectations of a quick solution. One thing is for certain, the Siniora Plan will not be easily implemented, but in the meantime the world is still looking for a fair resolution so that the cease-fire of the Israeli and Lebanese conflict can be realized at the earliest possible opportunity.

BRITAIN ON 'RED ALERT'

On August 11, 2006, British police foiled the worst airline terrorist plot since the fatal September 11. Had they not uncovered the suspected plot, police fear that it would have caused mass murder on an unimaginable scale. It is believed that the suspects were just a few days from making a dummy run, and possibly only a few more days before they carried out the real terror attack. If they had succeeded in taking down multiple aeroplanes, carrying hundreds of people, it would have a catastrophic loss of innocent lives.

It is believed that al-Qaeda may have been involved in the plan to hide explosive gel or liquid in a sports drink bottle. The plan was for the terrorist to dye the explosive liquid red to match the sports drink sealed in the top half of the bottle. The bottom half would have been a false compartment to hide the explosive gel. The detonator they intended to use was possibly as simple as an innocent flash from a disposable camera. The aim was to blow up planes while in the air, rather than attack any individual city. The plot involved flights to an undetermined number of US cities, which included New York, Washington, Los Angeles, Chicago and Boston.

England was immediately put on 'red alert' and security was tightened on British airports. There was mass chaos as flights were cancelled, security measures increased and all hand luggage was banned. Passengers, whose flights were permitted to leave, were told that they could only take on board the bare essentials such as passports and wallets, which had to be carried in a clear plastic bag.

British police started an immediate search of houses where suspected terrorists lived, and around 24 people were taken into custody for further questioning. The arrests were a culmination of a major covert counter-terrorist operation which had been going on for several months, and it is thought that the subsequent investigations will be very complex and lengthy. The country's terrorist alert was immediately raised to maximum level – critical – and New Scotland Yard said that Britain was definitely facing its most serious threat of a terror attack.

REBEL ATTACK
IN TURKEY

In August 2006, terrorist bombers carried out a 24-hour wave of attacks on innocent victims in Turkey. The Kurdistan Freedom Falcons, which is a hard-line militant group thought to be linked to the Kurdistan Workers' Party (PKK) terrorist organization, claimed responsibility for the latest attacks. The bombing campaign was aimed at destabilizing Turkey and trying to damage its economy by hitting at its tourist industry. Britons were attacked, not for Islamist or nationalist reasons, but simply as a way of scaring away other foreigners from Turkey. It is a well thought out plan, and one which worked with devastating effect in Egypt in 1997, when Islamic militants shot and killed 56 tourists in Luxor which crippled their country's tourism industry for years.

Turkey has been the subject of 20 bomb attacks in 2006, eight of which occurred in the month of August, which was planned to coincide with the peak month when millions of British holidaymakers head for the sun. The terror group sent out a warning to tourists that their spate of bombings was not over, and told them that they should not travel to Turkey.

The worst of the attacks occurred in the resorts of Antalya. Antalya, is one of Turkey's principal holiday resorts in the Mediterranean region of ancient Pamphylia, and is an attractive city with shady palm-lined boulevards, and a prize-winning marina. Following a blast in the old marketplace on the afternoon of August 28, three people died.

There were three more explosions in Marmaris, another one of Turkey's biggest holiday resorts. The town of Marmaris is located at the meeting place of the Aegean Sea and the Mediterranean Sea, and is one of the largest natural harbours in the world. Ten Britons and 11 Turks were injured when a minibus was blown up in the early hours of the morning. The bomb was placed under one of the seats, but miraculously none of the British tourists on the bus were killed, most suffered from burns and shrapnel wounds to their legs.

A family who were having a meal in a nearby café ran out onto the street when they heard the explosion. They were shocked by the scene of the tangled bus and bodies lying everywhere and, fearing that there would be a further blast, they ran away from the scene.

At the same time there were two other blasts after explosive devices were placed in rubbish bins on the main boulevard in Marmaris. Although it is a popular tourist area lined with bars, clubs, cafés and restaurants, there were no serious injuries connected with these blasts.

Six people were injured in a suburb of Istanbul when a bomb exploded in the garden of a school. Witnesses said the blast caused panic, with people covered in blood running away from the scene, and glass and debris flying through the air.

NOT HELPING THEIR CAUSE

The Kurdistan Freedom Falcons made it obvious that although they were targeting Turkey's tourist industry, the real reason was to further its separatist cause for the country's sizeable Kurdish minority. The explosions coincided with the installation of Turkey's new military chief of staff, Yasar Büyükanit, who had announced an unyielding fight against the terror attacks of the Kurdish extremists. The PKK, who ended a cease-fire in 2004, has used violent means to fight for their political rights for more than 20 years. More than 30,000 people lost their lives during a guerrilla war which took place in Turkey between the years of 1984 to 1999.

The Kurds do have reason to be bitter, due to their history with the three states of Iran, Iraq and Turkey. Over the years Iraqi Kurds have been brutally massacred by Saddam Hussein. However, the Kurds are not helping their cause especially at a time when Turkey is endeavouring to join the EU. By targeting civilians, the so-called 'Freedom

Falcons' are only making things worse for the people they claim to represent. Ordinary Turks, who are enraged at the latest spate of violence, are now calling for firm action to crush the Kurdish rebels once and for all.

To take action, however, would only bring about further bloodshed. It would do nothing to bring about a lasting settlement and would only do more serious damage to the Kurdish cause.

APPENDIX

A–Z OF TERRORIST GROUPS

Abdullah Azzam Brigades

Leader/s	Founded	Base	Aim	Attacks
Not known, but group named after Islamic militant Abdullah Yusuf Azzam	1987	Egypt	To establish an Islamic state in Egypt	Claimed responsibility for bomb attacks on the Old Market and Ghazala Gardens Hotel in the Egyptian resort of Sharm el-Sheikh on July 23, 2005, which killed 88 people and injured more than 150

Abu Nidal Organization (ANO)

aka The Arab Revolutionary Brigades, Black June, Black September, The Fatah Revolutionary Council (FRC), The Revolutionary Organization of Socialist Muslims

Leader/s	Founded	Base	Aim	Attacks
Abu Nidal ('father of struggle'). Born Sabri Khalil al-Banna 1937, died August 2002. The Iraqi government declared his death a suicide, but Palestinian sources suggest that he was shot by members of the Iraqi secret service	1974	Operations in Iraq, Syria, Egypt and Libya	Initially, the liberation of the Palestinian people, but mainly to destroy the state of Israel	Responsible for major terror attacks in over 20 countries, killing and injuring over 900 people. These include, among others: hijacking of TWA Flight 841 in 1974; Gulf Air Flight 771 in 1983; EgyptAir Flight 648 in 1985; and Pan Am Flight 73 in 1986. Also assassinated the deputy leader of the PLO in 1991

Abu Sayyaf Group (ASG)

Founder	Founded	Base	Aim	Attacks
Abduragak Abubakar Janjalani	1991	Southern Philippines	To promote an independent Islamic state in western Mindanao and the Sulu Archipelago – areas which are heavily populated by Muslims. They are renowned for using terror for financial profit	Kidnappings for ransom, bombings, beheadings, assassinations and extortions. First large-scale action was a raid on Ipil in Mindanao in April 1995. In February 2004 they bombed SuperFerry 14 in Manila Bay, killing 132

Allied Democratic Forces (ADF)

Leader/s	Founded	Base	Aim	Attacks
Jamil Mukulu, and consists of former members of the National Army for the Liberation of Uganda	1995	Western Uganda and eastern Congo	Initially set up in opposition to the government of Ugandan President Yoweri Museveni	Kidnapping and murder of civilians to create fear in local population and undermine confidence in the government. Suspected to be responsible for dozens of bombings in public areas and brutal attacks on tourists

Ansar al-Islam (AI)

Founder	Founded	Base	Aim	Attacks
Abu Abdallah al-Shafi'i and Mullah Krekar after a merger between Jund al-Islam and an Islamic Movement splinter group	2001	Northern Iraq	Aims to create an Islamic state in Iraq; known to be allied with al-Qaeda	Razing of beauty salons, burning schools for girls, murdering women in streets who refuse to wear the burqa. Seized a Taliban-style enclave of 4,000 civilians. Responsible for ambushing and killing 42 Kurdish soldiers. Responsible for assassination in 2001 of a senior official of the KDP, Franso Hariri, and for attempted killing of Burhan Salih, head of the PUK-led Iraqi Kurdistan regional government.

al-Qaeda

Leader/s	Founded	Base	Aim	Attacks
Osama bin Laden, millionaire son of Saudi Arabian family	1980s	al-Qaeda is a loose group of independent cells, or units, operating at various times in Afghanistan, Saudi Arabia, Bosnia, Sudan, Iraq, the USA and the UK	Initially formed to support the anti-Soviet Mujahidin in Afghanistan, bin Laden went on to speak out against the presence of American troops in Saudi Arabia, issuing a 'fatwa', or religious edict, to kill all Americans and their allies	Responsible for dozens of terror attacks around the world beginning in 1992. Major attacks include: the bombing of the World Trade Center in 1993; the bombing of US embassies in Africa in 1998; the bombing of the *USS Cole* warship in 2000; and most spectacularly, the 9/11 attacks on the USA in 2001. Since then, thought to have masterminded many more attacks, in collusion with other Islamic groups, including: the Bali bombings of 2002 and 2005, the Sharm el-Sheikh bombings of 2005, and the July 7 London bombings of 2005

Armed Islamic Group
(aka Groupe Islamique Arme – GIA)

Leader/s	Founded	Base	Aim	Attacks
Cherif Gousmi	1992	Algeria	To overthrow the Algerian government and replace it with an Islamic state	Conducted a series of horrifying civilian massacres during the 1990s. Also targets Europeans living in Algeria. Responsible for car bombings, kidnappings and assassinations, and is known for its brutal tactics, including slitting victims' throats

Army for the Liberation of Rwanda (ALIR)
(former Armed Forces of Rwanda – FAR)

Leader/s	Founded	Base	Aim	Attacks
Not known; but definitely ex-FAR or Interahamwe	1994	Mostly Republic of Congo and Rwanda, some in Burundi	To topple Rwanda's Tutsi-dominated government and reinstate Hutu control	In 1994 the FAR carried out the genocide of over 50,000 Tutsis. In 1996 the ALIR threatened to kill the US Ambassador of Rwanda and other US citizens. In 1999 they kidnapped and killed eight foreign tourists including two US citizens in a game park on the Congo-Ugandan border. In the current Congolese war, the ALIR is allied with Kinshasa against the Rwandan invaders

Aum Shinrikyo

Leader/s	Founded	Base	Aim	Attacks
Asahara Shoko (born Chizuo Matsumoto)	1986	Japan, Russia	Doomsday cult whose teachings are based on tenets borrowed from Hinduism and Buddhism, and who claim that the USA will start WWIII with Japan	Tokyo sarin gas attack in 1995 (12 dead and 5,500 injured); Matsumoto Nagano Prefecture sarin gas attack in 1994 (7 killed and 600 injured); kidnapping and murder of Tsutsumi Sakamoto and his wife and infant son; kidnapping and death of Kiyoshi Kariya in 1995; lynching of Kotata Ochida in 1994; and illegal production of various drugs

Baader-Meinhof Gang
(aka Red Army Faction or Fraction)

Leader/s	Founded	Base	Aim	Attacks
Andreas Baader, Ulrike Meinhof, Gudrun Ensslin	1968	West Germany	To mount a left-wing campaign against what it saw as the repressive policies of the police, the government and the state in Germany	Active during 1970s and 80s: bombings of military, police and media targets, kidnapping and murder of prominent German figures, hijackings. Thirty-four killed and many more wounded

Babbar Khalsa

Leader/s	Founded	Base	Aim	Attacks
Founded by Sukhdev Singh Babbar (now deceased) and Talwinder Singh Parmar	1978	India, UK, Canada	To establish an independent Sikh state, Kalistan ('Land of the Pure') in India	Assassination of Punjab Chief Minister Beant Singh 1995; bombings of cinemas 2005; alleged to have bombed Air India Flight 182 in 1985, but members acquitted in 2005 trial in Canada

Basque Fatherland and Liberty
(*Euzkadi Ta Askatasuna* – ETA)

Leader/s	Founded	Base	Aim	Attacks
(former leaders) Francisco Mujika Garmendia and José María Arregi Erostarbe	1959	Primarily in the Basque region of northern Spain and south-western France	To create an independent socialist state for the Basque people	In 1973, they killed Admiral Carrero Blanco, apparent successor to Francisco Franco. In 1995, a car bomb killed José María Aznar, leader of the conservative Popular Party. Since then have been involved in several low-level bombings in Spanish tourist areas, killing a total of 850 people and injuring hundreds more. ETA use car bombs, kidnapping and extortion, and kill victims with a gunshot to the nape of the neck

Community Party of the Philippines/
New People's Army (CPP/NPA)

Founder	Founded	Base	Aim	Attacks
José Maria Sison	1969	Rural Luzon, Visayas and parts of Mindanao. Has cells in Manila	Targets Philippine security forces, politicians, judges, government informers and former rebels who wish to leave the NPA. Opposes any US military presence in the Philippines.	Assassinations, murders and attacks on US personnel. Assassinated 2 congressmen from Quezon in May 2001 and Cagayan in June 2001.

Egyptian Islamic Jihad

Leader/s	Founded	Base	Aim	Attacks
Ayman al-Zawahri	1970s	Egypt, Afghanistan, Pakistan, Sudan, Lebanon, Yemen, UK	To overthrow the Egyptian government and establish an Islamic state in its place. The group has strong links with al-Qaeda	Helped to instigate uprisings against Egyptian government, killing hundreds; bombed Egyptian Embassy in Islamabad, Pakistan; assassinated Anwar Sadat

Gama'a al-Islamiyya

Leader/s	Founded	Base	Aim	Attacks
After split into 2 factions in 1997 – Mustafa Hamza and Rifa'i Taha Musa	1970s	al-Minya, Asyut, Qina and Sohaj Govern-orates of southern Egypt	Aims to replace Egypt's government with an Islamic state	Armed attacks against Egyptian security and government officials, Coptic Christians and Egyptian opponents of Islamic extremism. Attacks on tourists in Egypt, most notably in November 1997 at Luxor. Claimed responsibility for attempted assassination of Egyptian President Hosni Mubarak in Addis Ababa.

Hamas (Harakat al-Muqawama al-Islamiyya, Islamic Resistance Movement)

Leader/s	Founded	Base	Aim	Attacks
Founded by Shaikh Ahmed Yassin	1987	West Bank, Gaza Strip	To destroy the state of Israel and to establish an Islamic Palestinian state in its place	Accused of suicide bombings and other attacks against military, security and civilian Israeli targets. In 2006, Hamas became the democratically elected government of the Palestinian people but is still listed as a terrorist organization by the USA and other countries

Harakat ul-Mujahidin (HUM)/Harakat ul-Ansar

Leader/s	Founded	Base	Aim	Attacks
Fazlur Rehman Khalil, Farooqi Kashmiri	1985	Muzaffarabad, Rawalpindi and several Pakistani towns. Militants trained in Afghanistan and Pakistan.	Targets Indian troops, Kashmiri civilians and Western interests	Linked to militant group al-Faran that kidnapped and killed 5 Western tourists in Kashmir in July 1995. Hijacked an Indian airliner on December 24, 1999.

Hezbollah (Party of God)

Leader/s	Founded	Base	Aim	Attacks
Sayyed Hassan Nasrallah	1982	Southern Lebanon	To fight the Israeli incursions into Southern Lebanon	Accused of kidnap, torture and murder of Western military personnel and media figures; 1985 hijacking of TWA Flight 847; bombing of Israeli targets in Beirut 1992, 1994; rocket attacks against Israel in 2006. Hezbollah deny the attacks

Islamic Movement of Uzbekistan (IMU)

Leader	Founded	Base	Aim	Attacks
Tohir Yoldashev	1991	South Asia, Tajikistan, Iran	Opposed to Uzbekistani President Islom Karimov's secular regime and aim to remove Karimov to establish an Islamic state.	Attacks on US and Coalition soldiers in Afghanistan and Pakistan and plotted attacks on US diplomatic facilities in Central Asia. Blamed for explosion in city of Osh that killed 1 police officer and 1 terrorist. Responsible for explosions in Bishkek in December 2002 and 5 car bombs in Tashkent in 1999. Foreign hostages taken in 1999 and 2000, including 4 US citizens, 4 Japanese geologists and 8 Kyrgyzstani soldiers

Japanese Red Army

Leader/s	Founded	Base	Aim	Attacks
Fusako Shigenobu until her arrest in Japan in November 2000	1970	Unknown, but possibly based in Syrian-controlled areas of Lebanon	To overthrow Japanese government and monarchy and help instigate world revolution	Carried out a series of attacks around the world, including the massacre in 1972 at Lod Airport, two Japanese airliner hijackings and an attempted takeover of the US Embassy in Kuala Lumpur. In April 1988, JRA operative Yu Kikumura was arrested with explosives apparently planning an attack to coincide with the bombing of a USO club in Naples, which killed five, including a US servicewoman

Kahane Chai (Kach)

Founder	Founded	Base	Aim	Attacks
Rabbi Meir Kahane	1994	Israel, West Bank, particularly Qiryat Arba' in Hebron	Aims to restore the biblical state of Israel	Organized protests against the Israeli government. Harassed and threatened Arabs, Palestinians and Israeli government officials. Vowed revenge for death of their leader and his wife. Suspected of involvement in a number of low-level attacks

Khmer Rouge/
The Party of Democratic Kampuchea

Founder	Founded	Base	Aim	Attacks
Pol Pot	1970s	Outlying provinces in Cambodia, particularly in the northwest along the border with Thailand	Overthrow the Cambodian government	Infamous for their state-sponsored massacre of between 1 and 2 million Cambodians

Moroccan Islamic Combatant Group (GICM)

Founder	Founded	Base	Aim	Attacks
Not known	1990s	Western Europe, Afghanistan and possibly Morocco	Wish to create an Islamic state in Morocco and support of al-Qaeda's jihad against the West	Working with other North African extremists they engage in trafficking falsified documents and possible gun-running. 2003 terrorist attack on Casabalanca and 2004 Madrid bombing

National Liberation Army

Leader/s	Founded	Base	Aim	Attacks
Marxist insurgent group inspired by Fidel Castro and Che Guevara	1965	Colombia, Venezuela	Targets foreign employees from large corporations	Kidnapping, hijacking, bombing and extortion. Annually conducts hundreds of kidnappings for ransom, often targeting foreign employees of large corporations, especially in the petroleum industry. Frequently assaults energy infrastructure and has inflicted major damage on pipelines and the electric distribution network. In 2003, kidnapped eight foreign tourists, but they have all since either escaped or been released

Popular Front for the Liberation of Palestine (PFLP)

Leader/s	Founded	Base	Aim	Attacks
Founded by Dr George Habash	1953	Syria, Lebanon, Israel, West Bank, Gaza Strip	Targets Israel's 'illegal' occupation of Palestine and also opposes negotiations with Israel	Gained notoriety in the late 1960s and early 1970s for a series of armed attacks and aircraft hijackings, including non-Israeli targets; since 1978 several attacks against Israel and moderate Arab targets. It has stepped up its operational activity since the start of the current *intifadah*, with at least two suicide bombings since 2003, multiple joint operations with other Palestinian terrorist groups and assassination of the Israeli Tourism Minister in 2001

Provisional Irish Republican Army ('Provos')

Leader/s	Founded	Base	Aim	Attacks
Not known	1969	Northern Ireland, Irish Republic, Great Britain, Europe	To establish a united, self-governing Ireland independent of British rule	Bombings of military and civilian targets, both in Ireland and on the British mainland, killing a total of about 1,800 people between 1969 and 2005. Their activities also include assassinations, kidnappings, punishment beatings, extortion, smuggling and robberies

Qibla and People Against Gangsterism and Drugs (PAGAD)

Founder	Founded	Base	Aim	Attacks
Zahida Parveen	Qibla 1980s PAGAD 1996	Cape Town, South Africa	Qibla: To establishan Islamic state in South Africa PAGAD: To fight drug lords in Cape Town. Both groups promote a greater political voice for South African Muslims	Suspected of carrying out hundreds of bombings and other violent actions. Qibla protests through its own radio station 786

Revolutionary Armed Forces of Colombia (FARC)

Leader/s	Founded	Base	Aim	Attacks
Manuel Marulanda (aka Tirofijo), Jorge Briceno and 6 others	1964	Colombia	Oldest, largest, most capable and best-equipped insurgency of Marxist origin, whose goal is to overthrow government and ruling class	Bombings, murder, mortar attacks, drug-trafficking, kidnapping, extortion, hijacking as well as guerilla and conventional military action against Colombian political, military and economical targets. Executed 3 US Indian rights activists in 1999, captured and held 3 US contractors and killed 1 American and a Colombian when plane crashed in Florencia

Revolutionary United Front (RUF)

Leader/s	Founded	Base	Aim	Attacks
Founder, Foday Sankoh	1991	Sierre Leone, Liberia, Guinea	To put an end to the corrupt rule under the dictatorship of Siaka Stevens, and alleviate the widespread desperation in Sierra Leone	From 1991–2000 the RUF used guerrilla, criminal and terror tactics such as murder, torture and mutilation to fight the government and intimidate civilians. In 2000, they held hundreds of UN peace-keepers hostage; they have also been accused of attacks in Guinea at the behest of President Taylor

Salafist Group for Call and Combat (GSPC)

Founder	Founded	Base	Aim	Attacks
Hassan Hattab, a former Armed Islamic Group (GIA) regional commander	1996	Algeria	To overthrow the Algerian government and impose fundamentalist Islamic theocracy	Continue to conduct operations aimed at government and military targets, primarily in rural areas, although civilians are sometimes killed. A faction within the GSPC held 31 European tourists hostge in 2003 to collect ransom for their release. Believed to have allegiance to a number of jihadist causes and movements, including al-Qaeda

Sendero Luminoso ('Shining Path' aka Communist Part of Peru)

Leader/s	Founded	Base	Aim	Attacks
Abimael Guzmán (captured 1992)	Late 1960s	Andean highlands of Peru	To overthrow the government of Peru and establish a communist regime	Known for its extremely violent attacks, including brutal massacre of peasant communities, from 1980 to the present. Uses car bombs, sabotage, arson and other methods to created maximum disruption, both in cities and villages

Tamil Tigers
(The Liberation Tigers of Tamil Eelam – LTTE)

Leader/s	Founded	Base	Aim	Attacks
Velupillai Prabhakaran	1976	Northern and Eastern parts of Sri Lanka	To establish independence for the Tamil people of Sri Lanka	Accused of major terrorist attacks in India and Sri Lanka, such as the assassination of Rajiv Gandhi and other political figures, including rival Tamil activists, and of bombing civilian targets e.g. trains, banks, temples, etc. Also accused of recruiting child soldiers

Zviadists

Founder	Founded	Base	Aim	Attacks
Not known	1990s	Georgia, especially Mingrelia and Russia	Extreme supporters of deceased former Georgian president Zviad Gamzakhurdia. To overthrow Gamsakhurdia's successor Eduard Shevardnadze's rule	Conducted bombings and kidnappings. Attempted 2 assassinations against Shevardnadze in August 1995 and February 1998. Took UN personnel hostage following the attempt in February 1998 but released them unharmed